WORKPLACE WRITING

Workplace Writing: Beyond the Text draws together a wealth of research into different aspects of writing in workplace settings, creating a comprehensive picture of workplace writing and covering factors and activities that go far beyond the text. In a full analysis of the challenges facing the student writer transitioning from the academy to the workplace, this book:

- Covers topics ranging from intertextuality and collaborative writing practices to considerations of power and politeness, and the impact of organisational culture and processes of socialisation.
- Brings together the multiple, often interlinked factors that surround and impact on the process of workplace writing and the texts produced in professional settings.
- Takes a close look at the pedagogical implications of the various issues relating to workplace writing.
- Serves as a resource for teachers who want to go beyond potentially simplistic accounts of writing in the workplace and to provide students with a richer picture of what happens there.

Workplace Writing will be essential reading for any students, pre- and in-service teachers and researchers with an interest in professional and business discourse and language teaching for specific purposes.

Stephen Bremner is an Associate Professor in the Department of English at City University of Hong Kong.

WORKPLACE WRITING

Beyond the Text

Stephen Bremner

Routledge
Taylor & Francis Group

LONDON AND NEW YORK

First published 2018
by Routledge
2 Park Square, Milton Park, Abingdon, Oxon OX14 4RN

and by Routledge
711 Third Avenue, New York, NY 10017

Routledge is an imprint of the Taylor & Francis Group, an informa business

© 2018 Stephen Bremner

British Library Cataloguing-in-Publication Data
A catalogue record for this book is available from the British Library

Library of Congress Cataloging-in-Publication Data
A catalog record for this book has been requested

ISBN: 978-1-138-19383-3 (hbk)
ISBN: 978-1-138-19384-0 (pbk)
ISBN: 978-1-315-10475-1 (ebk)

Typeset in Bembo
by Deanta Global Publishing Services, Chennai, India

KV 06.20.2019 0735

CONTENTS

PREFACE

This book is an attempt to bring together in a coherent way the research and teaching that I have been engaged in over the last ten years or so. Throughout this period most of my colleagues, if asked, would have been hard pushed to say exactly which area of applied linguistics I work in. In my department there have been people who are closely associated with particular areas that are well defined and recognised: business communication, critical discourse analysis, World Englishes, English for Specific Purposes, conversation analysis and so on. When I am asked what I do, I struggle to find a recognisable label that could account for my work: over those ten years I have published articles relating to topics such as genre analysis, politeness theory, textbooks, collaborative writing, intertextuality and socialisation. The aim of this book is to pull these and my teaching together around a unifying theme.

Perhaps the best way to characterise the work that is discussed in this volume is to see it as situated at the interface between the academy and the workplace. Each of the areas addressed is a facet of workplace writing that affects the way in which texts are created and shaped, and that successful writers need to take account of, and that by implication can be addressed at some level pedagogically. This volume does not cover every conceivable feature of workplace writing, but a number of central elements that I believe to be influential. Nor is each chapter an absolutely comprehensive look at the issues covered, rather it is a discussion of certain features, and an attempt to show the ways in which they are key factors in workplace writing and to consider how they could be addressed to help students transitioning from the academy to the workplace. Wherever possible the points raised in the various chapters are illustrated or supported with examples from my own research. I hope that what emerges from these chapters is a clear and coherent picture of what is involved in workplace writing and of the challenges that this presents to our students, and at the same time I hope to stimulate thinking and discussion about how these challenges can be addressed. It is possible too that writing this book may also serve in helping define more clearly my own identity as an applied linguist.

From the outset, I would like to stress the necessary vagueness of the term "workplace". Much of the work discussed in this book could easily be placed under the umbrella of business communication, which is an established and largely recognised field that dominates the instructional landscape with its proliferation of textbooks, nearly all of which – perhaps of necessity – include the term "business communication" in their titles. However, to use this term would be to implicitly restrict the role of writing to that of an activity harnessed to the making of money. Despite the fact that financial considerations are never far away, evidenced, for example, in the gradual blurring of the notion of university as an institution of learning and as a corporate enterprise, there are nevertheless a range of functions achieved through writing in work settings that are less obviously directed towards money making. For this reason, the label of business communication is seen as potentially limiting. (See Darics (2015) for a different take on this issue.) The term "professional communication" has wider scope and applications, and while some researchers (e.g. Schnurr, 2013) see this as a "broad umbrella" that can include the factory floor, more traditional views of the term "professional" are still somewhat restrictive. Thus, the catch-all term "workplace" is preferred. Having said that, the work that is addressed in this volume should be seen as applicable to all areas of communication in workplace settings; the fundamental underlying principles and concerns are largely the same for writing and communication practices, whatever label is used to describe them.

A similar explanation should be made in relation to potential learners, particularly in respect of whether they are L1 (first language) or L2 (second language) users. As will be seen in the studies discussed in the different chapters, research and teaching have been conducted in a huge range of contexts, and while certain approaches to teaching workplace writing (e.g. English for Specific Purposes) are primarily targeted at L2 language users, and some (e.g. the New Rhetoric) place greater emphasis on other aspects of the writing process, this book will consider the distinction between L1 and L2 scenarios only when it is seen as pertinent, on the basis that the underlying issues and principles that relate to workplace writing are applicable in most situations, irrespective of the L1 of those involved.

A final point: it will be noted that the thrust of this book is largely instrumental, in that the aim of workplace writing is to get things done, and alongside this it can be seen that the thinking that underpins this book and my research more generally is largely informed by the university as a context for teaching and learning. However, I do not wish to suggest that the university is the only environment in which attempts to facilitate newcomers' transition into the workplace can or should be made; more importantly, without engaging in a wider discussion of the role of the university in society, I do not wish to imply that the primary role of universities is to provide workplace-oriented training.

ACKNOWLEDGEMENTS

I am grateful to Professor Anthony Paré for his insights and comments, and for very generously hosting me for a term at the University of British Columbia while I was writing this book. I have also benefited considerably from discussions with my former supervisor and co-editor, Professor Vijay Bhatia, and with my colleague Dr Christoph Hafner, both of whom took time to read chapters from the book. I am also indebted to the work of Katherine Miller, whose excellent book *Organizational Communication: Approaches and Processes* (2015) has been an enormously valuable source of information and stimulus in both my thinking and teaching relating to organisational culture and its relationship with communication.

1

THE WORKPLACE AND THE ACADEMY

Introduction

This book is founded on two premises. The first of these, as the title implies, is that in attempting to understand the nature of writing in workplace contexts, we need to look beyond the text: workplace writing is a complex business, requiring writers to consider a wide range of factors as they construct texts. The second is that despite the huge amount of related research that has been carried out in recent decades, much of this has failed to make its way into practical considerations of how workplace writing can be taught.

The complexity of workplace writing can be seen in the wealth of research that has been conducted over the last thirty years or so. There have, for example, been several important collections of papers that examine the socially constructed nature of workplace texts; in-depth studies of collaborative practices in specific organisations; investigations of organisational culture and its influence on communication practices; longitudinal studies of novice writers being socialised into different workplaces; genre analyses of sets of texts in specific professional contexts; examinations of the rich intertextual relations that characterise workplace writing, as well as studies of a number of other practices and phenomena relating to writing in professional settings. In combination, the complexities of writing addressed in this body of research add up to a substantial challenge for the student writer attempting to make the transition from the academy to the workplace, as well as for the teacher helping prepare students for this transition.

However, this rich trove of research is to a considerable degree fragmented, and has thus far not been pulled together to give a comprehensive picture of the challenges of workplace writing, as researchers have tended to focus on individual areas such as genre analysis, collaborative practices or socialisation processes, to name a few examples. This is perhaps an understandable consequence of the need on the part of researchers to investigate manageable elements of this highly involved process, but it can have the effect of implying that these are discrete phenomena, when in fact they are to a large extent interconnected. The presence of inter-textuality found in most workplace writing, for example, is very much linked to collaboration in that so much writing involves the appropriation of other people's texts, while an understanding of discourse community and organisational culture can be seen as an integral part of the socialisation process. There is, then, a need to bring together in one volume an account of the multiple factors that surround and impact on the process of workplace writing and the resulting textual products, and to give a sense of how these are interrelated.

The second premise for this book relates to the pedagogical perspective: text-books that address workplace writing can tend to overlook many of the factors that shape texts in the workplace, often adopting reductive approaches that see texts as standalone entities, free of any context. This book not only aims to provide an account of the various factors and issues that influence and shape workplace writing, but also to consider their pedagogical implications. Having said that, this volume is not intended to be a course book, nor is it intended to be prescriptive; rather, it is hoped that it can serve as a point of reference for anyone who wants to look beyond potentially simplistic accounts of workplace writing, whether researchers, teachers or students or even practitioners.

It should be stressed that although this book is about workplace writing, the central focus is not so much on text itself, but on the contextual considerations and activities surrounding the construction of texts. Bhatia (2010), in discussing the relative degrees of attention that have been given by researchers to text on the one hand, and context on the other, talks of "text-internal" and "text-external" fac-tors or resources: a focus on text alone would take into account the former, while research that sees context as having a key role would also look at the latter. Bhatia (2010, p. 34) notes that text-internal resources "have been well-researched within discourse and genre analytical literature", and this is certainly borne out by the substantial body of studies that have analysed texts in a variety of workplace settings.

In seeking to assign greater importance to context in his analysis of professional genres, Bhatia (2010, p. 33) proposes a model which takes account of various levels of context, and suggests that in addition to looking at the lexico-grammatical, rhe-torical and organisational resources of a given genre and its conventions, we need to consider the practices and culture of the relevant profession, discipline or institu-tion, saying that "any instance of professional communication simultaneously oper-ates and can be analysed at (these) four levels, as text, as representation of genre, as realization of professional practice, and as expectation of professional culture".

This book also acknowledges the significance of context but differs from Bhatia in terms of its motivations, in that it is more overtly concerned with the implica-tions for teaching and learning. There are of course tacit pedagogical implications in any enquiry that seeks to understand why workplace practitioners write in the ways that they do, which is the aim of much contemporary analytical investigation of genres in professional settings. But in taking a more directly pedagogical perspective, this work considers additional contextual factors which contribute to the construction of workplace texts that are pertinent to the transition from the academy to the workplace, such as collaborative practices and socialisation processes.

Given this book's concern with the challenges that the complexities of writing in the workplace pose for pedagogy, one area that is considered at the outset is the fundamental difference between the workplace and the academy, and this is addressed in the next section.

The workplace and the academy: a comparison

As Mabrito (1999, p. 105) explains, "We will never be able to exactly duplicate in our classrooms many of the constraints and pressures that writers experience in the workplace". There is little doubt that the two contexts differ in a number of ways: they represent and function as very distinct communities, with different cultures, aims and patterns of interaction. This section outlines ways in which the two contexts differ, and in effect will serve as a preview of the various elements of workplace writing that will be addressed in greater detail in subsequent chapters.

In describing and explaining aspects of these two contexts for writing, there is a risk of presenting them as binary entities with exclusive practices, and that attempting in one (the classroom) to prepare students for the other (the world of work) represents an almost impossible project. This would do a disservice to the many instructors who make considerable efforts in their teaching to somehow reduce the gap between the academy and the workplace. We see many reports in the literature of courses and projects that attempt to replicate features of workplace practices, with varying degrees of success – the work of Freedman, Adam and Smart (1994) representing just one example. Similarly, it is important to acknowledge that teaching and learning, both formal and informal, can take place in either context at various moments; as Roberts (2010, p. 211) points out: "The boundaries between education and work are no longer patrolled by time, with a period of formal education leading seamlessly to work." It should also be emphasised that there is considerable variety from workplace to workplace, and from classroom to classroom. Nevertheless, there are certain elements of the two contexts which are fundamentally different, and which have an unavoidable impact on the ways in which writing takes place, lending strength to Mabrito's somewhat gloomy contention, and it is these elements that are explained and discussed below.

Communities and cultures

The first consideration is the reason or basis on which the respective communities are formed, and the function that writing serves for them: workplace communities are constituted for the purposes of getting things done, whether it is manufacturing and selling a product for profit, managing a government department, running a charity or any other enterprise. Writing in these organisations serves to further those instrumental goals and might involve promoting, reporting, persuading or myriad other functions. Academic communities, on the other hand, are primarily constituted for the purpose of learning, thus most of the writing that takes place in these is intended to help develop writing skills or for the display of knowledge (Freedman and Adam, 1996) i.e. to demonstrate whether learning is taking place.

Closely connected to this is the kind of culture that will evolve in a given community – every workplace has its own specific culture, both professional and organisational, and with this culture come certain traditions, practices, expectations and so on. The culture of the classroom also has its own dynamic, and its own disciplinary influences and expectations. Of course, there will be variety from one classroom context to the next, but given that the central aim in such contexts is teaching and learning, however these are conceived and managed, these classroom cultures will generally be very different from those seen in the world of work.

This fundamental difference between the two communities and their cultures has an impact on many other elements of the workplace writing process, the composition of the different communities and the levels of diversity found in them being a major factor. Within workplace communities, differences among members can be seen in several respects. First, there is the role they play within the organisation, and the department or unit they represent, with the attendant interests and motivations; Dautermann (1993, p. 103), in her study of a hospital community, gives a sense of this kind of diversity: "Within the writing group, each writer represented a unit, a specialty, a hospital role, or a level of commitment to the hierarchy." Second, there will be varying levels of knowledge and experience. The third – often related – area of potential difference is that of status, which may be the result of a formal position or of social abilities, explained respectively by Bargiela-Chiappini and Harris (1996, p. 637) as "inherent status", which "results from holding a powerful position ... acknowledged by all members of the ... community and beyond", and "relative status", which is "enjoyed as a result of the power an individual can exercise in an inter-personal relationship".

Classroom communities, on the other hand, tend usually to be made up of students of a similar age and status, offering similar levels of knowledge and experience. It is perhaps overly simplistic to suggest that students are largely uniform in terms of what they bring to the classroom: there are likely to be differences among them in areas such as interest, motivation and, to some extent, knowledge and experience; greater differences might be seen among postgraduate student groups when compared with undergraduate groups; language proficiency, disciplinary background, culture and personality will all have a part to play too. Nevertheless, it is reasonable to posit that the degree of homogeneity in a student community, particularly in relation to workplace writing competence, is higher than would be seen in its workplace counterpart, a homogeneity that is strengthened by the students' shared aims when it comes to writing.

The different makeup of the communities in terms of these elements leads in turn to different types of interaction and varying contributions to the writing process. Contributions and inputs may be based on particular knowledge or skills that are possessed by participants in the process. The power and status that derive from position, experience and knowledge also play a part here. In this regard, Bhatia (2004) talks of the "participatory mechanisms" that can be found in workplaces, which in effect regulate who can contribute – and what they can contribute – to the writing process, a point considered by Yates and Orlikowski (2002, p. 17) in their discussion of "who is not empowered to initiate or receive certain genres" This question is related to motives for instituting collaborative writing groups in an organisation. Often, for example, the contributions of participants in a collaborative process are decided by management, so that best use can be made of individual talents, knowledge and experience. At the same time, organising people into teams can act as a form of control. However, as noted, writers may have different goals and interests according to their position or department, and this can add an extra dimension to interactions, requiring the negotiation of textual content and organisation, with the attendant possibility of conflict.

Meanwhile, by contrast, students generally share the same goals, offer similar levels of knowledge and experience, and for the most part enjoy similar status. The main reason that they collaborate is that they are required to – often as part of the assessment process. In most cases, they can decide themselves how they divide up tasks, and this division can be based on a number of factors (cf. Bremner, Peirson-Smith, Jones and Bhatia, 2014), perhaps relating to particular skills they might have, such as editing or design, if, for example, the written output is multimodal in nature. A further dimension to student collaboration is that the lack of status differentials can often result in interactions in student groups depending on personality and social skills alone, rather than external factors.

A major difference in the two contexts relates to the audiences for the written product. Workplace texts, with their instrumental "real world" goals are intended either for an audience within an organisation or for external readers, who are expected to take appropriate action on the basis of what they have read. The production of workplace-like texts in classroom contexts, however, although often similar in terms of language and content, usually has the display of knowledge as its goal, and most student output is only read by teachers, primarily for evaluative and developmental motives. These motives contrast with those of readers of texts created in real workplaces, as explained by Freedman *et al.* (1994), who say that in workplace writing "the prime concern is for what the reader can get from the text, not for what the writer got out of the process of writing" (p. 206). One other potential by-product of the objective of displaying knowledge and understanding on the part of the student writer is the inclusion of information that would not normally be expected or necessary in a workplace setting (Dovey, 2006).

Resources for writing

Not only do the two communities have different goals and audiences for their writing, but they also have access to and draw on different resources in constructing texts. This key difference is tied up with the notion of intertextuality, the "explicit and implicit relations that a text or utterance has to prior, contemporary and potential future texts" (Bazerman, 2004, p. 86). It is largely accepted that texts composed in professional settings draw on – and are shaped by – other texts in a variety of ways, whether referring specifically to other documents, taking shape within chains of emails or other interactions, incorporating the work of colleagues as part of the collaborative process, or being informed by the templates, practices and traditions that are specific to an organisational setting and which have evolved as a result of its institutional history.

Students, on the other hand, often have no other documents to refer to when doing their assignments. Rather, they work with a "scripted context" (Bremner, 2008) which tells them who they are and what they think and gives guidelines as to what to write. Indeed, despite the many studies that have identified the ways in which intertextuality plays out in professional contexts, there is little evidence that the fruits of this research are being applied in the classroom. Many course books, for example, appear to overlook this feature of workplace writing, treating texts as standalone, decontextualised entities, rather than components in wider systems of activity (ibid.).

Learning and socialisation

Finally, there is the question of learning and socialisation and how these are effected. Given the different aims and composition of communities in workplace and academic settings, it is to be expected that the two function quite differently as contexts for learning (Freedman and Adam, 1996). Every workplace organisation has its own specific goals that relate to the nature of its activities, and although these goals are paramount, learning does take place as newcomers engage in the organisation's work – this may be the incidental outcome of the interactions that surround the business of getting things done, or it may be the outcome of more considered schemes whereby newcomers and junior employees learn from colleagues with particular skills or experience (cf. Lave and Wenger, 1991). The diversity seen among employees is often the reason that such outcomes are possible. The academy, on the other hand, is set up with the primary goal of learning, but sources of information and guidance tend to be different in nature from those found in workplace settings, and are often restricted to textbooks and instructors. A key difference between the workplace and the classroom as contexts for learning is that in the former, skills are being acquired in the situations for which they are needed, while in the latter, skills are being acquired for future, as yet unspecified situations and purposes. Thus, the very nature of what is being learnt is different, and in the case of the classroom, often intentionally so.

As can be seen from this brief sketch of the differences between the workplace and the academy as contexts for writing and learning, there is a considerable gap in terms of expectations, opportunities, affordances and constraints, and this gap presents a challenge to students intending to make the transition from the classroom to the real world of work – and to teachers trying to help them make this transition. This book, by looking in detail at the various activities and related demands that surround workplace writing, is intended to provide a picture of what it takes to be a competent writer in the workplace, and to open up a little wider the discussion as to how the challenges relating to the transition from the academy to the workplace can be met.

Scope of the book

The book will consider a range of different factors that influence both the process of writing in the workplace and the textual outcomes of that process. However, it has been necessary in planning this volume to limit the scope of its examination. In selecting the factors to address, I have focused on those that I believe to be more closely and immediately linked to the writing process, and which represent concerns that relate to any workplace.

Inevitably, there will be areas omitted here that some readers may feel deserve coverage, and perhaps the most obvious of these is the question of the influence of culture upon writing, in the sense of national culture, as discussed in the work of Hall (1976), Hofstede (1983, 2001) and Scollon, Scollon and Jones (2011), in general terms and more specifically in workplace contexts by a host of researchers (e.g. Babcock and Du-Babcock, 2001; Bargiela-Chiappini, Bülow-Møller, Nickerson, Poncini and Zhu, 2003; Du-Babcock and Babcock, 1996; Nickerson and Van Nus, 1999). On this topic, Bhatia (1993), discussing the findings of Hofstede's (1983) study of national cultures in relation to genre, says that "Genre, after all, is a socio-culturally dependent event and is judged effective to the extent that it can ensure pragmatic success in the business or other professional context in which it is used" (p. 39), and in this way points to the potential influence both of expectations among readers in different cultural settings and of cross-cultural input in the workplace.

However, while there is little doubt that workplace interactions among multicultural workgroups will be influenced by the different cultural backgrounds of the individuals involved, it is less clear the extent to which this influence will feed into the documents that they produce. There are, of course, other types of culture that have an impact on the way in which participants in text construction interact and write, most obviously those which relate to the organisation or the profession that they are connected to. As will be seen in the coming chapters, notably Chapters 4 and 8, organisations have their own ways of doing things, and these are often made manifest in texts that writers are expected to produce, whether tacitly understood or more explicitly seen in templates prescribed by the organisation.

This begs the question of whether organisational culture has a greater influence on writing practices in workplace settings than the national culture of individual writers. Certainly, there is some debate as to the constraints that national culture will place on organisational communication practices (Gerhart, 2009; Hofstede, 2001), and Poncini (2003), considering this issue in the context of workplace interactions, suggests that "cultural values may be less useful when actual interaction is of interest, especially when individuals from a range of cultures are involved" (p. 76).

She goes on to talk of multicultural meetings which "seemed to have their own culture or sense of groupness not necessarily linked to national cultures" (p. 79). A similar point is considered by Nickerson (2003, p. 78) in relation to the evolution of business English as a lingua franca, a phenomenon whereby organisational members with different L1s (first languages) use English as their commonly held language to communicate. She cites Rogers (1998) in suggesting that "English has come to lead a life of its own as an ergolect, or work language, and has become largely disassociated from national culture", adding strength to the notion that national culture may be a lesser influence than that of the specific organisation on the communication practices found there. Thus, while recognising the importance of national culture as a factor in workplace interaction, this book will not deal with this issue specifically, taking the view that the influence of organisational culture is likely to be a more potent influence on the ways in which texts are constructed, and also acknowledging that there is already a considerable body of research relating to inter-cultural and cross-cultural communication.

It is of course not possible to provide exhaustive coverage of every issue relating to workplace writing, but it is nevertheless hoped that the key issues are covered in sufficient depth, and that the discussion of these can open up routes for further enquiry. The next section gives a brief outline of each chapter and the particular aspect of workplace writing that it looks at. It should be remembered that these different aspects of workplace writing are interconnected in many ways; addressing them in separate sections is a convenient way of structuring the book, but there will inevitably be a degree of overlap.

Structure of the book

A central issue relating to workplace writing is that it takes place in professional communities which have their own particular ways of writing: thus accountants, engineers or lawyers, for example, will take different approaches to writing as they deal with the demands of their respective jobs. Chapter 2 considers the relationship between workplace writing and the discourse communities in which it is produced. It also discusses an important related consideration, a central tenet of the social constructionist view of writing and more particularly genres – namely, that the texts which emerge from these professional groups play a role in shaping the communities in which they are produced, i.e. text and context have a mutually constitutive relationship in that each helps shape the other in a dynamic manner.

It is axiomatic that texts produced in workplace contexts are written with particular purposes and audiences in mind. Indeed, purpose is central to an understanding of workplace writing, and this is closely associated with the notion of genre. Chapter 3 considers the nature of genres and how they are viewed from the perspective of North American rhetorical genre studies and by proponents of analytical approaches espoused by the English for Specific Purposes school of thought. Genre analysis as an approach to understanding how workplace texts are constructed is also discussed in this chapter. This discussion goes beyond the consideration of text to the professional and socio-pragmatic factors that influence the ways in which texts are shaped (cf. Bhatia, 2004). The question of intended audience is also considered – whether the audience is internal or external, known or unknown, expert or non-expert will have an impact on the choices a writer will need to make with respect to language and register.

Workplace writing is not an isolated event; rather, it is a complex, intertextual process, whereby any text produced is the outcome of a set of interactions with other texts, both written and spoken. Much of the writing produced in the workplace is intertextual in that writers are responding to other texts or drawing on the work of their colleagues in using organisational templates or previous instances of a given genre (Devitt, 1991, 2004). This aspect of workplace writing and its implications for the ways in which practitioners approach the writing process are discussed in Chapter 4. The different ways in which intertextuality is perceived in the academy and the workplace – and the implications of this – are also examined.

Related to this is the idea that writing involves other people; indeed, as much as 75% to 85% of workplace writing is collaborative in nature (Burnett, 2001). Texts are typically contributed to by multiple writers, either directly or indirectly. This phenomenon is rendered more complex by the fact that participants often have different levels of knowledge, status and different motives for writing – a point made earlier in relation to the workplace and the classroom as contexts for writing. The collaborative nature of workplace writing makes a range of demands on writers, in that it involves interacting with colleagues and managing relationships. Chapter 5 highlights the importance of collaboration as a central feature of workplace writing, and discusses the findings from some significant studies conducted in recent years. It also looks at the differences between collaborating in the workplace and collaborating in academic contexts, and considers what implications these might have for the teaching of collaborative writing practices. This aspect of the writing process highlights the close relationship between writing and speaking in professional settings, again reminding us of the intertextual nature of this form of writing.

Chapters 6 and 7 look at the kinds of choices that writers face when composing in workplace settings, examining first the linguistic considerations that are tied up with power relationships between writers and readers, and then the question of channels of communication. Power relationships between writer and reader have a considerable impact on the writing process, particularly on the register (Halliday and Hasan, 1976) of a text, and most notably in the levels of politeness that writers deploy to achieve their aims in relation to a particular audience. There is a substantial body of research relating to power and politeness, and while much of this is concerned with spoken language, the underlying theories have also been applied to writing, although to a lesser extent. Chapter 6 looks at some of the work done in this area and considers what impact this can have on writers and people learning to write in professional settings. An important element of the discussion in this chapter is the notion that the enactment of power and politeness in workplace writing is a dynamic process in which text and context have a mutually constitutive relationship (Bremner, 2006; Holmes and Stubbe, 2003).

Choosing a channel of communication has an impact on the way a message is received, and on the process of crafting the message. Chapter 7 considers the factors affecting such choices, looking at issues such as the relationship between media richness and the complexity or ambiguity of a message, and reasons why writers and organisations more generally choose a particular medium to communicate. It also looks at the challenges that are posed by composing in different channels, as well as the skills that are necessary to deal with the affordances and constraints of new media, such as the ability to rework text to fit into digital formats, or to handle multimodal text.

Chapters 8 and 9 are concerned with organisational culture and socialisation processes and the ways that these are interlinked components of the assimilation of a writer into a particular workplace. An issue addressed in Chapter 2, workplace writing takes place in discourse communities that have their own way of viewing and doing things. This also applies to individual organisations – every organisation has its own culture, the result of particular values and beliefs about how things should be done, and which is evidenced in artefacts and behaviours ranging from office layout and dress codes to communication practices such as decision-making and conflict management. Writing, then, needs to be understood and acquired with reference to an organisation's culture. Chapter 8 highlights the various elements that can contribute to the culture of an organisation and discusses the importance of understanding this phenomenon from the perspective of a new entrant to the workplace, in that effective participation in an organisation depends to a considerable extent on an ability to read its culture and thereby to produce appropriate discourse.

Socialising into an organisation can be a long and often complex process, involving the acquisition of understanding and skills that are particular to the organisation in question. It is generally understood that a central element of becoming an accepted member of a workplace community is acquiring the discourse of that community (Li, 2000). Chapter 9 compares the academy and the workplace as contexts for learning to write, considering the contentious issue of whether specific writing skills can be effectively acquired outside the contexts in which they are to be used. It goes on to discuss the growing body of studies that have investigated socialisation processes in professional contexts, as well as considering the various factors that can contribute to or hinder effective socialisation.

The final chapter draws together the various features of workplace writing that make it such a rich process, and which make it so distinctive from other types of writing. It revisits and discusses the implications these features and differences have for the teaching and acquisition of workplace writing. More specifically, it looks at the kinds of activity that are on offer in textbooks aimed at writing in the workplace, and considers their merits and limitations before going on to outline in general terms possible approaches and activities that might help students in the transition from the academy to the workplace.

2

WORKPLACE COMMUNITIES AND WORKPLACE WRITING

Introduction

Chapter 1 outlines the key differences between the academy and the workplace, and in so doing makes clear that these are fundamentally distinct contexts and communities with very different goals. It is now necessary to delve deeper into the nature of workplace communities and explain why an understanding of what happens there is a crucial element of the process of preparing students for the transition from their own community to that of the workplace.

The challenge that faces students as they make the bid to transition from one community to another is famously and eloquently captured by Bartholomae (1985, p. 134):

> Every time a student sits down to write for us, he (sic) has to invent the university for the occasion – invent the university, that is, or a branch of it, like history or anthropology or economics or English. The student has to learn to speak our language, to speak as we do, to try on the peculiar ways of knowing, selecting, evaluating, reporting, concluding, and arguing that define the discourse of our community.

While this is concerned with what it takes to be a student in a university, the essence of the issue remains – every group, every institution, every discipline, every profession, every organisation has its own way of doing things, its own way of thinking, its own way of working towards its goals, and its own way of speaking and writing about them, and to become a successful participant in a community, it is necessary to acquire the ways of doing things that are specific to that community. What underlies this is the idea that language and community have an interlinked, mutually constitutive relationship, and that the key to entering a workplace community rests to a considerable extent in learning its particular language and its ways of thinking. Three central notions and their implications are explained and discussed in this chapter, namely social constructionism, discourse community and genre.

As explained previously, the various factors that impact on workplace writing are very much interconnected, and there is a potential overlap between this chapter and other chapters in this volume, most notably Chapter 3, which looks at genre analysis, Chapter 8, which is concerned with organisational culture, and Chapter 9, which looks at processes of socialisation. This chapter will be mainly focused on the nature of professional and disciplinary communities and the close relationship between language and community, introducing the concept of genre. Chapter 3 develops the idea of genre, looking at approaches to genre analysis and related issues; Chapter 8 is concerned with the culture that is evidenced through the artefacts and behaviours that can be seen in different organisations; while Chapter 9 will refer to issues discussed in Chapters 2 and 8, focusing primarily on how the knowledge, skills and awareness required to enter and participate successfully in communities and cultures can be acquired.

The three key notions addressed in this chapter are so interconnected that it is difficult to disentangle them from one another for the purposes of discussion. Nevertheless, this chapter will attempt to do so, first by providing a brief explanation of each and an account of how they function together, before going on to discuss each concept in more detail, citing studies that have illustrated this interrelationship in various workplace settings. The discussion will look at why these concepts are so central to the business of preparing students for the world of work, and will consider the implications for the classroom, highlighting the gap that inevitably exists between academic and workplace communities in this respect, and finally will tackle the oft-visited question of how specific we should be when it comes to teaching the language of discourse communities.

As mentioned, the three notions are interdependent. Generally speaking, a discourse community is a group with shared aims that produces and interacts around texts intended to serve those aims; these texts are known as genres and, as the product of the shared-group enterprise, can be seen as socially constructed. It should be pointed out that although the focus of this book is workplace writing, concepts such as those discussed here relate to workplace communication more generally – they are not specifically or exclusively related to writing, but they have considerable ramifications for our understanding of writing in workplace settings and for the practice of writing itself.

Social constructionism

Social constructionism, as the name implies, is the notion that texts and many other elements of a group that have come together for a particular purpose, whether disciplinary or professional or even recreational, are constructed by and are an integral part of that group and its practices. Bruffee (1986) explains that taking a social constructionist position "assumes that entities we normally call reality, knowledge, thought, facts, texts, selves, and so on are constructs generated by communities of like-minded peers" (p. 774), going on to explain that "Concepts, ideas, theories, the world, reality and facts are all language constraints generated by knowledge communities, and used by them to maintain community coherence" (p. 777). The social constructionist view of genre, according to Blyler and Thralls (1993), "focuses on community, viewing communal entities as the sources of knowledge maintained by consensual agreement ... and as the bodies to which non-members must – through collaboration – be acculturated" (pp. 13–14). This contention highlights two key issues: the centrality of community to the construction of texts, and the idea that these communities represent a target group to which outsiders wishing to become insiders must aspire, becoming proficient in the texts and practices of the community in the process. This second point will be addressed later in this chapter.

Discourse communities

The idea of community in relation to both disciplinary and professional contexts has been the source of much interest and has generated a variety of terms and definitions. Kwan (2014), in an extensive discussion of the relationship between communities and discursive practices, identifies three commonly deployed categories of community, namely, scientific community, discourse community and community of practice. These categories differ in their emphasis and highlight certain features over others, the "result of their epistemic origins and orientations" (Kwan, 2014, p. 447), but at the same time share a number of attributes, including a coherence that derives from joint goals, norms and values, which in turn engenders a repertoire of "knowledge, techniques, tools, semiotic resources, communicative mechanisms, which are all essential to the sustenance of the community" (ibid. p. 447).

The notion of scientific community (Kuhn, 1977), pertaining as it does to scientists rather than a broader field, will not be considered in this chapter, which will focus on the term discourse community. As for the term "community of practice" (Lave and Wenger, 1991), this is connected to the idea that newcomers to an organisation learn through participation in the community and through interaction with old-timers there. Kwan (2014) explains the term as not just a theoretical concept, but "shorthand for the social theory of learning that Lave and Wenger (1991) attempted to develop" (p. 446). A very important and relevant concept for the question of socialisation into workplace communities, the community of practice will be examined and discussed at greater length in Chapter 9.

"Discourse community" as a term has been the subject of much discussion, without any consensus being reached as to its definitive nature. Kent (1991) sees a cline of views, contrasting "thick formulations that depict a community as a determinate and codifiable social entity" with "thin formulations that depict a community as a relatively indeterminate and uncodifiable sedimentation of beliefs and desires" (p. 425); Hyland (2016) contends that the term is "one of the most indeterminate in the writing literature" (p. 26), while Kwan (2014) observes that the various terms for community discussed in her article are often used loosely and interchangeably.

Swales (1990), as a genre and discourse analyst, has offered a detailed attempt at defining the idea of discourse community, and it is worth examining this in that it raises several important points relevant to the thrust of this chapter. In seeking to narrow down the definition of what he saw as an uncertain concept, he suggests a number of characteristics, including an agreed set of common goals, mechanisms for communication among members for the provision of information and feedback and a threshold level of members who have sufficient content and discourse knowledge. He also stresses the centrality of active communication in saying that it is not sufficient simply to belong to the same profession – basically, if you don't communicate then you're not a member of the discourse community. A very pertinent characteristic for the purposes of this chapter is the stipulation that the community "utilizes and hence possesses one or more genres in the communicative furtherance of its aims" (p. 26) i.e. not only do these communities have their own agreed goals and practices but they have their own language for realising these.

As Kwan (2014, p. 446) explains, this definition "underscores shared discursive conventions and norms as the major criteria used to define a discourse community". However, it would seem from a reading of Swales' (1990) explanation of this slippery concept that his focus is primarily on what happens *within* the professional community i.e. on the communication that takes place among the members who either have the requisite knowledge and expertise or those who seek to acquire these, be they engineers or doctors or accountants or any other group. This perspective implies a relatively tight conception of the notion of discourse community, and also a potentially restricted view of the discourse that its members use to go about their business, a point raised by Bex (1996) and Devitt, Bawarshi and Reiff (2003) in their discussions of the asymmetry that can be seen in communications between expert members of a community and addressees who are not part of that group. Certainly, much of the work and communication that characterises a community takes place within that community, but there is increasing recognition of the fact (e.g. Hafner, 2014) that many professional communities are required to communicate their ideas and stances to a wider audience that does not necessarily share the genres or technical language of the discourse community in question.

This requirement is explained by some of the professional informants interviewed in the final section of Bhatia and Bremner's (2014) *Handbook of Language and Professional Communication*. The banker, for example, explains that members of the profession "need to understand the technical language, which is used in banking documents, and they should have the ability to transform that banking information into simple language for a layman (sic), for an individual investor who is not hugely qualified to understand the jargon" (p. 536). Similarly, a public relations (PR) informant in Hong Kong talks about public engagement as part of a practitioner's work: "the audience is Joe Chan, on a public housing estate, so you've got to de-jargonise everything – plain 'lay language' is king" (ibid., p. 568).

If, as seems evident from these observations, the ability to communicate in non-specialist language with "laypeople" is part of a professional's repertoire, then speaking and writing to people outside the immediate professional group should not be regarded as communicative activity that is outside the purview of the discourse community. As the banker in Bhatia and Bremner (2014) explains, a member of his profession needs "the ability to suggest and explain the kinds of products or schemes that your clients may find attractive" (p. 535). This, of course, will entail language that is accessible to the layperson, rather than what might be considered specialist discourse or jargon. But there will, in the banking community, be accepted ways of selling products to lay clients that have been developed over time, and these will be seen as established genres in the discourse community in the same way that internal documents dense with specialist lexis will be. Similar situations are seen in a range of areas, a notable example being that of healthcare, as has been extensively reported in, for example, Sarangi and Roberts (1999), Sarangi and Candlin (2003) and Iedema (2007), although much of this is concerned with spoken rather than written discourse. Also, noteworthy in this regard is the work of Harris (2003), who looked at a selection of sites of institutional discourse, namely magistrates' courts, doctors' surgeries and the reception area of a police station.

There may also be a need to communicate with other specialists who have their own discourse communities. Smart (2006), for example, in his study of the practices of the Bank of Canada considers the genres employed by the bank for communicating externally with outside groups such as the government and the business sector. Meanwhile, Palmeri (2004) reports the interactions among attorneys, nurse consultants and writers in a law firm as they collaborated to produce various documents, and highlights the issues and conflicts that emerged as members of these different communities, with their own "beliefs about appropriate discursive conventions, epistemological standards, and definitions of technical terms" (p. 38) came together.

The preceding discussion raises the question of whether a discourse community can be as narrowly defined as Swales (1990) implies. Barton (2007, pp. 75–6), for example, prefers a more inclusive definition that comprises both writers and readers:

> A discourse community is a group of people who have texts and practices in common, whether it is a group of academics, or the readers of teenage magazines. In fact, discourse community can refer to the people the text is aimed at; it can be the people who read the text; or it can refer to the people who participate in a set of discourse practices by both reading and writing.

Such a definition widens the net of those who might be considered to be community members, and also reminds us of the lack of consensus regarding the exact nature of discourse communities. Ultimately, though, there may be no need to pin this notion down definitively – however broadly or narrowly conceived the term is, the idea that there is a relationship between discourse communities and texts is widely accepted, and the focus should be on the value of this idea and how it can help in our understanding of writing practices.

Indeed, as Hyland (2016) intimates, the fact that the concept of discourse community is somewhat fuzzy does not necessarily diminish its power as an explanatory tool. It has been useful in academic writing to show how different disciplines within the larger academic community have their own ways of writing particular genres, such as essays and reports, and that "the ability to produce them does not involve generic writing skills" (p. 27). A lab report for a biology class, for example, will display different features from those seen in its counterpart in a business context.

A simple – and early – illustration of the value of highlighting variation found in different disciplines i.e. discourse communities, can be seen in Flowerdew (1993); adapting material from Tribble (1991), he shows through the use of a concordance how the word "say" is used in the disciplines of history and engineering respectively. In the former, it is used most often to report, as in "it is a facile answer to say that Elizabeth ought ...", whereas in the latter it is more commonly used to exemplify, as in "An infinite heat source of, say, 300 degrees ..." (1993, p. 311). There is much value in work of this kind, and many other studies have examined variation in research papers across academic disciplines, either looking at particular sections, such as Introductions (Samraj, 2002) or Discussion Sections (Peacock, 2002), or at more specific linguistic features. Peacock has been particularly active in this regard, with his analysis of the use of boosters (Peacock, 2006) and adverbials (Peacock, 2010) across a variety of disciplines, to mention a couple of examples. Studies that show the ways in which language serves the needs of workplace communities are discussed later in this chapter.

Genres and communities

A central point that was touched upon above in explaining the basic notion of social constructionism is the idea that the various constructs and communicative resources that make up the repertoire of a particular community are not simply elements that belong to the community, but contribute in a mutually constitutive way to the shaping of the community. As Hyland (2016, p. 25) explains: "Through notions of community we can see writing as a means by which organisations actually constitute themselves, and how individuals signal their membership in them." This idea is seen in Bruffee (1986), who talks of the language generated by communities being "used by them to maintain community coherence" (p. 777), while Kwan (2014) points to community repertoires as being "essential to the sustenance of the community" (p. 447).

This leads on to the question of what form these linguistic repertoires take, i.e. the key notion of genre. Hyland (2016, p. 26), echoing Pogner (2003), says that "it is the routine practices and conventions they use which turns groups into communities". A community's texts do not appear overnight, rather they develop over time (Swales, 1990), and as they develop into recognised ways of carrying out the work of the group, so the community forms, constituted by its genres.

To consider more specifically how these texts or genres come to be, an invaluable point of reference is Miller's (1984) article "Genre as social action", in which she characterises genres as "typified rhetorical actions based on recurrent situations" (p. 159). In other words, genres evolve from the responses that different groups make to particular social needs. A very basic example of a genre might be that of the postage stamp, which evolved from the need for a text that showed that an appropriate sum of money had been paid for a letter or package to be delivered, the result being a very simple (usually adhesive) text that displays the information needed to meet this objective, i.e. the name of the country of origin (or, in the unusual case of the United Kingdom, an image of the head of the monarch) and the price paid. This is an example of a genre that stabilised relatively quickly, and one which has not changed much since the early stamps of the mid-nineteenth century. Another example is the air ticket, which illustrates a genre that has retained the basic information seen as necessary by the community, while its shape has evolved in line with developments in mediational tools – it still includes much of the same information (passenger's name, airline, flight number, point of departure, destination, time, etc.), but has changed more noticeably in form, developing in recent years from a small paper booklet containing carbon copies to an electronic document.

The texts, then, that emerge as responses to these recurrent situations are the products of particular social contexts in which a group has come together to meet the exigencies of the situation. But in seeing writing as a socially constructed activity (Miller, 1984), we are not looking down a one-way street, and this is a crucial point – not only does the social context influence the shape of the genres that emerge, but these genres also contribute to the construction of those social contexts and communities. It is a mutually constitutive relationship in which genre and context are inextricably linked and by extension should not be studied independently of each other. This point is demonstrated by Pogner (2003) in his study of a discourse community of engineers, in which he looks at the ways in which certain texts evolved within the community, showing that the production and revision of these texts by the engineers:

> are not only cognitive problem-solving and communication processes … but also means of negotiating professional standards and roles; defining strategic functions of texts and genres; establishing, maintaining, or changing social and professional relationships; and contributing to changing the text's and interaction's context by helping the readers/users of the text carry out their own complex technical and business tasks.
>
> *(p. 865)*

In other words, as Pogner goes on to explain, the processes of drafting and revising various texts are shaped by the community, but also play a part in constructing the community through the acts of "reifying, reproducing, negotiating, modifying, or changing" (ibid., p. 865) its norms and conventions.

The second important feature of genres is their fluid, dynamic nature. As Berkenkotter and Huckin (1993, p. 481) point out, the world changes and individuals bring their knowledge of the world to the interpretation of genres; these factors, they suggest, mean that genres "are inherently dynamic, constantly (if gradually) changing over time in response to the sociocognitive needs of individual users".

The example of the air ticket explained above is an illustration of the changing nature of genre realisations. Key studies in academic contexts, which look at the dynamic nature of genres, include Bazerman (1988), who demonstrates how the experimental research article has changed, and Dudley-Evans and Henderson (1990, 1993), looking at economics articles. As for workplace contexts, Yates and Orlikowski (1992) in a much-cited article examine the development of the office memo as it is shaped by changes in management philosophy. Their approach is partly based on structuration theory (Giddens, 1984), which "involves the production, reproduction and transformation of social institutions, which are enacted through individuals' use of social rules" (Yates and Orlikowski, 1992, p. 299). Swales (1990) and Bhatia (1995) also suggest that genres take time to evolve, the latter saying that genres are "often not recognisable till they become somewhat standardised" (p. 1).

Genre: a definition

As mentioned in the Introduction to this chapter, the next chapter will examine genres and genre analysis. Specifically, it will look at the development of approaches to understanding and analysing genres, as well as factors to consider when conducting a genre analysis. For the purposes of this chapter, the following definition of genre is offered: "Genres are recognizable communicative events, characterized by a set of communicative purposes identified and mutually understood by members of the professional or academic community in which they regularly occur" (Bhatia, 2004, p. 23). This particular definition, which in some respects derives from an earlier and more extensive definition offered by Swales (1990), is by no means comprehensive and certainly does not represent the depth of analysis that Bhatia has applied to an enormous range of texts over a long career of genre analysis, but it will serve as a working definition for the remaining sections of this chapter and beyond. In keeping with the discussions here, the definition clearly acknowledges the relationship between genres and the communities in which they are found, as well as the idea that genres are the outcome of recurring responses to particular needs.

The view of genres and communities represented in the foregoing discussion has important implications for those preparing to make the transition from the academy to the workplace. If we take the position that genres are the socially constructed outcome of the interactions of discourse communities, then the key to entering these communities is through gaining an understanding of how they function, and of how their genres are constructed. Berkenkotter and Huckin (1993) suggest that the acquisition of genre knowledge is the outcome of participation in communicative activities, claiming too that we can learn much about the norms and ideologies of a discourse community from the conventions of a genre. They talk of genre knowledge as "a form of 'situated cognition' which continues to develop as we participate in the activities of the culture" (p. 478).

From a pedagogical perspective, the first route towards understanding and acquiring the necessary genre knowledge mentioned by Berkenkotter and Huckin

(1993) – participation in the communicative activities of the target community – presents the obvious challenge that bedevils the teaching of workplace writing, and which will become something of a theme and lament as this book proceeds: the simple fact that the context afforded by the academy, and the community within it, is far removed from its counterpart in the workplace. Mawer (1999) implicitly highlights this almost intractable difference between the two contexts, suggesting in her discussion of workplace language and literacy programmes that, "To a large extent, the workplace itself becomes the curriculum, with its particular explicit and implicit dynamics, purposes and methodologies" in that "the communicative context of the workplace shapes what needs to be learnt" (p. 60).

If participation in the activities of the target community is not a feasible option, the second point made by Berkenkotter and Huckin (1993), namely, that the conventions of a genre can provide insights into the norms and ideologies of a discourse community, offers another route to understanding and acquiring genre and community knowledge. The wealth of related research available is very helpful in opening up this route, as genres have been studied in a wide variety of workplace settings. However, it should be stressed that while the study of genres offers a potential way into uncovering the norms of a discourse community, it is important to look beyond the text alone. Indeed, for a fuller sense of a community's practices, texts should not be considered standalone entities, either from an analyst's or writer's perspective; they are components in much larger cycles of activity and need to be understood in that way. Every community has not only its own texts, but its own ways of putting those texts together, and there is still a great deal to be learnt about this aspect of workplace writing. Kwan (2014) voices some concern about this issue, suggesting that a "predominant focus on discoursal attributes of specific genres in specific communities seems to have overshadowed work that deals with other less pursued and yet important aspects of the writing practices in some communities" (p. 449). It is fair to say that there is a large body of studies that have focused primarily on the discoursal features of texts (e.g. Ghadessy, 1993), but there is also a growing collection of papers that have examined disciplinary and workplace writing practices through a wider lens, taking into account many of the contextual factors and processes that contribute to the construction of genres in particular communities. Elements of workplace writing activity that are being increasingly investigated include the ways in which texts combine with other texts to serve the goals of the community, and the ways in which people work together to create texts, i.e. the phenomena of intertextuality and collaboration. These are touched on in the studies discussed in this chapter, but are addressed more fully in Chapters 4 and 5 respectively.

Studies of discourse communities

This section references a variety of collections and studies focused on particular communities or workplaces, and looks at one or two areas in greater detail to illustrate the explanatory power of this kind of research.

A substantial number of studies have been conducted within the perspective of the New Rhetoric, a view of genres that embraces the tenets of social constructionism, and which will be discussed at greater length in Chapter 3. Well-known early examples that focus on disciplinary communities include Bazerman's (1988) study of scientific research articles and Myers' (1990) analysis of the writing of biologists. As for the workplace, Miller's (1984) conception of genre as a form of social action can perhaps be seen as the catalyst for several collections of papers looking at the nature of workplace writing and its relationship with social contexts, for example, Bazerman and Paradis (1991); Bishop and Ostrom (1997); Freedman and Medway (1994a, 1994b); Odell and Goswami (1985); Spilka (1993).

In addition to these, there has been a considerable number of studies located in specific communities. Notable early examples include Devitt's (1991) examination of the function of text in the tax accountancy community and Yates and Orlikowski's (1992) investigation of office genres. More recent work has looked at engineering (Pogner, 2003), the academic community (Hyon and Chen, 2004), tax accountants (Flowerdew and Wan, 2006), land surveyors (Cheng and Mok, 2008) and PR (Bremner, 2014a). The last three studies are revisited in Chapter 4, as, in addition to providing insights into the communities under study, they also highlight issues relating to intertextuality.

Some of the most illuminating research into different communities has come from longitudinal studies, an interesting example being Swales's (1998) textography of a small university building in North America, in which, as Bazerman (1998, p. ix) puts it in his introduction, "Through analysis of text, of textual forms, and of systems of texts, we are shown the lives, life commitments, and life projects of people deeply embedded in the literate culture of the university". Other examples include Nickerson's study of the communicative practices of a multinational in the Netherlands (1998) and Winsor's (2003) examination of the writing processes of engineers. Also worth mentioning is the work of Cross (1994, 2001), which is discussed more fully in Chapter 5, given its focus on collaborative writing practices, and of Beaufort, who looks at the writing activities in a US job resource centre (1997, 1999, 2000) and in so doing provides insights into what a writer needs to know to participate in the community. Her research has provided a major contribution to our understanding of socialisation processes, and is revisited in Chapter 9.

The work of Graham Smart in relation to the Bank of Canada (1993, 1998, 2000, 2006) merits particular attention, not only because it is the result of more than twenty years' research and association with the institution, but because it is a powerful illustration of the concepts discussed in this chapter. Smart explains his methodology – interpretive ethnography – as a powerful means of investigating the ways in which professional communities construct specialised knowledge, going on to state that central to his study are "current views on the indivisible, mutually constitutive relationship between discourse ... and disciplinary knowledge" (2006, p. 10) and "the socio-rhetorical notion that it is through their discourse practices that members of professional organizations collaborate in creating and applying the specialized knowledges they need for accomplishing their work" (2006, p. 11).

Drawing on activity theory (Engeström, 1987; Russell, 1997) he shows how the knowledge-building and policy-making that take place in the bank are mediated by four "cultural tools" (i.e. genres), also demonstrating that these cultural tools can evolve and be modified as community members go about the business of construct-ing knowledge. This captures the key idea underpinning social constructionism, namely that there is a reciprocal and dynamic relationship between the community and its communicative repertoire, which Smart sums up in this way: "professional organizations advance in their work by building achieved knowledge into their tools, which are then in turn used to engender new knowledge" (2006, p. 107).

A discourse community: the PR industry and its practices

The theme of this chapter, underpinned by the three interlinked notions of social constructionism, discourse community and genre, is that every profession, dis-cipline, group, organisation and so on has its own way of doing things and of speaking and writing about them. This is very evident in the world of PR, and a brief account of recent studies of this industry is presented here to make this point regarding the particularity of discourse communities, and also to highlight the importance and value of researching practices in different workplaces, on the basis that understanding these offers a potential way into their communities.

Like any other industry, PR has its own way of constructing knowledge, draw-ing on certain genre configurations and engaging in particular patterns of interac-tion to achieve its goals. At the heart of much of the activity in the PR industry sits the press release, and as one of its central genres this has been the focus of a number of studies, which have looked variously at its different communication purposes and multiple receiver roles (Catenaccio, 2008), its text structure and generic fea-tures (McLaren and Gurău, 2005; Tench, 2003), contextual factors that shape the genre (Catenaccio, 2008; Lindholm, 2008) and the processes surrounding its pro-duction and promulgation (Bremner, 2014a; Sleurs and Jacobs, 2005).

What is particularly interesting about the press release is the issue of its intended aim and audiences. The central idea behind the genre in its original conception is that it will be repackaged in some way by journalists for their own readers. How-ever, it is largely accepted that press releases, given that they are nowadays readily accessible on the internet and through other channels, have an audience beyond the press. Thus, this genre, according to Jacobs (2006), is characterised by a special "participation framework", in which the target audience is a "more general reading public" as well as journalists, resulting in "a kind of indirectly targeted, projected discourse" (p. 200).

The issue of multiple potential readers, aside from raising questions about the composition of discourse communities (see the discussion above regarding the definitions proposed by Swales (1990) and Barton (2007)), has considerable impli-cations for the ways in which press releases are framed. If one of the writer's inten-tions is for the content of the release to be repackaged by journalists for their readers, then a central aim would be to make that task as easy as possible for the journalist; the perfect press release, then, could simply be transferred verbatim into the medium that the journalist worked with. This is, of course, a highly unlikely scenario, but press release writers would nevertheless be looking at ways to make this transfer easier. This leads to the phenomenon of "preformulation" (Jacobs, 1999), explained as working towards "a news style that requires little or no reworking on the part of the journalists who receive them" (Jacobs, 2006, p. 201). A related practice is the use of "pseudo-quotes" (Sleurs, Jacobs and Van Waes, 2003), in which direct speech is attributed to someone associated with the issue, but which was not actually uttered by that person (Bell, 1991). These pseudo-quotes lend a 'newsy' feel to the text, and the fact that the manufactured speech is often attributed to an authoritative voice indicates the intention of giving credibility to the story. Another noticeable feature of press releases is that the protagonists, even though they are writing about themselves, will refer to themselves in the third person rather than the first, as this also eases the possible transition from press release to news article.

Thus, it can be seen that certain textual practices are specifically connected to the needs and aims of the PR industry, demonstrating the central thesis of the chapter, namely, that discourse communities have their own ways of doing things, and – equally important – their own reasons for doing them in these ways. But as explained earlier, looking at a text – in this case the press release – in isolation to try and understand how and why particular practices are enacted is not enough, and studies which investigate the processes surrounding the construction of these texts, and the ways in which they combine and interact with other texts, can give us a fuller picture of the community's way of doing things.

My own work in this area (Bremner, 2014a) was carried out with this in mind, building on a number of the studies referenced above, with the aim of going deeper into the community to look at the processes surrounding the construction of press releases. The study was based primarily on the daily journal of an intern working with a PR company for three months. During this period, she was closely involved in the process – from beginning to end – of producing and pitching press releases, and her journal of around 150 pages provides a detailed account of how this process is enacted, along with insights into practices that are specific to this process and the industry more generally.

Zachry (2000a) suggests that "organizational participants rely on long chains of more-or-less routine, genre-mediated communicative exchanges" (p. 63), and these emerged as the intern described and explained three pivotal cycles of activity in the production and promulgation of a press release, namely, brainstorming, drafting/revising and media pitching, which together form what Bazerman (1994) describes as a "typical sequence". The study identified different associated genres and collaborative interactions, along with certain distinctive features. The first is that the process was very dynamic in nature and the writing highly recursive, as the press releases underwent multiple drafts. This was not simply a case of finetuning a constant message, but of incorporating new information and updates from the client, accommodating input from colleagues, and making modifications to orient the release to different audiences. Once the written text was finalised, it would then need to be pitched orally to the press, requiring further repackaging of the information for the telephone pitch. The second notable feature of the process was the high levels of intertextual influence – the releases drew on a variety of texts, including previous client-related work, the client's website, and promotional texts previously produced for other clients of the agency. (The incidence of intertextuality in relation to press releases is also observed by Lindholm (2008), Pander Maat (2008) and Sleurs *et al.* (2003), and is revisited in Chapter 4.) Finally, the process was very collaborative in nature, with multiple inputs coming from both the client and colleagues.

The findings suggest that a prominent feature of PR practice is the need for writers to rework and repackage information, adapting it to the requirements of different audiences and communication channels. Thus, the study uncovers aspects of writing in the PR community and the underlying reasons for the process playing out in a particular way that perhaps could not be identified through the examination of discoursal features alone (cf. Kwan, 2014). An extra dimension to the research is that it gives us the perspective of an intern, i.e. a newcomer, thus providing insights regarding how they feel on entering the community and engaging with its practices, and also how they negotiate the early stages of participation in its activities, which, as noted earlier, Berkenkotter and Huckin (1993) see as a necessary means of acquiring the community language. In taking this approach, the study concludes by suggesting what it might take to work successfully with press releases: the ability to manage a constantly evolving and interconnected process, and above all the ability "to rework and repackage information on a regular basis, an activity that requires an understanding of the relationships between mode and audience and text" (Bremner, 2014a, p. 275).

The study addressed just one aspect of the writing activities of the PR industry, albeit a central one, and it is hoped that the findings have added, if only infinitesimally, to the growing body of understanding of this particular discourse community, and that it can help address what Hyland calls "the imperative to inform classroom decisions with knowledge of the language features, tasks and practices of particular communities" (2002, p. 386). As explained above, the study is described here in order to help illustrate the point that communities have specific writing practices that are the outcome of their particular needs and purposes.

Conclusion

Several issues relating to community membership and community knowledge need to be raised before this chapter concludes. The first is that the dynamic nature of genre development and the changing nature of the workplace (which are not unconnected) necessitate ongoing investigation of the communicative practices of different communities. To take the banking industry as an example, our own everyday experience of accessing account information, of buying foreign currency, of paying our bills, to name a few examples, have all seen gradual changes as banking has developed, particularly as it has moved online. Meanwhile, an illustration of the ways in which new genres can evolve within a community comes from an interview with a banker in Bhatia and Bremner (2014), in which he explains a mode of communication that has developed as an alternative to email because of the volume of email that arose from copying groups into every message:

> there are systems and ways by which bankers started doing the internal chat system. So we have an inter-enterprise chat system whereby … if I need just to deal with you … I would work on the chat rather than sending an email. That is also a genuine mode of communication … that's also stored and recorded.
>
> *(p. 542)*

The ways in which bankers – and other workplace discourse communities – managed their communicative goals thirty years ago, even ten years ago, may be very different from the ways they do this today, and as researchers we need to revisit these different professional sites regularly to see how they are changing.

The second point is that we should not view communities as hermetically sealed entities with their own monolithic discourse. Kwan (2014) talks of their "porosity and overlapping nature" (p. 453), and this has implications both for the discourses found in different communities, and for the members of these communities as they interact both within and outside the community. One phenomenon that has been increasingly observed is that of interdiscursivity, which "can be viewed as appropriation of semiotic resources across genres, professional practices and disciplinary cultures" (Bhatia, 2008, p. 162). This is a potentially problematic notion from a research perspective, in that it implies that certain discourses "belong" to particular professional or disciplinary communities, and the issue of how to account for interdiscursively appropriated discourse, for instance, whether it should be considered as part of a community's practices or as a particular "discourse mode" (Bax, 2011) is one that needs further questioning (and this will be addressed in Chapter 3). Nevertheless, the very phenomenon of interdiscursivity lends strength to the idea that discourse communities are porous in nature.

It is also necessary to dispel the idea from the perspective of aspiring community members that there is a single community discourse that needs to be mastered – practitioners need to be able to communicate in multiple ways and with a variety of audiences. On the one hand, they do need the ability to communicate with fellow specialists, as the lawyer in Bhatia and Bremner (2014) explains: "A good attribute for a lawyer … is the ability to skillfully interact with other lawyers. Many conflicts (between lawyers) can be resolved through discussions and through conciliation and mediation" (p. 548). But on the other hand, as has been discussed, the ability to mediate their work to non-specialists and to specialists in other communities (Hafner, 2014; Palmeri, 2004; Smart, 2006) is also an important attribute, an issue addressed by Beaufort (1997, 1999). It is also important to recognise the need to be able to operate in a range of social environments. The challenge inherent in this is expressed by Hyland (2002, pp. 389–90) in relation to academic contexts, but it applies equally to the workplace: "Such epistemological, ontological, social and discursive border-crossings pose enormous challenges for students and teachers alike, but a good starting point is to recognise the literary practices that help mark off these borders."

Throughout this chapter I have made every attempt to stress the value of understanding the communicative practices of different discourse communities. However, whether and how this kind of knowledge and understanding of the practices of specific discourse communities can be effectively transmitted to students is a matter of some discussion. In the context of writing in academic disciplines, the question has centred to some extent around the degree of specificity in teaching. Spack (1988) famously asked how far we should go when attempting to initiate students into the academic discourse community. Her main concern related to whether English teachers should be teaching the language of specific disciplines, and she concluded that this should be left to teachers who work in the specific disciplines and who therefore have the necessary knowledge. Hyland (2002) revisits this question, but is primarily concerned with the question of generic and discipline-specific skills. He makes a strong case for specificity, concluding that "we must go as far as we can" (p. 394).

To some extent, the concerns that apply to the teaching of discipline-specific language also apply to the teaching of workplace writing, but, as noted, the latter has its own particular challenge, namely, the vast differences between the workplace and the academy as contexts for writing and learning to write. But in seeking to initiate our students into the genres and practices of particular workplace discourse communities, we also need to ask ourselves how far we can go. This thorny problem is discussed in Chapter 9.

3
GENRES AND GENRE ANALYSIS

Introduction

This chapter is centred on the premise that an understanding of genres is a key component of workplace writing ability. In the previous chapter, genres were characterised as "typified rhetorical actions based on recurrent situations" (Miller, 1984, p. 159), and it was suggested that genres are strongly associated with different discourse communities in that they evolve as responses to the needs of those communities, and that there is a mutually constitutive relationship between genre and community. It was further argued that if genres and communities are linked in this way, then – logically – the way into those communities will be provided through an understanding of the relevant genres. This chapter moves the discussion forward by considering the ways in which this understanding might be effected, primarily through an examination of theories of genre and approaches to genre analysis.

Students need to understand why texts are written in the ways they are in order to be able to produce similar texts for their own purposes. Swales (1990) sees genre analysis as a valuable tool in this regard because of its "clarificatory" power, while Hyland (2007, p. 150) contends that genre pedagogies can offer "a means of presenting students with explicit and systematic explanations of the ways writing works to communicate". Meanwhile Dias *et al.* (1999) look beyond the text in their championing of genre studies as a means of understanding writing, considering not only regularities seen in text and context, but also the associated practices of composing and reading, and the roles of those involved in these processes. Chapter 3 develops this line of thinking and begins with a discussion of theories of genre and approaches to genre analysis, and these are considered in relation to the challenges of preparing writers for the workplace. As will be seen, the notion of purpose takes central stage as a privileged criterion in much of the discussion of genre issues, and the impact this has on texts is examined and exemplified. The related issue of audience as an influence on text creation is also briefly discussed – workplace texts are addressed to a range of readers, external and internal, known and unknown, expert or non-expert, and these different intended audiences will be a factor in the choices that writers make in terms of language and register.

Ultimately, it will be argued, rather than simply teaching different genres that we anticipate our students will need, we should be concerned with raising awareness of genres and providing the necessary tools to analyse them. Such tools require an understanding of the nature of genre knowledge and expertise, areas which have received growing attention as research into workplace writing practices has progressed. The chapter will briefly consider ways in which the study of genres has extended its ambit before moving on to focus on the various professional and socio-pragmatic factors beyond the text (Bhatia, 2004) that influence genre creation. As our understanding of the nature of genre creation expands, so our work as teachers becomes more wide-ranging, and in identifying the various elements of the workplace that contribute to the construction of genres, this chapter flags issues such as intertextuality and collaboration that are dealt with in greater detail later in this book. The chapter concludes with a discussion of the implications that a thicker description (Geertz, 1983) and fuller understanding of genres might have for the classroom.

Approaches to genre and genre analysis

In the field of applied linguistics, genre is defined as "a particular class of speech events [texts as well] which can be considered to be of the same type" (Richards, Platt and Platt, 1992). In this basic conception, genre is commonly understood in the sense of its being a recognisable rendering of some kind of goal, however broadly or narrowly conceived. However, genre as a concept has been considered and applied in a variety of distinct contexts, and different theories and approaches have developed which relate to those contexts and the motivations of researchers and practitioners working within them. These distinctions have most famously been examined by Hyon (1996), who talks of genre in three "traditions", namely, English for Specific Purposes (ESP), the New Rhetoric and Systemic Functional Linguistics (SFL). The evolution of these has been influenced to a large extent by beliefs about the relationship between language and society and about language learning and teaching; geography and target learning group have also played a part in this evolution. The term "traditions" implies a greater sense of longevity and fixity than exists in what is a still evolving field of study, and is clearly one that other researchers are slightly uncomfortable with: Flowerdew (2002), for example, talks of "worlds" of genre scholarship, while Johns (2011) uses the term "camps". I will be referring to them for the most part as approaches.

Any reader looking through genre-related literature will see that the three labels (ESP, SFL, New Rhetoric) continue to be commonly used in discussions of approaches to researching and teaching writing. However, it will be seen that a certain amount of overlap already exists among the three, and the distinctions are becoming increasingly fuzzy as researchers and teachers take on and combine elements from the different approaches in their work. There is, of course, a danger if we persist with these labels of reinforcing perceived distinctions. Nevertheless, like many other researchers, I shall use the labels as a convenient point of departure for explaining – with the help of Hyon's (1996) much cited paper – the various approaches to understanding and analysing genres, before going on to consider ways in which the boundaries between them have blurred and suggesting how their concerns and principles might usefully be applied to the study and teaching of workplace writing.

As mentioned, the geography and target learning group have been influential in the development of the different approaches: ESP is often thought of as having its genesis in Britain, with non-native speakers (NNS) of English at universities as the target audience; the New Rhetoric is largely based in North America and is concerned with the teaching of writing at university level and, increasingly, professional writing; SFL, sometimes referred to as the Sydney School because of its provenance, has largely been concerned with literacy in schools, initially in Australia but subsequently in many other parts of the world and also with adult migrants.

Proponents of ESP, in which the work of John Swales and Vijay Bhatia is regarded as particularly formative, see genre as a tool for the analysis and teaching of both written and spoken language that NNS need in academic and professional settings, although it is perhaps fair to say that the bulk of analysis carried out in ESP relates to written language. Genres are understood – and named – in terms of their purposes, e.g. reports, advertisements, proposals, applications and so on. Analysis of such genres in its most basic form typically involves looking at the organisation of a text, breaking it down into its constituent moves, each move representing a distinct communicative act that serves the larger purpose of the genre; the organisation of these moves is referred to as the "schematic structure" (Swales, 1990) of the genre. The next stage of the analysis involves going deeper into the text, examining the relationship between function and linguistic form, and attempting to identify instances of text patterning and common lexico-grammatical features. In unpacking the structure and linguistic features of different text types, this type of genre analysis is intended to make these available to learners such that they can reproduce similar texts in their writing or speaking in different disciplines and professions. The utility of this approach to genre analysis will be illustrated later in this chapter.

SFL is "concerned with the relationship between language and its functions in social settings" (Hyon, 1996, p. 698), and is derived to large extent from the work of Michael Halliday. Halliday's early work *Language as Social Semiotic* (1978) served as a launch pad for what has become a highly developed and increasingly popular approach to understanding and teaching genres. The focus of SFL is for the most part on primary and secondary school genres, and non-professional workplace texts (rather than academic and professional writing). Fosen (2000) points to some of the motivating factors underlying this approach, suggesting that the attention of those involved in genre debates in Australia "is to school as a site of social change, where underprivileged groups gain access to the dominant academic discourse, and therefore discursive power" (p. 4), an assertion supported by Johns (2011). Genres in SFL, defined by Martin and others as "staged, goal-oriented social processes", are conceived and labelled in a slightly different way from those dealt with in ESP, in what is seen as a "more context-driven approach to linking genre naming to text structures" (Johns, 2011, p. 59). Eight "Key Genres" have been identified by researchers from the Sydney School, namely *recount, information report, explanation, exposition, discussion, procedure, narrative* and *news story* (Macken-Horarik, 2002, pp. 21–22).

Research that looks at workplace writing from the perspective of SFL seems to be somewhat thin on the ground, but this is not to suggest that SFL is an inappropriate framework for analysis of workplace writing, rather that, as noted, most teachers and researchers working with that approach are focused on a different target student group. Bax (2011, p. 51) also suggests that "many real-world texts cannot easily fit straightforwardly" into the kinds of classificatory schemes such as recounts, descriptions, protocols and so on as proposed by Martin and Rose (2008), and that we probably need to look beyond frameworks of this kind for analysis of texts outside the educational domain. Having said that, the notion of register (Halliday and Hasan, 1976), a concept from SFL which accounts for the relationship between text and context in terms of field, tenor and mode, has the potential to serve as an illuminating explanatory tool in studies of workplace texts. A recent study by Forey (2014), for example, of language in the business process outsourcing industry applies notions of field, tenor and mode to good effect in outlining "differences between written and spoken discourse, with the aim of building a bridge between what we know within applied linguistics and how language is understood in the workplace" (p. 383). The importance of register in relation to tenor is examined in greater detail in Chapter 6, in the discussion of issues relating to power and politeness.

Both ESP and SFL are aimed at uncovering rhetorical patterns and their linguistic realisations, and showing how these are harnessed to serving the purposes of a given genre. In this way they offer insights into the features of written text with a view to presenting them in classroom contexts. Where they differ, according to Hyland (2007), is that SFL places a greater emphasis on language, while ESP "stresses the importance of the situatedness of genres in particular contexts through rhetorical consciousness-raising" (p. 154).

The views of the New Rhetoric (also known as Rhetorical Genre Studies) in relation to genre were touched upon in Chapter 2, with the work of Miller (1984) in particular being noted as highly influential. Research and teaching in this approach have mainly been concerned with L1 (first language) teaching of composition studies, rhetoric and professional writing. This concern evolved as a reaction to the then predominant model of teaching composition, which focused on the product, or form of writing, rather than factors such as audience and context, or the notion of writing as a socially constructed activity. The focus in the New Rhetoric is more on the institutional contexts in which genres are found than on forms; there is strong emphasis on the social purposes and actions fulfilled by these genres. This position is stressed by Miller (1984): "a rhetorically sound definition of genre must be centered not on the substance or the form of discourse but on the action it is used to accomplish" (p. 151). A further important point, also raised in the previous chapter, is that the social constructionist perspective which underpins the New Rhetoric's view of genres sees them as contributing to the construction of social contexts as well as being responses to these contexts, leading to the conclusion that they should not be studied independently of one another. New Rhetoric research often uses ethnographic (as opposed to linguistic) methods for analysis, as it seeks to describe contexts and the actions performed by texts found in those contexts. Thus, genre theory in this approach is intended to help students and workplace entrants understand the relationship between genres and their surrounding contexts and the functions they serve within those contexts.

Viewing these three approaches to genre through the prism of Hyon's (1996) work is a convenient means of accounting for their genesis and helps to highlight the basic principles and motivations associated with each "tradition". Indeed, her work continues to serve as a springboard for discussion of approaches to genre and genre-based instruction, as evidenced by the number of times her paper has been cited. Nevertheless, Hyon's thesis has been subject to some questioning, most notably from Bloor (1998), who in her discussion of the work of John Swales suggests a higher degree of overlap among the three approaches than is implied by Hyon. More importantly, however, as these different approaches to understanding genre and genre analysis have matured, there is increasing evidence of interaction and cross-fertilisation among researchers and practitioners, a situation recognised by Flowerdew (2011) with his observation that there has been some convergence between ESP and the New Rhetoric, something also noted by Bhatia and Bremner (2012). Indeed, for some time now there has been growing focus on the role of social purposes in relation to genres among many working in ESP genre theory, for example Bhatia and Swales, for whom communicative purpose is the key criterion in identifying genres. Certainly, it would be misleading to suggest that the adherents of the different approaches are locked in silos, impervious to each other's thinking and methodologies, and the field has reached a stage whereby the distinctions, while useful as a theoretical point of reference, are less clear and less real, and perhaps less significant.

To sum up, these different approaches have emerged as a result of different motivations and from different pedagogical settings, but very importantly they all bring valuable elements to the table that can enhance our understanding of genres, both as researchers and teachers. There is no clear reason for particular elements to be confined to the settings in which they were conceived, rather we should select, adapt and combine those which make most sense for our particular teaching situation. My own teaching, for example, which involves L2 (second language) undergraduate writers working on professional discourse, combines a consideration of contextual factors (field, tenor, mode) and how they combine to influence register (from SFL); analysis of schematic structure, looking at moves and how these are organised and realised in lexico-grammatical terms (from ESP); and examination of the wider context, whether professional or organisational, along with other influences on texts and writing processes, such as intertextuality and collaboration (from the New Rhetoric).

Widening the scope of genre analysis

The convergence and overlap among the approaches discussed in the previous section is to be welcomed if we wish to develop investigative frameworks that might lead to a fuller understanding of why workplace practitioners write in the way they do. The limitations of a narrow research focus on textual analysis, and the need to look beyond the text – not only at purpose – are now largely recognised. Indeed, more than twenty years ago Bhatia (1993) suggested that historical development in the field of linguistic and discourse analysis indicates a clear progression from "pure surface description to a thicker description of various aspects of texts or genres" (p. 11). He has subsequently characterised this as a shift from textualisation (a concern with the surface features of text, e.g. at sentence or sub-sentence level) through organisation (examining texts and attempting to discern patterns in the ways in which they are organised) to contextualisation, which takes account of a wider range of factors, requiring multi-dimensional and multi-perspective analyses of genres (Bhatia, 2004). In this framework, he explains, discourse is manifested in different forms: discourse as text, discourse as genre, and discourse as professional and social practice. Thus, just as textual analysis has widened its sphere from looking at isolated features of text (for example, Barber's (1962) analysis of scientific writing), to looking at patterns of discourse, so researchers in genre analysis have moved from working with texts alone to the examination of the factors surrounding the creation of the text under investigation, evidence of some convergence of thinking from the different approaches outlined by Hyon (1996) and alluded to earlier.

Genre knowledge

A full account of a given genre, then, would require an examination not only of the text itself, but of the processes surrounding its construction, i.e. the "particular processes of producing, distributing and consuming texts" (Fairclough, 1992, p. 126), along with an investigation of the social or professional context in which these take place. Beaufort (2000) gives an idea of the range of areas that an expert writer might take into account, suggesting five areas of context-specific knowledge acquired by old-timers in her study, namely, discourse community knowledge, subject matter knowledge, genre knowledge, rhetorical knowledge and task-specific procedural knowledge (p. 203). As can be seen, such a view of genres and writing would extend well beyond the text the conceptions of genre knowledge that we wish to impart to novice writers; the basic elements of this knowledge are enumerated below.

Genre knowledge at the level of text would include a grasp of the communicative purposes of the genre, and how these relate to the typical themes, content and meanings carried by texts; the typical organisation pattern, or "schematic structure" (Swales, 1990) of the genre; and the ways in which the moves of the genre are realised in linguistic terms, i.e. the predominant lexico-grammatical features. In addition to this, a writer would need to understand the context in which genre consumption is likely to take place, i.e. the target readers and how and where they would use the text: consider the difference, for example, between a train timetable, which would be scanned for specific information and therefore designed to facilitate that kind of reading, with a legal document that requires close attention to every element of the text. Attention would also need to be given to other issues relating to the audience, such as the levels of shared knowledge among writers/speakers and readers/ listeners – by way of illustration, the explanation of a new banking instrument to trained economists would be framed very differently from the text that marketed the same instrument to members of the public with a less developed understanding of financial products. An understanding of the relationship between writers/ speakers and their audience would also entail the consideration of power relations and how these could be successfully be managed in terms of register.

As well as understanding how the genre will be used, the writer or speaker would also need to have a knowledge of the typical production procedures relating to a genre, and this is very closely connected to the notions of discourse community and organisational culture, that is to say the genre producer would need to develop an awareness of the ways in which things are done in particular professions or organisations. Knowledge of practices and conventions could involve an understanding of how organisational members work together to create target genres, and of the texts that they might draw upon in the process of genre production.

How deeply we delve into these aspects of genre depends on how thick an account of genres and genre-related practices we want to provide, and this will be based on a variety of factors: the teaching context, the target student group, the aims of the curriculum and possibly the beliefs of the teacher. It will be seen, though, that the foregoing discussion is at the heart of this book, in that it has outlined the key aspects of genre knowledge beyond the text that can be considered as desirable components of a genre producer's armoury, and these are dealt with in greater depth in other chapters in the book. The study of an intern in a PR company presented in Chapter 2 (Bremner, 2014a) is intended as an illustration of the very specific ways in which particular professions or discourse communities go about their business, and the reasons for which they do so. This phenomenon is further considered in the discussion of organisational culture in Chapter 8. As for production practices relating to the use of other texts and to collaboration, these are addressed in Chapters 4 and 5 respectively, while the issue of audience in respect of power relationships is discussed in Chapter 6. This chapter now moves to the issue of purpose, which is a primary consideration when looking at how genres are constructed.

Genres and purpose

Purpose is a potentially complex and highly influential factor in genre creation that can operate at a number of levels: rhetorical (e.g. requesting, persuading, reporting, etc.); institutional or organisational as an element of broader community goals; and individual in the sense that the writer may also be exploiting the conventions of the genre for their own personal ends.

It was pointed out above that an important criterion in identifying genres is purpose, and to get a sense of how central this is to an understanding of genres and their role in discourse communities, we need look no further than the detailed definition of genre proposed by Swales (1990, p. 58):

> A genre comprises a class of communicative events, the members of which share some set of communicative purposes. These purposes are recognized by the expert members of the parent discourse community, and thereby consti- tute the rationale for the genre. This rationale shapes the schematic structure of the discourse and influences and constrains the choice of content and style. Communicative purpose is both a privileged criterion and one that operates to keep the scope of a genre as here conceived narrowly focused on comparable rhetorical action. In addition to purpose, exemplars of a genre exhibit various patterns of similarity in terms of structure, style, content and intended audience.

As can be seen from this, it is proposed that purpose not only constitutes the ration- ale for the genre, but also influences its shape. Accepting this view has considerable ramifications for the study and teaching of genres: it underpins the thinking at the core of ESP genre analysis, namely, that there is value in investigating the rela- tionship between purpose and schematic structure in samples of texts with similar purposes, as this may open up the possibility of identifying broad commonalities in patterns of textual organisation and rhetorical strategy use in such genres.

A classic example of how this can work is seen in Bhatia (1993), in which he analyses two text-types, which are conventionally seen as somewhat different – the sales promotion letter and the job application letter – and demonstrates through his genre analysis that the two share similar schematic structures, for the very reason that they share the same communicative purpose of promoting something, in the first case a service and in the second an individual applicant. As he (1993, p. 59) explains: "The emphasis in genre analysis on the shared communicative purpose on the part of the participants makes it possible for us to view sales promotion letters and job application letters as close cousins".

Bhatia's (1993) study has lent strength to the notion that genres sharing the same purposes and context of use are likely to have similar sets of rhetorical moves and to deploy similar strategies to achieve these, and his work on this particular genre type has been used as the basis for other research into genres that have promotion as their central purpose. The move structure that he developed for sales promotion letters has been used in a range of studies looking at that particular genre (e.g. Barron, 2006; Cheung, 2008, 2010; Upton, 2002; Vergaro, 2004). As for work on application letters, this has also seen a variety of studies based on Bhatia's original schematic structure, often identifying extra elements that relate to the specific context, but essentially retaining the basic structure (e.g. Al-Ali, 2004, 2006; Connor, Davis and De Rycker, 1995; Gillaerts, 2003; Henry and Roseberry, 2001; Soroko, 2012; Upton and Connor, 2001). Gillaerts (2003) is very clear in explaining why he sees Bhatia's framework as valuable, saying that "it is the most articulated, based on corpus research and without prescriptive aims" (p. 108).

Further illustration of the utility of Bhatia's (1993) work analysing promotional genres can be seen in a recent study of my own, conducted with a colleague (Bremner and Phung, 2015), in which we examined the "Summary" sections of profiles on the networking site LinkedIn. This site serves as a platform on which professionals and job seekers can promote themselves, and for that reason it was expected that the Summaries would share rhetorical features with application letters, which also have the central purpose of self-promotion. This turned out to be the case, as it was indeed found that the Summaries displayed many of the obligatory moves identified by Bhatia (1993), and also identified in studies of application letters as mentioned. Where there was divergence, this related to the specific context of the genre, most notably the channel through which it was mediated. The study demonstrates once more the centrality of purpose as a factor in shaping genres, leading us to conclude that "the model continues to serve as a valuable analytical framework that can be applied to other examples of promotional genres" (2015, p. 379).

Taking a genre analytical approach of the kind deployed in the studies discussed above is helpful not only for researchers but for students – if they can use this analytical model to investigate groups of genres with similar purposes to draw conclusions about commonalities in terms of schematic structure, this can move them along the road to understanding how and why the genres under analysis work in particular ways, a point made by Flowerdew (1993) and Bremner and Phung (2015), among others.

Genre colonies

The importance of purpose in respect of genre analysis cannot be underestimated. As a key influence on the shape of genres, it serves both as the initial point of investigation and also as the basis for genre analysis. Moreover, if, as has been demonstrated in the discussion of studies presented above, genres with similar purposes tend to display similar schematic structures and other discoursal features as a result of the shaping influence of that purpose, then it would seem reasonable to group genres together in terms of their shared purposes, and assume that all members of that group will have a degree of similarity in terms of rhetorical organisation and features.

This possibility has been captured by Bhatia (2004) with his notion of genre colonies, which are clusters of genres with a common communicative purpose. The colony of promotional genres, for example, would include texts such as advertisements, job applications, reference letters, travel brochures, book blurbs and so on. Genres within these colonies can be designated as primary, secondary or peripheral, depending on the degree to which they adhere to the shared communicative purpose. In the case of promotional genres, an advertisement would be seen as a primary instance of the genre, while a book review would be secondary in that while it has the potential to serve a promotional purpose, it can also function as an opinion piece, which would also make it simultaneously a member of another colony that might include genres such as editorials.

While the primary or prototypical genres belonging to a particular colony are likely to display similar rhetorical structure and features, secondary or mixed genres may also draw on discourse associated with other genres or communities to achieve their goals. This could be seen as an instance of interdiscursivity in action, i.e. the appropriation of semiotic resources from other professional practices and disciplinary cultures (Bhatia, 2008), a phenomenon touched upon in Chapter 2. A rich illustration of this practice of interdiscursive appropriation is provided by Bhatia (2008, 2010) in his study of the production of corporate annual reports, in which he shows how the writers of these documents incorporate discourse from accounting, economics, public relations and law in order to achieve their communicative goals.

Discourse communities and interdiscursivity

As intimated in the brief discussion of interdiscursivity in Chapter 2, there is an implicit assumption in this concept that certain types of discourse belong to or are at least associated with particular professional communities, and by extension that there is such a thing as PR discourse, accounting discourse and so on. As an idea, this needs to be approached with some caution: it is perhaps convenient for us to think of PR practitioners as using a particular discourse to go about their work, and most of us would intuitively characterise this as in some way promotional; similarly, we might conceptualise accountancy discourse as being associated with numbers and reports. However, such views of communities and their particular discourses may be somewhat restrictive, presenting only a partial picture of what practitioners in these professions do.

Moreover, as professional communities evolve, their members are often required to take on roles as writers that have not been traditionally associated with the profession in question. As academics, for example, few of us operate solely within the confines of the traditional genre set (Devitt, 1991, 2004) of academia – lectures, research papers, conference presentations and so on. Many of us are involved in a variety of other activities that reflect the realities of the contemporary university, such as marketing programmes to international students, writing reports that account for our activities to management or funding bodies, or drawing up financial plans and projections, all of which makes it difficult to set the boundaries of what can be considered the discourse of academics. It may be, then, that the increasingly diverse roles taken on by writers in professional communities have undermined the explanatory power of community-specific labels such as "PR discourse" or "accountancy discourse", and this leads to the broader question of how closely we can or should associate particular discourses with particular communities.

According to Bhatia (2010) interdiscursivity "refers to more innovative attempts to create various forms of hybrid and relatively novel constructs by appropriating or exploiting established conventions or resources associated with other genres and practices" (p. 35). When a new genre such as the corporate annual report is formed, it is understood that initially the writers are appropriating recognisable semiotic resources from other communities or genres to create it, but ultimately it can be seen that the corporate annual report has evolved into a genre in its own right, i.e. a recognisable response to a recurring need, that displays a particular rhetorical structure. What has happened is that the semiotic resources appropriated from elsewhere have been repurposed in their new context. Interdiscursivity as a concept helps to explain this phenomenon, but perhaps has more value as a theoretical construct that can be used by researchers to make sense of the ways in which genres and writing practices more generally continue to develop, than as a tool for instruction.

Given that different groups tend to have a variety of rhetorical aims in their writing practices, witnessed in the concept of mixed genres and evidenced in specific examples such as the corporate annual report, it may be more helpful to view the make up of such genres in terms of the functional stretches of discourse that contribute to the genre, such as description, explanation, instruction and so on, what Bhatia (2004) calls "generic values" and Bax (2011) terms as "discourse modes". A restaurant review, for example, requires a combination of description, narrative and evaluation in order to achieve its goals – to break a text down in this way seems to offer a way for novice writers to understand how language is harnessed to purpose at both the genre and sub-genre level, and may be more illuminating as an approach to genre analysis than characterising discourses with reference to the communities which they apparently come from.

As can be seen from this somewhat lengthy foray into the role of purpose in relation to genre, it plays a powerful role, not only as the rationale and a shaping influence on the text, but as an explanatory tool in accounting for what writers are trying to do as they create increasingly hybridised texts in order to achieve their goals, as demonstrated, for example, by Bhatia (2008, 2010) in his analysis of corporate annual reports and Bhatia, A. (2012) in her study of the CSR report.

The evident creativity seen in the construction of genres such as the corporate annual report or the CSR report, raises the issue of the extent to which writers are constrained by the conventions or integrity of a given genre, and how writers can manipulate or exploit these to achieve their goals, whether organisational or individual. In this regard Bhatia (1999) discusses the relationship between what he calls "socially recognised communicative purposes" and private intentions, the latter notion representing a writer's attempts to achieve a particular objective within the accepted framework of a particular genre. An example of this would be the way in which a journalist might report an event such that they lent a particular slant to a story that on the face of it appeared to be a straightforward news item, through the organisation or omission of elements in the narrative, foregrounding or backgrounding of participants, choice of particular lexis to characterise participants, and so on.

The tension between these private intentions and the recognised purposes of a genre can play out in a number of ways. This is particularly true of workplace writing, which tends to be less predictable than academic writing, with Bhatia going so far as to contend that genres in professional settings "rarely, if ever, serve a single purpose" (1999, p. 25). Genres such as news items, as already explained, are a common arena for the exploitation or manipulation of generic conventions to particular ends. Mixed genres, such as the corporate annual report, also display evidence of manipulation in the sense that while they are ostensibly accounts of the year's activity, presenting an objective set of facts as implied by the term 'report', they typically contain a number of promotional elements, and like news reports are prone to exploitation through the foregrounding or backgrounding of information, along with other linguistic strategies.

Achieving one's own particular goals as a writer in workplace settings requires a considerable amount of skill, but what is absolutely key in the manipulation of genres is that they should retain their generic integrity, i.e. a genre should look like the genre it is supposed to be. If attempts to bend a genre, whether through mixing or embedding or any other means, put it out of shape to the extent that it is no longer recognisable, then the writer may be considered to be working with a text other than the target genre, and therefore may fall short of their particular goal.

To a large extent, the exploitation of genres in workplace settings is writing that is being carried out by the writer on behalf of the organisation, i.e. writing in the service of the organisation's goals, as in news or PR writing, or in the construction of reporting genres with promotional elements. This is pointed out by Dias, Freedman, Medway and Paré (1999), with their observation that "Rhetorical intentions, long considered the author's prerogative, are more accurately located in the workplace community's collective aspirations and goals" (p. 115). There are, however, situations in which writers will be concerned with attending to their own individual interests as well as trying to serve community goals, i.e. balancing their needs with those of the organisation, an issue considered by van Nus (1999), who explains that "the purpose of a genre is a social purpose, a way through which a society's activities are performed, and through which communicators can achieve their own individual purposes" (p. 183).

My own research in this area (Bremner, 2006, 2012b) looked at the experiences of writers tasked with carrying out work on behalf of a university administration, much of which required them to make demands of their colleagues, mostly by means of email, asking them to attend workshops, produce different documents, meet deadlines and so on. The lack of "inherent status" (Bargiela-Chiappini and Harris, 1996) or real power enjoyed by the writers presented a considerable challenge, and this was compounded by the expectation that all writing relating to this project would be copied to the administration. The dilemma that faced them was that while on the one hand they wanted to be seen by management as doing their job, on the other they were concerned about how they would be perceived by their colleagues. More specifically, they were worried about the possibility of being evaluated or held accountable on the basis of the texts that they produced, but also wanted to avoid being seen as lackeys of the administration. Their goal, then, was to try and steer an appropriate line between the two audiences, and in so doing meet the objectives of the institution while satisfying their own individual objectives.

To achieve this goal, they adopted a number of strategies: the deployment of politeness strategies, particularly those aimed at negative face; upbeat justifications of the various tasks that were demanded; impersonal constructions (e.g. "the plan is", "the idea is") that distanced them from the requests that they were making, given their concern about the degree to which they appeared committed to particular views or positions in the eyes of their colleagues; careful use of personal pronouns so as to obviate the perception that they were instigators of the initiatives they were helping to implement. But the important point is that all of this was effected within the recognised and accepted parameters of the genres they were working with, i.e. they understood how these genres worked, but were making "use of what is conventionally available to a discourse community to further (their) own subtle ends" (Bhatia, 1995, p. 3).

From this discussion and explanation, it will be seen that genres, once they are considered in relation to their context and to the purposes of those who work with them, are a complex business, with the corollary that the acquisition of genre knowledge is also a challenge of some substance. To become a competent writer, it is not simply a question of mastering particular genres, but of learning how to manage the many aspects of genre that go into constructing them: an understanding of the needs and practices of the relevant community; the ability to tailor one's writing to meet the needs and expectations of different audiences, whether superior or subordinate, internal or external, specialist or non-specialist, single or multiple readers and so on; an understanding of purpose and its impact on the ways in which texts are structured and realised; and the ability to work within the accepted boundaries of genres while achieving one's goals as a writer. As Hafner (2013) explains, "genre knowledge is ... seen not only as a matter of understanding available generic structures and their textualizations, but also in terms of aligning with the underlying assumptions of the relevant disciplinary culture, in order to participate more fully in the professional community" (p. 140).

Genre and pedagogy

The final issue to be tackled in this chapter is the question of how the complexities of genre and the processes surrounding genre construction can be approached in classroom settings. A considerable challenge in this regard lies in the fact that the workplace and the academy are very different as contexts for both writing and for learning. This point is raised in Chapter 1 and addressed in some detail in Chapter 9, which looks at socialisation processes. The discussion here is restricted to the question of what aspects of genre should or could be addressed in the classroom, the differences in context notwithstanding.

Johns (2011) draws a distinction between genre acquisition and genre awareness, the former involving the teaching of particular text types that are seen as common examples of genres, and the latter looking at how texts, their purposes and the contexts in which they are found interrelate. That is not to suggest that it is a case of one or the other. Indeed, Johns herself (2011, p. 60) proposes an approach "that takes into consideration writer processes, systems of texts, and the varied contextual influences upon them" as well as teaching text formats. But it is important that we recognise the limitations of teaching particular text types to learners. It may be possible to identify certain genres that are produced in some form in different workplaces, but if we accept the view that genres are very much the products of particular communities, a view taken throughout this book, then as teachers we must be wary of suggesting that learners can take these directly into the workplace. Indeed, in the recent study of LinkedIn and its potential applications as described above (Bremner and Phung, 2015) we stressed that our goal was not to propose a prescriptive approach to composing LinkedIn Summaries, but to provide insights into the ways in which expert résumé writers went about this task that might serve as a reference point and springboard for students when creating their own profiles. This is very much in keeping with Bhatia's (1999, p. 38) point that we should consider generic conventions more as a resource than a "blueprint for further replication in similar rhetorical contexts". Our job then is to make learners aware of how these resources can be exploited once they reach the workplace. In the meantime they can be exposed to a wide range of genres on the understanding that it is the principles that inform the construction of these genres that should be taken away for application in a new setting, rather than a rigid set of texts. Alongside this, we need to raise awareness, through the examination of genres in their professional settings, of the ways in which purpose, context and all the other related factors enumerated in this chapter work together to create these genres.

A final point, which will be revisited in Chapter 9, is that while acknowledging the power of the workplace as a context for learning, we should not defer completely to this power. As Hyland (2007, p. 151) explains, "genre-based writing teaching can short-cut the long processes of situated acquisition" and we should recognise that there is much that can be done in the academy to assist students in their development as writers. Ultimately, though, the way that genres are handled in classroom settings should be based on the understanding that whatever is learnt and understood will be a basis for reflection and will need to be adapted to the needs and expectations of particular workplaces. Genre analysis can provide a gateway to an awareness of the multiple aspects of genres and the contextual elements and processes that contribute to their construction, and as an analytical tool it can serve not only instructors but learners themselves (Bremner and Phung, 2015; Flowerdew, 1993), one that they can deploy to make sense of the new genres that they encounter in the workplace.

4

INTERTEXTUALITY

Introduction

At the heart of this chapter is the understanding that texts produced in the workplace are connected to and shaped, both directly and indirectly, by other texts. This is explained as "intertextuality", a term coined by Kristeva (1980) in relation to literary criticism, but one that has made its way into considerations of how texts interact with another in professional and disciplinary settings to the extent that it is now a well-established concept. Indeed, Swales (2004, p. 21) suggests that it "has now become so imbricated in modern academic thought as to no longer require extensive textual discussion and citation", going on to say that "We are all admitted intertextualists now, both in theory and practice". It is fair to say that in respect of workplace writing, intertextuality has been investigated from a variety of perspectives and in a range of settings, but crucially, a question hangs over the extent to which the findings from these investigations have made their way into pedagogical considerations and this concern will be addressed in the chapter.

This chapter first looks at how intertextuality has been defined and categorised, and the ways in which genres interconnect and work together to achieve organisational goals. It goes on to consider the multiple ways in which it plays out in workplace settings, before moving on to a discussion of more recent research that has taken intertextuality as its central focus in examinations of workplace discourse. In particular, it addresses the notion that intertextuality plays a significant role in the creation of coherent texts and the corollary of this, namely that the ability to manage intertextuality is an important component of workplace writing competence. The prevalence of intertextuality in workplace writing has implications for writers and the teaching of writing, and these concerns are examined in the second half of the chapter, looking in particular at the extent to which pedagogy has taken active note and account of this feature of text construction in the workplace.

The final section of the chapter introduces a recent study that attempted to introduce intertextuality into student writing assignments, discussing the challenges this initiative posed for students and the implications for task design.

Genres and Intertextuality

Intertextuality has been variously defined, but no discussion of this concept should omit to mention the work of Kristeva (1980) or Bakhtin (1986), who broadly see all discourses as intertextual in that they are in some way connected to prior or predicted texts. But it is to the work of researchers concerned with disciplinary and workplace discourse that this chapter turns for its definitions, citing two in the first instance to show how different aspects of intertextuality can be highlighted. Bazerman (2004, p. 86), for example, as noted in Chapter 1, explains it as the "explicit and implicit relations that a text or utterance has to prior, contemporary and potential future texts", in effect placing an emphasis on the ways in which texts are both backward and forward looking in their textual reference, and the idea that this is an ongoing process. Fairclough's (1992, p. 84) definition, meanwhile, considers the degree of tactical intent on the writer's part, explaining intertextuality as the property texts have "of being full of snatches of other texts which may be explicitly demarcated or merged in, and which the text may assimilate, contradict, ironically echo, and so forth". Fairclough also makes a distinction between "manifest intertextuality", where there are overt traces of other texts in evidence, and "interdiscursivity", in which the writer draws on the conventions of other genres. (Interdiscursivity, which is one particular realisation of intertextual links, is discussed in greater detail in Chapters 2 and 3.) Bazerman and Fairclough are only two among a number of researchers who have investigated the nature of intertextuality, and it will be seen over the course of this chapter that many others have engaged in different ways with this concept.

The importance of intertextuality in the workplace rests in the fact that texts are not standalone entities that appear from nowhere, created out of nothing, but are the outcome of ongoing interactions with other texts. As Candlin and Maley (1997, p. 203) explain, any given text is derived from a "plurality of sources", while Zachry (2000b) warns of the dangers of thinking of genres such as the annual report or the résumé "as if they existed autonomously" (p. 100). Indeed, research that examines the role and influence of intertextuality in workplace contexts is predicated on the understanding that texts should not be viewed in isolation. Freadman points out that genre "is more usefully applied to the interaction of, minimally, a pair of texts than to the properties of a single text" (2002, p. 40), and there is now a considerable body of work that sees workplace genres as components of larger networks of interrelated activity, describing these variously as "genre sets" (Devitt, 1991, 2004), "systems of genres" (Bazerman, 1994), or "genre repertoires" (Orlikowski and Yates, 1994). Berkenkotter (2001, p. 327) stresses the importance of recognising the interconnected nature of writing in workplace settings: *"the professions are organized by genre systems and their work is carried out through genre systems"* [emphasis in original].

Essentially, then, genres combine together in different ways to achieve the goals of an organisation; this collective function is explained by Fairclough (1992, p. 126) thus: "a society, or particular institution or domain within it, has a particular configuration of genres in particular relationships to each other, constituting a system". The key point to make here is that the resulting intertextuality is more than just a link between texts, it is a phenomenon that helps shape other texts, and as genres combine to achieve different goals, they contribute to the development of new genres as they are recontextualised (Linell, 1998), a process "whereby parts of a specific prior text becomes (sic) a part of other texts in a coherent manner" (Warren, 2016, p. 27).

It should also be stressed that if we look at genres through the social constructionist lens discussed in Chapter 2, which sees genres and contexts as inherently dynamic and mutually constitutive (Berkenkotter and Huckin, 1993; Goodwin and Duranti, 1992; Smart 2006), we are obliged to consider the ways in which genres will influence other genres in the systems of which they are a part.

Intertextuality in workplace settings

Intertextuality can reveal itself in a number of ways in the workplace and Devitt (1991) has identified three different types that she terms referential, functional and generic. Referential intertextuality can be seen when a text refers directly to another (e.g. "In your letter of 23 March, you mentioned …" or "As explained in Section 2b of the Terms and Conditions"). This category is very similar to Fairclough's notion of "manifest intertextuality". Functional intertextuality is seen when a text is shaped by other texts in a system or exchange: for example, an adjustment letter may be influenced by the complaint to which it is responding, by in-company guidelines for writing such letters and so on. As for generic intertextuality, this is the outcome of drawing on previous texts that have been produced in response to a particular recurring need. Examples of this would be seen when writers make use of templates or standard letters that have been written previously within an organisation to deal with situations similar to the one at hand. This is reported by Flowerdew and Wan (2006) in their study of tax computation letters produced by tax accountants, leading them to observe that "intertextuality both defines and serves the needs of the accounting community" (p. 150). A lawyer informant in Bhatia and Bremner (2014) also reports similar practices, explaining that "today, for most transactions, you work off precedents, you work off documents you have, so it's adaptation … (p. 552). Bhatia (2004), meanwhile, has developed Devitt's notions of referential and functional intertextuality, coming up with more detailed categories: "texts providing a context" (p. 126), "texts within and around the text", "[t]exts explicitly referred to in the text", "texts implicitly referred to in the text", "texts embedded within the text" and "texts mixed with the text" (p. 127).

There are many ways in which intertextuality can be seen in action in workplace settings. One of the most prevalent is the textual relations that emerge from interactions between groups or organisations. Bazerman, as noted, uses the term "systems of genres" to talk about such interactions, explaining them as "the full set of genres that instantiate the participation of all the parties – that is the full file of letters from and to the client, from and to the government, from and to the accountant" (1994, p. 94). Thus, a chain of correspondence between such groups would display intertextual links, in particular referential and functional (Devitt, 1991) as writers responded to and built on the dialogue, whether it related to an order, a complaint or any other workplace transaction.

A common form of intertextual influence comes from the organisation itself, in the sense that there is usually a body of practice and of texts that writers can draw upon, consciously or otherwise, and which will shape the texts that are produced for a given purpose. As discussed in Chapter 2, every community has its own ways of doing things, and these can be seen explicitly in prescribed templates, in previous examples of texts used for recurring purposes (Devitt's generic intertextuality) or in tacitly recognised norms, part of what Berkenkotter (2001, p. 338) refers to as "historically sedimented practices". In addition, input and influences will come from the work of colleagues – workplace writing is essentially intertextual in that writers are collaborating, building on and revising each other's work in the process of knowledge making (Prior, 2004; Reither, 1993). These organisational and collegial influences are pointed to by Freedman *et al.* (1994) with their assertion that "workplace writing is resonant with the discourse of colleagues and the ongoing conversation of the institution" (p. 210). (The collaborative element of workplace writing referred to by Reither (1993) and Freedman *et al.* (1994) is dealt with more explicitly in Chapter 5.)

The issue of appropriating the work of colleagues as an intertextual practice has implications for the classroom, in the sense that in an academic context, to do this would be considered plagiarism. It raises the question of what constitutes an acceptable level of borrowing from colleagues. Bremner (2012b) describes a workplace where writers regularly used report templates created by other colleagues, and notes that this practice was not considered problematic. Freedman *et al.* (1994) report a similar lack of concern about originality or the appropriation of colleagues' ideas. As noted, they see the workplace as "resonant with the discourse of colleagues" and go on to explain that "The etiquette for citing is complex and political, but the fact of such intertextual borrowing is a reality and a perceived good" (1994, p. 210). It would seem, then, that the kinds of proscriptions with regard to using other writers' work in the academy do not apply in the workplace. The practices reported in Flowerdew and Wan's (2006) study of tax accountants, for example, illustrate how writers made use of standard letters previously produced by other colleagues. Thus, the task for the student in such situations is not about whether copying is sanctioned, but about understanding what is generic (Devitt, 1991) and what needs to be changed to meet the exigencies of the specific issue they are dealing with in their writing – essentially they need to balance these in order to produce a text that would be seen as appropriate to the particular reader.

An important point in relation to intertextuality is that influences on written text will come from spoken as well as written discourse. Debs talks of texts being "surrounded by talk" (1991), while Gunnarsson (1997) describes the "continuous interplay" between spoken and written discourse in the workplace. Spoken input and influences can come from a range of sources: discussions with colleagues about the content, structure and wording of a text; exchanges at a meeting; phone calls and messages. Studies by Cheng and Mok (2008), Evans (2012) and Nickerson (2002), for example, show how writers of email draw on spoken texts such as meetings as well as other emails when constructing new texts.

As can be seen from this discussion, the presence, indeed the prevalence, of intertextuality in workplace writing and the ways in which it influences and shapes the texts that are produced in professional settings, strongly suggest that for an understanding of how workplace writing works we cannot rely on looking at texts in isolation, but must look at them in relation to other texts, as has been argued by Berkenkotter (2001), Warren (2013, 2016) and many others. As Zachry (2000a) explains, genres exist "as part of larger networks of activities that help organizations realize objectives" (p. 61), and the textual relationships that help form these networks are an integral part of how writing functions.

The purpose and function of intertextuality

It is equally important to understand that these textual relationships are not static, rather that workplace writing is an "ongoing, dialogic process" (Bremner, 2008) and that this process helps shape "potential future texts" (Bazerman, 2004). This aspect of intertextuality comes through very clearly in a number of studies of workplace writing in which the focus has been on the process rather than the text alone. Notable examples can be seen in the context of the PR industry: Sleurs *et al.* (2003) talk about the texts that the writer in their study of press release writing has at his disposal, while Lindholm (2008) similarly discusses intertextuality as a feature of press releases. A more recent study of the process of writing press releases (Bremner, 2014a), discussed in Chapter 2, demonstrates the degree to which the press release as a genre is intertextually embedded in a large genre system. This study tracks the discourse associated with the construction and deployment of press releases, from the key messages to the iterative writing and revising of the release itself, to the media-pitching process and onto the media coverage, and in doing this provides strong evidence of intertextuality as a presence throughout the process.

Other studies have considered the issue of intertextuality and its role in workplace writing more specifically. Cheng and Mok (2008), for example, investigating communication practices in the land surveying professions, illustrate how intertextuality works in a discourse flow of land survey project management, showing connections between and among invitations to tender, tender proposals, meetings, minutes, notes, emails and reports. Their study reports "heavy use of referential intertextual links" (p. 68) and cites examples of language use to signal these links, such as "referring to" and "further to". Most importantly, this research highlights the key role that intertextuality plays in the management of writing, and in this regard they suggest that novice land surveyors need to acquire various skills, including "the ability to refer to and accurately reference prior discourses; the ability to summarise prior discourses and then succinctly revise specific aspects of them; a heightened awareness of all of the parties involved in a particular discourse flow" (Cheng and Mok, 2008, p. 70).

Email and intertextuality

One area of workplace writing where the dialogic relationship among texts is very much in evidence is email. The role of intertextuality in the writing of emails has been the subject of a number of studies which, while looking at different aspects of this phenomenon, reinforce our sense of its ubiquity in the workplace and the vital part it plays there. Evidence of the prevalence of intertextuality in workplace settings can be seen in Kankaanranta (2006), who looked at company internal email communication and genres in a multinational organisation, noting the high incidence of "referencing to other communicative events" (p. 218). Indeed, over half of her data were what she terms "Dialogue genres", which explain information about company-related issues and which "always contained manifest intertextuality" (p. 219). Meanwhile, Evans (2012) studying email practices in white-collar workplaces in Hong Kong with a view to considering the implications for task design, also found intertextuality to be widespread, as well as observing the interplay of email with other types of texts in the workplaces he looked at. He highlights the importance of intertextuality to email communication, explaining that "email plays a crucial role in binding together flows of internal and external activities that are directed towards the resolution of problems, the formulation of plans or the execution of decisions" (Evans, 2012, p. 210).

Warren (2013, 2016) goes deeper into workplace texts to look at more specific features of intertextuality and the way that it is achieved linguistically. His study of email messages of two professionals (an IT professional and a merchandiser) examined certain realisations of intertextuality seen in their discourse, finding that these are influenced "by profession-specific communicative contexts and goals" (2013, p. 12). This finding takes us back to the notion discussed in Chapter 2, namely that each professional community has its own way of doing things, a point that will be revisited later in this chapter. In his 2013 study, Warren is concerned with the question of directionality, i.e. whether elements of the email refer backwards, forwards or both. As with so many studies of workplace writing that consider intertextuality, Warren's email data are shown to be interconnected with other types of discourse such as meetings, phone calls, informal discussions and so on. He found that intertextual elements accounted for the largest proportion of the emails he analysed, saying that "every single text contains intertextual elements providing contexts within which the current text is to be interpreted" (p. 21). Warren's later study (2016) also examines the contribution of intertextuality to a text's coherence, looking at how writers make use of recurrent words and phrases to signal intertextuality in business emails. Like the earlier study, it considers directionality, specifically whether the words and phrases in question are signalling prior or predicted texts, but also looks at power relations as an influence on the choice of signal. In this latter regard he notes, for example, the use of imperative forms such as "check" or "confirm" that might be used by writers with higher status than that of the reader, as opposed to phrases such as "please find" and "please see attached" that might be deployed by writers with lower status.

A slightly different perspective on workplace email is taken by Gimenez (2006) in his study of the phenomenon of "embedded emails", which consist of two types of messages – the "main messages and subordinate messages which rely on the main messages to make sense" (p. 159), again showing the intertextual links that can be seen in these types of workplace data. Importantly, he considers what this embeddedness means for those involved in the writing process, explaining that writers "need to be capable of not only recognizing contextual information provided by the first message the chain initiates, but also identifying whom to call on as witness to the communication event" (p. 167). The fact that multiple writers, often in different geographical locations, are involved in the production of such embedded emails, means that different members of a group are able to participate in the decision-making process. At the same time the practice of including previous emails in an email helps make a group accountable for decisions made, while phrases like "as agreed", referring to a meeting or discussion, would help in establishing this kind of accountability.

Ho (2011) also considers intertextuality from the writer's perspective, focusing on instances of intertextuality and interdiscursivity found in request emails exchanged by a group of English language teachers in Hong Kong, and showing how these two features of writing can be used strategically. In his study, it can be seen that the deployment of intertextuality performs functions such as diverting resentment, convincing others, emphasising roles and managing support. Ho concludes that "the strategic incorporation of intertextual and interdiscursive elements could effect a higher chance of request compliance" (p. 2, 545). Intertextuality, it would seem, needs to be managed because it serves a rhetorical purpose and can lead to more effective writing.

A number of points come out of these studies of intertextuality in workplace email. The first two relate to the importance for researchers of understanding the nature of the professional context. In relation to the broader picture, as noted briefly, Warren (2013) sees the contexts and goals that are specific to a particular professional community as having an influence on the ways in which intertextuality is managed, a point also made by Ho (2011). Warren also talks of intertextuality "often conveying participant and organizational identities and ideologies" (2013, p. 13), referring to the work of Tekin (2008) in this regard. But there is also a need to work with the more immediate context when analysing email chains. On one level, there is the need to carry out email data analysis within the context of related discourse flows (Warren, 2013), but there is also an unarticulated context that needs investigation. As Evans (2012, p. 209) explains, "chain initiators", i.e. the initial email messages that set off a chain of messages, do not "fall suddenly from the clear blue sky". They set a dialogue in motion, but there is very often already an established relationship between the writer and reader, whereby the background and corporate context are understood. For this reason, such analysis benefits from professional informants (cf. Sarangi, 2002), because of their understanding of the organisational and professional context, and also of the more specific local context in which elements are often understood tacitly rather than articulated explicitly.

Perhaps the most important point that emerges from the review of recent research in the preceding paragraphs, is that intertextuality is a more or less ubiquitous but above all *purposeful* feature of workplace texts. It is not simply a theoretical construct to be discussed in the abstract, rather it is a feature of workplace writing that gives texts their coherence in relation to the contexts in which they are produced and in relation to other texts that pertain to the issue at hand, whether one is considering a chain of emails, a set of documents concerning a sales negotiation, or a decision-making process carried out by a group of colleagues. It follows from this, and this is being increasingly demonstrated in the various studies discussed, as well as earlier work (Candlin and Maley, 1997; O'Connor, 2002), that the management of intertextual relations in texts is a key aspect of workplace writing competence. This point is made explicitly by Cheng and Mok (2008) and Ho (2011), as noted, while Warren (2016, p. 35) explains that the ability to signal instances of intertextuality is an "important aspect of discourse coherence". Elsewhere, this time in the context of the law, Hafner (2013) shows how using intertextual references appropriately "can be seen as a way for the writer to display expert membership of disciplinary and professional communities" (p. 134). For these reasons, the very specific ways in which intertextuality plays out, and the question of whether these can be identified and subsequently incorporated into teaching activities are areas that warrant investigation.

Intertextuality and pedagogy

Despite the increasingly acknowledged importance of intertextuality as a feature of writing, and also the need for writers to be able to manage it, there is thus far little evidence that it is being addressed as a specific component of professional literacy in classroom contexts. There has been some acknowledgement of its centrality in the context of academic writing (e.g. Holmes, 2004; Hyland, 2004), but aside from some of the studies discussed, notably Evans (2012), the pedagogical aspects of intertextuality have not been addressed in anything more than an implicit way.

My own work in this area (Bremner, 2008) has included an extensive survey of business communication textbooks to find out the extent to which they engage with the concept of intertextuality, whether implicitly or explicitly, looking also at the amount of intertextual support that is given to accompany sample texts and written tasks. The study looked specifically at a number of aspects of the texts, explanations, tasks and activities found in eight popular textbooks including:

- the planning process, looking at the extent to which writers are asked to refer to and incorporate other previously written documents during the process;
- the collaborative nature of writing – whether this is addressed as an interpersonal event or an intertextual event, or both;

- referring and responding to other documents – how explicitly this is addressed, and whether it is treated as an influence on the shape of the document to be written;
- templates, layouts, organisational conventions – whether there is any discussion of what influences these and how they in turn shape the text to be written;
- plagiarism as an issue or practice;
- whether writing as a dynamic, dialogic process is acknowledged or discussed;
- whether there are any intertextually situated tasks which require the writer to refer to other texts.

Interestingly, the word "intertextuality" is not mentioned in any of the books analysed in the study. The existence of other texts is to some extent acknowledged, but there is little discussion of the ways in which these might influence the shape of target texts that are under construction. Moreover, the writing tasks in the books have little in the way of what could be termed "intertextual surround" that might be helpful to students, and that would be normally found in a comparable workplace context. Similarly, what one finds in terms of practice tasks does not really resemble the kind of writing activity one might find in a workplace, where writers would be drawing on and referring to other texts such as organisational templates, previous examples of similar texts written by colleagues and texts that form part of a larger ongoing dialogue. Instead, the textbooks provide help with the writing of the task, but this often comes in the form of "scripted context" (Bremner, 2008), which explains to the writer what has happened and what they need or want to do. It is worth citing an example (previously cited in Bremner (2008)) to illustrate this:

> The auditors from Lindsay & Associates are due to arrive Monday to begin the interim audit of FTE Enterprises. As FTE's controller, you just learned today (Wednesday) that a group of business executives from Moscow will arrive on Monday to examine your accounting systems. Previously you had agreed to assist this group in implementing similar accounting strategies in their country whenever they could arrange to be in Milwaukee. Because the visitation involves not only you but the entire MIS Department and several employees in the Accounting Department, you must arrange for the interim audit to be rescheduled.
>
> *Lehman and DuFrene (2002, p. 274)*

As can be seen, there are a number of potential implied texts in this situation, but none of these is available for the student writer to refer to or draw upon. This example is not untypical, and illustrates the point that although the existence of other texts is tacitly but very broadly recognised in these books, this recognition does not translate into explanations and tasks that bring to the fore the realities of intertextuality and its role in binding texts together in a coherent manner. An important point is that this kind of scripted context in effect tells the writer who they are and what they want, thus removing any need on the student's part to make the kinds of decisions relating to content and purpose that they would expect to face in the workplace. This is also a reductive approach to writing practice in that it can encourage students to think of and create workplace texts as standalone entities, rather than components in wider processes of communicative activity. This potential problem is in fact noted by Evans (2010, p. 165) in the context of his own research: he explains that in "compartmentalising the various linguistic codes, media and skills, the study fails to capture ... the interdependence of reading, writing, speaking and listening in the production of professional discourse".

In concluding this examination of business communication textbooks, I note the dangers of treating texts as isolated, decontextualised events, rather than components in larger genre systems, and call for the provision of "a richer discursive environment, and one which would give students the opportunity to make more authentic rhetorical responses to different situations" (Bremner, 2008, p. 307), a call echoed by Evans (2012) and Ho (2011).

Tackling intertextuality in a classroom setting

In the light of these concerns, a colleague and I (Bremner and Costley, 2016) have been working on the production of classroom writing tasks that might make the kinds of intertextual demands on students more closely resembling those they could expect in the workplace. It has been seen from the foregoing discussion of workplace writing that email – "the primary medium of internal and external business communication" (Evans, 2012, p. 203) – has the potential to make considerable intertextual demands on writers, and that it could also serve as an arena in which to situate tasks that would require students to draw on multiple texts as they write. While there has been research on email writing in academic contexts, much of this has looked at student-instructor emails, considering the impact of power relationships on the ways in which requests are framed and register is managed (e.g. Biesenbach-Lucas, 2007; Chen, 2001, 2006; Economidou-Kogetsidis, 2011). (The question of how power relationships affect workplace writing is considered in Chapter 6.) Moreover, these studies have tended to deal with emails as standalone texts rather than components in discourse flows, and thus do not address many of the issues that have been discussed thus far in this chapter in respect of intertextuality.

To help students experience the demands involved in managing intertextuality, I have suggested the need for "the provision of more complex sets of intertextually linked texts" (Bremner, 2008, p. 307), while Evans (2012, p. 206) is more specific, stressing the "desirability of embedding email messages in activities which involve the processing and use of spoken and written input". It is with these calls in mind that we set out to design tasks that would provide the necessary discursive environment. Following the point that students "should not be writing in a vacuum, but producing texts as responses to previous and current situations" (Bremner, 2008, p. 310), the plan was to provide a set of texts that the students would need to read and process before composing emails themselves. In giving them these tasks, which represented a departure from the typical task types – the "scripted contexts" – that they had previously encountered in their classes and textbooks, the aim was to look at how they coped with the challenges posed by the intertextual nature of these new and relatively unfamiliar tasks.

The study was carried out in a Hong Kong university with a group of undergraduate English majors taking a course in business communication. The assessments consisted of three email tasks, all of which required the students to engage in the types of communicative activities they might find themselves being required to undertake in workplace contexts, such as responding to information, making a request and delivering bad news. Although the tasks differed in terms of communicative function and focus, they made use of the same context and writer identity and were therefore part of ongoing and interconnected communications.

The first task required students to write an email requesting information from a client their manager had previously been in contact with. They had to process a chain of emails between their manager and a client regarding an order for merchandise, as well as a related voicemail message. In the second task they had to write a response to a company supplier to clarify and confirm information regarding an order. To do this they were given an email received from the supplier and subsequently annotated by their manager. In both of these tasks the students were asked to take over the communications. The third task asked the students to draft a "bad news" email on behalf of their manager, explaining to a client that their order had been affected by a warehouse fire. The students received a message from their manager which included key points the email needed to consider. This task was linked to the previous context, and as with the first two tasks, required the students to make decisions about the extent to which to draw, implicitly or explicitly, on the previous emails and other texts.

What distinguishes these tasks from the more common standalone tasks that are found in textbooks is that the writer is being asked to enter an already existing relationship in which the writer's manager and client have previously communicated about the topic at hand. This recalls the point made earlier that often the context for writing has elements tacitly understood by the writer and reader (Evans, 2012). The task for the new writer is to make appropriate decisions about how to enter the dialogue, and how much information they will need to include in their email, and which information should be prioritised. An additional component of the third task was that students were able to discuss possible ways of writing the email with classmates, with the idea that this could reflect the "talk about text" (Debs, 1991) that is a common feature of workplace practices (Gunnarsson, 1997).

The analysis of the emails showed three interrelated themes emerging as being potential issues and challenges for the students, namely, the length of the email and the amount of information included, the degree of explicitness in referring to other texts, and the management of the dialogue or relationship.

In general, it was seen that there were problems relating to the length of the emails, as most of the writers were unsure as to how much information they needed to include to reach their communicative goals. The upshot of this was that many of the emails were longer than necessary, containing considerable amounts of information that the reader would already have known. This was particularly evident in the third task, in which students followed textbook models of mediating bad news rather than locating their emails in the context of what would already be known and understood by the reader. Research using authentic email data (e.g. Warren, 2016) suggests that the length of individual emails within a discourse chain can be quite short, in contrast with the texts produced by the students in the study.

The second challenge related to how explicit writers felt they needed to be from the reader's perspective – how much information to include, and how to refer to it in a way that made sense in terms of what the reader already knew. This caused problems not only in terms of the amount of information they included, but also how this was handled linguistically. A number of specific illustrations of the students' attempts to deal with these tasks are presented, as they go a long way to highlighting the problems they experienced and the challenges that these pose for classroom teaching.

Some writers assumed too much existing knowledge on the writer's part, as shown in this example taken from the third task, in which the fire that has affected the client's order is introduced:

> due to the fire accident which happened yesterday at our warehouse, 25 white T-shirts are going to be replaced by green and blue T-shirts.

The writer's job is to gently break the news of the fire and mitigate it in some way, yet this opening has a somewhat abrupt effect, but most problematically, it also suggests that the reader is aware of the fire already.

The next example, from the second task, is an attempt to discuss knowledge shared with writer and reader:

> I am writing on behalf of Mr Smith to confirm the details of your **order** of T-shirts for the charity football match. Regarding your **order**, we would like to confirm the details as the following:
>
> 1   Size: There is not any price difference for different sizes in your **order**.
>
> (Emphasis added)

In contrast with the preceding example, there is no element of surprise for the reader here, rather the text is overloaded with referents, which makes for a somewhat clumsy style.

As can be seen from the two examples, which were not untypical, writers struggled to find an appropriate position when balancing what the reader already knows with what they need to know. It is perhaps worth including here an example of a successful attempt in which the writer managed to make a brief, succinct reference to shared knowledge and to convey the necessary amount of new information:

> It would be great if we can receive your reply by the 21st, so that we'll have enough time to process the order and deliver the T-shirts by the 29th.

As mentioned above, writers also had certain linguistic difficulties when handling shared knowledge. One area to cause problems was the use or non-use of definite articles (although this may be in part attributed to the fact that the student population are L1 speakers of Cantonese, which does not have an article system). The next example, like the first example, surprises the reader by referring to an incident that would not be known to them, whereas the writer needs to introduce the story of the fire in a less obtrusive manner:

> *Your order was ready to be delivered as we experienced the unpleasant incident of the fire at one of our warehouses.*
>
> *(Emphasis added)*

Meanwhile the non-deployment of the definite article also caused problems, as shown here:

> *Please confirm if you are able to deliver (the) 100 T-shirts to us on 27th September.*

The omission of 'the' means that this appears to refer to a new order, but in fact should refer to the existing order.

Another linguistic problem in dealing with shared information that emerged from the data was related to the nominalised proforms that writers commonly use to avoid repetition – words such as *situation, matter, question, issue, information* and so on. The purpose of these, in common with other words and phrases used to manage intertextuality, is to achieve cohesion, yet what can be seen from the following examples are sentences that are vague in their reference, in situations where a certain degree of precision would be needed:

> *I am writing on behalf of Bob to reconfirm the information that you have given us in the previous emails in order to finalize everything.*

> *I am writing on behalf of my boss Bob to acknowledge our understanding on the situation but we have noticed that there are several points on the matter that have yet to be clarified.*

The third area that presented some problems for the student writers was the management of the dialogue and relationship. This was particularly challenging as they were not the initiators of the interaction and accompanying chain of emails but were entering a dialogue that was already in progress. The problems were most evident in the third task, in which writers were supposed to tell the client about a warehouse fire that had affected their order. What writers did in a number of cases was open with a line that acknowledged the relationship, but at a very general level, rather than suggesting that they were in an ongoing discussion of an order for T-shirts, as can be seen here:

> *Thank you for your continuous support for our company; it is our pleasure to work with you.*

> *Thank you for choosing our company. We are always excited to work with ambitious and energetic corporate organizations like your company, one of the best sellers in local market.*

This could be partly explained by the models for bad news writing that students may have been exposed to, whereby they are expected to introduce 'buffers' and to bury the bad news itself deep in the email. Nevertheless these examples are bereft of any intertextual references to the more immediate situation and relationship, and as a result do not really cohere to the context of the dialogue that has been taking place. This problem was also evident in the ways in which many of the emails in the third task were finished, again not really suggesting that a dialogue about a specific order was taking place:

> *Once again, thank you for choosing our company and we are looking forward to working with you in the coming future.*
>
> *I hope this does not affect your trust in our company. We hope to work with you again in the future. Thank you for your understanding.*

Another manifestation of the difficulties experienced in closing an email can be seen in endings such as this one:

> *To express our apology, we will only charge for the 75 T-shirts at a discount of 10% off. Please find the attached new PO useful. We thank you again for your purchase.*

While it may be a useful strategy for managing bad news in that it leaves the reader with little room for manoeuvre, it is not conducive to the maintenance of an ongoing relationship between buyer and seller, and is perhaps the consequence of the writer's seeing this email as a standalone text. This is in contrast with a more acceptable way of ending the email yet encouraging further dialogue:

> *Please get back to us and tell us what will be your decision, or if you want to have further discussion of other alternatives.*

What seems clear from this study is that many of the students had difficulty dealing with the demands of an ongoing intertextual dialogue. On the one hand, their uncertainty about how much information to include, and how much to refer to, specifically resulted in lapses in coherence and readability; on the other hand, the strategies and language used, particularly in the third task, were not always consonant with the dialogue and relationship that they were entering. Given the exploratory and small-scale nature of this study it would be difficult to account for these difficulties, but one line of speculation that needs to be followed up is the possibility that students may not have actively perceived the texts they were producing as being part of a wider system of texts or dialogue, which would underline the concerns voiced in the second part of this chapter regarding the tendency in pedagogy to treat texts as isolated entities.

Conclusion

This chapter has set out to show that intertextuality is a highly prevalent feature of workplace writing, something evidenced in the large number of studies that have addressed this phenomenon in the last thirty years or so, suggesting too that it is now an acknowledged and established element of writing-related research. Over this period, there has been an increased appreciation of its prevalence as a feature of workplace writing, but in addition to this, there is a growing understanding of its function, in that it is a tool that helps give texts coherence in relation to the contexts in which they and other connected texts are found. Alongside this is the recognition that the ability to manage intertextual relations when writing is a component of an effective writer's armoury.

As I have noted, students need to "see the texts they read and produce as part of a wider, ongoing system of intertextually related practice, grounded in a professional context" (Bremner, 2008, p. 319). Yet, there is little evidence of pedagogy engaging in any focused or systematic way with the implications of the findings from research. The small-scale study reported in this chapter has perhaps unearthed some potential problems that students might encounter when engaging with tasks that involve the management of intertextuality, but this merely represents the beginning of a research trajectory that needs to be pursued along two lines. The first is the need to build on the work of Cheng and Mok (2008), Evans (2012), Warren (2013, 2016) and others who are beginning to show how intertextuality works as a cohesive tool and the ways in which it is realised linguistically; the second is to develop tasks that simulate more closely workplace writing tasks that make intertextual demands on student writers. In this way, we can build a fuller picture of how intertextuality works and is managed by experienced professionals, and of the challenges that students encounter when faced with tasks that replicate those found in the workplace. Swales's (2004) observation that we are all intertextualists may apply to the academic community, and it is fair to say that we are better informed intertextualists, but in the case of our students there is still a long way to go.

5
COLLABORATION

Introduction

The previous chapter deals with the idea that workplace texts are interconnected. One key element of this interconnectedness is that writers are constantly drawing on the work of others, directly or indirectly. Thus, much workplace writing is in effect a form of collaboration in that the inputs of different members of an organisation are being brought together to create new texts, while the fusion of different inputs from these writers is a form of intertextuality. It was noted in Chapter 1 that the various aspects of workplace writing are interconnected in many ways, and certainly it is difficult to disentangle intertextuality and collaboration for the reasons mentioned. The most basic distinction, however, is realised in the focus seen in Chapters 4 and 5. While Chapter 4 focuses on the interactions among texts, this chapter has as its focus the interactions among people as they collaborate to produce texts and, as will be seen, the pedagogical implications of addressing intertextuality and those of addressing collaboration are somewhat different.

It was observed in the opening chapter of this book that as much as 75% to 85% of writing in the workplace is collaborative in nature (Burnett, 2001). Collaborative writing, in its many forms, is an almost integral element of any organisation, and it has been the focus of considerable research interest over the last thirty years or so. This interest has come from a variety of disciplines, ranging from information systems to team management to business communication, to name but a few. This chapter looks initially at the ways in which collaborative writing has been defined and the taxonomies that have been generated to explain the ways in which it is enacted. Alongside these definitions and taxonomies, there have been a number of longitudinal ethnographic studies of collaborative writing, which suggest that the associated processes are less structured and ordered than we might hope. These studies are discussed in the next part of the chapter, and it will be seen that the processes involved are somewhat resistant to the attempts to pin them down that are implicit in work on taxonomies. Any bid to define the nature of collaborative writing is based on varying motives, whether relating to research or pedagogy, and the ramifications of differing approaches to defining and explaining collaborative writing are discussed, particularly in respect of their implications for teaching. Related to this is the issue of whether collaborative writing is a skill or a set of skills that can be taught: what does it take to be a successful collaborative writer? What options does the teacher have to help students achieve this? The chapter goes on to examine the ways in which collaborative writing has been approached in classroom contexts, discussing issues such as the teachability and portability of skills that relate to this important feature of workplace activity.

What is collaborative writing?

As noted, research relating to collaborative writing in the workplace is an established field. Since the pioneering work of Faigley and Miller (1982) and Paradis, Dobrin and Miller (1985), a substantial body of work has taken shape, ranging from studies that describe and categorise aspects of collaborative writing (e.g. Couture and Rymer, 1989; Ede and Lunsford, 1990; Lowry, Curtis and Lowry, 2004; Witte, 1992;) to ethnographies conducted in organisational settings (e.g. Cross, 1994, 2001; Wegner, 2004). Yet, this profusion of research has not led to a precise definition of collaborative writing; indeed, Gollin (1999) suggests that there is no generally agreed notion of exactly what it is, something she attributes to its "complexity and interactivity" (p. 287). This presents a challenge to both researchers and teachers seeking to describe, categorise and explain collaborative writing. In this regard, Bremner (2014b, p. 487) suggests "that collaboration is so imbricated in workplace activity that it is difficult to decide where the boundaries of collaborative writing lie for the purposes of analysis". This relates to the point made regarding the relationship between collaborative writing and intertextuality, a point fleshed out by Reither (1993, p. 198), who contends that "writing is 'social', 'collaborative', 'intertextual' in that authors challenge, modify, use, build on and add to the utterances of others to join in 'co-operative competition' with them in the process of text and knowledge making".

Attempts at defining collaborative writing have ranged in their level of detail and specificity. At one end, we see Ede and Lunsford, who describe it simply as "any writing done in collaboration with one or more persons" (1990, pp. 15–16), while what can be seen in the more fully elaborated explanations of collaborative writing are echoes of the idea discussed in Chapter 4, namely, that influences on written texts will come from both written and spoken discourses. Couture and Rymer's (1989) definition extends to activities surrounding the process and they talk about "discourse interactions" or the "oral and written communication pertaining to a document during the process of planning, drafting and revising it" (p. 79), saying that "it may be fair to conclude that significant writing is enveloped in talk" (p. 79). Jones (2005, p. 450) takes the intertextual influences further, defining collaborative writing as "interaction by an author or authors with people, documents, and organizational rules in the process of creating documents".

In many cases these definitions come across as implicit statements about what can or should be investigated when researching collaborative writing practices. The more precise and detailed definitions provided by some researchers hint at a belief that collaborative writing can be pinned down in some way and deconstructed to uncover a set of constituent skills and subskills that can be identified and possibly mastered, which of course has potential implications for pedagogy. For this reason, it is worth quoting in full the very detailed definition developed by Lowry *et al.* (2004: pp. 72–74):

> an iterative and social process that involves a team focused on a common objective that negotiates, coordinates, and communicates during the creation of a common document. The potential scope of CW goes beyond the more basic act of joint composition to include the likelihood of pre- and posttask activities, team formation, and planning. Furthermore, based on the desired writing task, CW includes the possibility of many different writing strategies, activities, document control approaches, team roles, and work modes.

Lowry *et al.*'s definition is based on their examination of a large number of studies of collaborative writing and it would seem that their goal is to provide a comprehensive explanation of this type of writing, along with a taxonomy and nomenclature. It is of course difficult to come up with a definition that could be applied to any workplace, because of the wide variety of ways in which collaborative writing can play out. But what comes through from this definition is an implied sense of order and collective purpose in collaborative writing that is not necessarily reflected in some of the group writing processes that might be labelled as collaborative (Bremner, 2014b).

Jones (2007) suggests that we should resist reliance on "a single narrow definition", rather we should see collaboration "as consisting of a rich, varied group of activities" (p. 290). Yet, if we are to understand how this highly pervasive feature of writing in the workplace functions, it can be argued that some kind of taxonomy is needed to achieve a common understanding among researchers, particularly given the fact that collaborative activity has been a focus of research interest in a number of different disciplines (Forman, 2004; Lowry *et al.*, 2004). It would not be possible in this chapter to do justice to all the work that has attempted to provide taxonomies of collaborative writing, but two or three important studies will be cited here to give a sense of the thinking behind these attempts.

An early example is the work of Witte (1992), who describes four categories of collaborative activity: in the "traditional" mode, two or more writers work together, sharing equally the responsibility for the final product; a variation on this is the "committee" mode in which the level of responsibility assumed by each writer can vary; "incidental" collaboration consists of "brief, often highly focused interactions … through any medium"; the final category is "covert" collaboration, which consists of interactions among writers, conscious or otherwise, by means of "both linguistic and non-linguistic texts" (1992, p. 296). These different modes capture much of the spectrum of what goes on, with the last category, "covert", similar to the notion of "occluded genres" discussed by Swales (2004), accounting for many of the less visible intertextual and organisational influences considered here and in Chapter 4. At the same time, this "covert" mode, in contrast with Lowry et al.'s (2004) definition, seems to include some of the less planned and controlled activity that can occur as part of a collaborative writing endeavour.

The work of Lowry et al. (2004) and Jones (2005, 2007) can be seen as a concerted attempt at understanding the ways in which collaborative writing functions. Lowry et al. (2004) propose a detailed taxonomy that has four overarching elements: writing strategies, activities, document control modes and roles. Writing strategies are described as "a team's overall approach for coordinating the writing of a collaborative document" (p. 74); activities, dynamic and iterative in nature, can occur throughout the process, from prewriting to postwriting, and can include elements such as socialisation, communication and negotiation; document control modes, as the term suggests, are the ways selected to manage the collaborative document; the fourth element is the various roles that participants play in the process. Lowry et al. (2004) also talk about "work modes", which refer to the degree of proximity and synchronicity that can be found in a collaborative writing group. This taxonomy, which is only described in the most basic terms here, represents a very full attempt to understand and categorise collaborative writing activity.

The other major effort in this regard can be seen in the work of Jones (2005, 2007), whose "Comprehensive Collaborative Continuum" describes three categories of collaborative interaction: contextual collaboration, which "involves the context of the organization itself" (2005, p. 451); hierarchical collaboration, defined in Ede and Lunsford (1990, p. 133) as "carefully, and often rigidly, structured, driven by highly specific goals, and carried out by people playing clearly defined and delimited roles"; and group collaboration, which "involves a collection of people who largely plan, draft, and revise together" (2005, p. 454). The Continuum is so called because the three categories are positioned along it according to the degree of overtness of the collaboration; contextual sits at the least overt end and group at the most overt.

Contextual collaboration is a helpful notion in that it accounts for the influence of the organisation on texts, in the shape of templates, practices, culture and so on. Winsor (1989, p. 271) explains this aspect of writing in a workplace setting very clearly: "any individual's writing is called forth and shaped by the needs and the aim of the organization, and . . . to be understood it must draw on vocabulary, knowledge, and beliefs other organization members share". The idea of writers drawing on previous texts (Jones (2005) refers to this as "document borrowing", Freedman et al. (1994) as "intertextual borrowing") and drawing on the practices of an organisation more generally is discussed in the previous chapter in the context of intertextuality.

Hierarchical collaboration is also a key concept in that it relates to power relationships in the workplace, in particular to the question of who is allowed to contribute to the collaborative process and when they can do this (cf. Bhatia, 2004). This issue is also discussed elsewhere (Cross, 1994; Gollin, 1999; Holmes and Stubbe, 2003); Hansen (1995) mentions it as a source of conflict, while Angouri and Harwood (2008) look at seniority levels within an organisation as a factor in collaborative writing processes. Bremner (2014a) also notes the hierarchical nature of collaborative editing in his study of an intern in a PR company, evidenced by the fact that texts were generally passed up through the organisation to be edited.

The third category, group collaboration, sits at the more overt end of his continuum, and here Jones (2005) talks of shared goals, a sense of group identity and the general view of the group that they are involved in a collective effort. As can be seen, this vision has something in common with features of Lowry *et al.*'s (2004) definition of collaborative writing, e.g. "focused on a common objective" and "team formation" (p. 72).

The research outlined – Witte (1992), Lowry *et al.* (2004) and Jones (2005, 2007) – effectively covers the gamut of collaborative writing activity. It should be noted that Lowry *et al.* (2004) are primarily concerned with providing a comprehensive taxonomy for researchers that takes into account the huge range of research from diverse disciplines that exists in the literature. But looked at from a pedagogical perspective, of the three approaches to describing and explaining collaborative writing outlined, Jones's (2005, 2007) model seems to be the most accessible, in that without being overwhelming in its provision of detail, its three categories clearly bring to the fore important issues about collaborative practices, namely, that there is a considerable degree of less visible collaborative influence that comes from the organisation, that hierarchical relationships play a large part in the management of collaborative practices and that collective purpose in collaborative endeavours is desirable.

It is worth dwelling briefly on the word "collaborative". While at various points in history the terms "collaboration" and "collaborator" have had fairly negative connotations, in the context of the workplace the term "collaborative writing" conjures up groups of colleagues of being on same page, harmoniously working together towards the same objectives. This is perhaps in keeping with Jones's (2005) category of group collaboration and some of the elements of Lowry *et al.*'s (2004) definition, and there is a certain sense of order and common purpose implied by these. However, it is important to note that there is plenty of evidence in the literature to indicate that collaborative writing is not as predictable, ordered or linear a process as some definitions and textbooks would have us believe; rather, it can be a fairly disordered process (e.g. Dourish and Bellotti, 1992; Winsor, 2000). The definition used in this book to explain collaborative writing attempts to be broad without being prescriptive and comes from an earlier study conducted by this researcher. The term is taken "to refer to all activity and communication surrounding the construction of texts by multiple contributors, whether written or spoken, and whether planned or incidental" (Bremner *et al.*, 2014, p. 2).

Collaborative writing in workplace settings

The possibility that collaborative writing can be less predictable and ordered than is implied by some definitions is linked to the fact that it takes place in specific workplace settings, each with its own constitution and dynamic. As Cross (1993) explains, "Culture, text, and process . . . are not discrete facets of collaborative writing" (p. 143), and much of the research that has investigated the nature of collaborative writing has taken a social constructionist perspective, viewing writing and the surrounding processes as intrinsically linked to the contexts in which it takes place. There has been a number of longitudinal studies of workplace writing in specific organisational settings; some consider collaboration as part of the broader process under investigation (e.g. Beaufort, 1997, 1999, 2000; Bremner, 2014a; Haas and Witte, 2001; Pogner, 2003; Smart, 2006; Winsor, 2003), while others focus more closely on the collaborative aspect (e.g. Cross, 1994, 2001, 2011; Gollin, 1999; Paradis *et al.*, 1985; Wegner, 2004; Yates and Orlikowski, 2002).

One important element of collaborative writing activity that can be seen in many of these studies – and this is evidence that the process does not always run smoothly – is the role of conflict. The possibility of conflict is increased when groups or individuals come from different workplace cultures or disciplines, an issue discussed by Burnett (1993, 1996), Gooch (2005), Palmeri (2004) and Spilka (1993). One researcher who has taken a particular interest in conflict in workplace writing is Cross (1994, 2000, 2001), whose research has provided some valuable insights into collaborative writing processes. His study of large-scale collaboration in a financial conglomerate (2000, 2001) illustrates what can happen when collaborative processes break down, and he goes on to describe the subsequent rescue and resurrection of the process, or what he calls the formation of a "collective mind" that can be "found in the heedful interrelation of group members" (2001, p. 79). It should be emphasised that conflict is not necessarily a problematic element of collaborative writing. Palmeri characterises it as "not inherently positive or negative" (2004, p. 60), and there are studies that indicate that substantive conflict (i.e. cognitive rather than emotional) has the potential for beneficial outcomes (Burnett, 1993; Dauterman, 1993).

There is a possible tension between accounts of collaborative writing practices in workplace settings, which can be "relatively unstructured" (Dourish and Bellotti, 1992) or "improvised" (Winsor, 2000, p. 172), and attempts to bring order to these processes through the development of taxonomies. Indeed, a reliance on taxonomies and prescriptive definitions risks the possibility of overlooking the more unstructured and incidental elements of the collaborative process. Of course, many collaborative writing processes run smoothly, but we do not want to give our students the impression that collaborative writing is always an ordered process that can be reduced to its constituent skills, which can then be taught in some way. This leads on to the question of how we can prepare our students for the challenges of collaborative writing in the workplace.

Teaching collaborative writing

There is a general consensus that collaborative writing is a sufficiently integral element of workplace activity to warrant our attention as teachers. As Nelson (2003) says "it is important to expose students to ... collaborative writing practices in the classroom if we want them to seek out these practices as professionals" (p. 274) – a point also made by Colen and Petelin (2004), Dovey (2006), and Gollin (1999). Bremner (2014b) identifies three issues that pertain to the question of how to approach the teaching of collaborative workplace writing in academic contexts: the difference between the workplace and the academy, the extent to which skills are transferable or portable from one context to another, and the degree to which collaborative writing should be actively taught.

The differences between the workplace and the academy are addressed in Chapter 1. These include the basis on which the community is formed; the professional, disciplinary and organisational culture of that community; the composition of the community in terms of the varied roles played by participants; the diversity of their background and experience; levels of knowledge and ability; the balance of power; the function of writing; the kinds of contributions allowed, expected and made by the different participants; and the kinds of texts that writers are able to work with and draw on, i.e. the levels of potential contextual collaboration (Jones, 2005). These differences are discussed in greater depth in Freedman *et al.* (1994), Freedman and Adam (1996) and Bremner (2010). Taken together the differences add up to two substantially different environments and contexts for writing, underlined by Freedman *et al.*'s (1994) contention that "the nature of the institutional context necessarily and inevitably shapes the writing in ways that cannot be altered" (p. 221).

So great are the differences between the two contexts, it would seem, that one might question the value of instituting collaborative writing in one, i.e. the academy, when it is so clearly different from the other. This leads to the second related issue – whether skills acquired in the classroom can be transferred to the workplace. The thinking among many researchers on this question is not particularly sanguine (e.g. Anson and Forsberg, 1990; Dias and Paré, 2000; Freedman and Adam, 2000), although recent work by Artemeva (2005, 2009) has suggested that it may be possible to teach domain-specific communication separately from the local context. A more in-depth handling of this question of the portability of skills can be found in Artemeva and Fox (2014).

Clearly any attempt to effect the transfer of skills and competencies relating to collaborative writing entails identifying those that can lead to success in this area. A number of studies have considered skills associated with teamwork in general and collaborative writing more specifically. In the context of the former, Newstrom and Scannell (1998, p. xi) have suggested that high-performance teams "usually exhibit an overall team purpose, mutual accountability, collective work products, shared leadership roles, high cohesiveness, collaborating in deciding task assignments and collective assessment of their own success". As can be seen, there are echoes here of Lowry *et al.* (2004), in that the notion of everyone working together in a purposeful way is emphasised. Meanwhile Rentz, Arduser, Meloncon and Debs (2009) mention listening to each other and trying not to dominate as being helpful in achieving successful writing as a group. But these goals, while certainly desirable, seem to represent general recommendations or exhortations rather than specific practices, and the ways in which they could be achieved would vary according to the context of collaboration.

More specific attempts to identify and break down team characteristics and translate them into something more specific can be found in the work of Chen, Donahue and Klimoski (2004), and Onrubia and Engel (2009). The former have built on the work of Stevens and Campion (1994), extracting five KSA (knowledge, skills and abilities) dimensions, namely, conflict resolution, collaborative problem solving, communication, goal setting and performance management, and planning and task coordination. The latter take a slightly different tack as they identify and evaluate the main strategies required "for collaborative elaboration of written products" (Onrubia and Engel, 2009, p. 1,260) in respect of the ways in which members of a collaborative writing group divide up and tackle the components of a task.

The sheer volume of work that has been conducted in relation to collaborative writing – and the studies reported here represent only a small proportion of this research – serve as an indicator of the importance of this feature of the workplace. At the same time, it is clear how complex it is and this complexity represents a considerable challenge for teachers of workplace writing. As mentioned, there is a certain consensus that students should be given opportunities to collaborate (Colen and Petelin, 2004; Dovey, 2006; Nelson, 2003), but at the same time it has also been claimed that not enough attention has been paid to this aspect of learning (Chen et al., 2004; Rentz et al., 2009). Hansen (2006) goes as far as to suggest that "it appears that the majority of faculty who place students into teams do nothing more than that" (p. 15), something also suggested by Snyder (2009).

A study of popular business communication textbooks that I conducted (Bremner, 2010) also supports the sense that collaborative writing is given insufficient emphasis from a pedagogical perspective. It was observed that in many cases the tasks provided are based on the idea that teamwork simply means working together, rather than attempting to take into account the complexities of collaborative writing that can be found in the workplace. This can be seen in some of the examples cited from these books, e.g. "Working in teams of three or four, assume the role of grievance committee of your union" (Ober, 2004, p. 201); "After you have completed your research, develop your collaboratively written report" (Roebuck, 2006, p. 217); "Formal report: Intercultural Communication … Write your report individually or in teams" (Guffey and Du-Babcock, 2008, p. 291). The incidence of task instructions of this nature only serves to reinforce Hansen's (2006) contention.

Bremner (2010) also contends that the textbooks offer a somewhat idealised vision of teamwork, where everything runs smoothly and everyone is on the same collective page, echoing to some extent the definition of collaborative writing proposed by Lowry et al. (2004). In addition, it was noted that a number of tasks are over scripted, with participants being told who they are and what they think. The consequence of this is that aside from the possibility that it prevents students from bringing their own thoughts and views to the collaborative process, there is little scope for different viewpoints, which in turn makes the possibility of conflict less likely. As explained in this chapter and noted in many of the business communication textbooks, conflict is often seen as an important element in collaborative writing. The study concludes that while these books provide explanations as to the nature of collaborative writing, they do not give students opportunities to practise it in a meaningful or realistic way, which, it is suggested, is "akin to explaining a grammatical structure without giving any opportunities for communicative practice" (Bremner, 2010, p. 130).

The question then is what form any attempts to induct students into the world of collaborative writing should take. The fact that much of the research examining the nature of collaborative writing takes a social constructionist position has an influence on the thinking in this regard. In light of this perspective, Storch (2005) suggests that "learners should be encouraged to participate in activities which foster interaction and co-construction of knowledge" (p. 154). Many other approaches to the teaching of collaborative writing have focused on the social aspect of the process, discussing the need to provide a community in the classroom (Doheny-Farina, 1986; Gollin, 1999) and opportunities for students to interact (Couture and Rymer, 1989) and play multiple roles (Dias *et al.*, 1999). Bremner (2010), meanwhile, looking at the positive role that conflict can play in collaborative writing, suggests that activities that capitalise on the possibility of difference in groups could be considered.

The degree of instructor intervention is an issue for some. Gollin (1999) says that "Collaborative writing is a complex activity and needs to be actively taught" (p. 289), a position also taken by Colen and Petelin (2004), and Dovey (2006). Fredrick (2008), citing Bolton (1999), suggests that it is not enough to simply provide students with opportunities to collaborate, rather that instructors need to work as facilitators. She proposes facilitation strategies such as actively teaching teamwork, which include getting students to read about collaboration and analyse and reflect on previous collaborative projects, grading teamwork, and self- and peer evaluation. Some work has looked at the effects of implementing collaborative writing processes in classroom settings (Baker, 1991; Bekins and Merriam, 2004; Hemby *et al.*, 2004), but this has not led to agreement on what might serve as a useful pedagogy. This can be attributed to the fact that the academy and the workplace differ in so many ways as sites of collaboration, as already discussed. The gap between the two contexts poses questions for the relationship between research and pedagogy. Fredrick (2008) claims that most research in professional communication "assumes that the teamwork strategies suggested for working professionals apply to students as well", and questions this assumption, saying that these strategies do not address "complicated authority issues" (p. 440), referring to the hierarchies seen in the respective contexts. Seibold and Kang (2008) also have concerns about this issue, suggesting that there is a mismatch between what is taught about teamwork and the realities of the workplace. They have doubts, too, about the value of lists of desirable teamwork skills: "At best, such lists provide students with templates ... At worst, they perpetuate the chasm between education and real workplace dynamics" (p. 435).

The picture that emerges from this account suggests that collaborative writing has generated research that is somewhat diverse in its aims – from exhaustive taxonomies to wide-ranging ethnographies. At the same time, there has emerged a multiplicity of approaches to dealing with it in the classroom, ranging from teachers who simply place students in groups to complete a particular assignment, to those attempting to facilitate collaborative activities that might engender something resembling "real workplace dynamics" (Seibold and Kang, 2008), to those who actively train students in the competencies that have been identified as conducive to successful collaborative work.

Clearly there is no consensus on how to manage the teaching of collaborative writing, but any approach that is taken should be informed by some sense on the instructor's part of what kinds of dynamic and interaction they want to foster in the student group. It could be argued that those teachers who simply place students in groups to perform a task or assignment (cf. Hansen, 2006) are not interested in helping develop collaborative writing skills but have organised groups for reasons of expediency. Certainly, there is ample anecdotal evidence from this writer's experience that many university courses include group assignments in order to reduce the grading load rather than because of any interest in collaborative writing as a practice to be encouraged. But if there is genuine interest in helping students experience something akin to the realities of workplace collaboration and a desire to help them develop appropriate skills, then something more considered than arranging students in groups is called for.

Task design and collaborative interaction

In relation to this Bremner *et al.* (2014) make a distinction between what they term "group work" and "collaborative work". They define the former as "work in which students are simply brought together to perform a task, and, for reasons possibly relating to the nature of that task or to other factors, they experience low levels of interaction" (p. 14). Such work does not involve much in the way of discussion and often many parts of the task are performed individually. As for collaborative work, this leads to students spending more time in brainstorming, discussion and the exchange of ideas: "they engage more with the task and with each other, and these higher levels of interaction increase the likelihood of their learning from the process" (ibid., p. 14).

If the intention is to involve students in collaborative work as described by Bremner *et al.* (2014), the selection and design of appropriate tasks becomes a crucial factor. In this regard, Fredrick (2008) stresses that "teachers should begin by critically questioning whether their assignments really value the *process* of teamwork" (p. 446, original emphasis), going on to explain that "Successful collaboration begins with a well-designed assignment that highlights the necessity and benefits of working as a team" (p. 447). The growing body of research noted in this chapter that looks at workplace-oriented collaboration in academic contexts (e.g. Baker, 1991; Bekins and Merriam, 2004; Fredrick, 2008; Hemby *et al.*, 2004; Snyder, 2009) tends to be more focused on the management of collaborative processes than on the features of the task. Similarly, surveys of work relating to collaboration and pedagogy (Hansen, 2006; Thompson, 2001; Wickliff, 1997) do not address in any depth the relationship between task design and collaborative interaction.

However, a recent study conducted by Bremner *et al.* (2014), addressed this very issue, looking at the impact that different task types had on the ways in which students interacted collaboratively in various assignments that were aimed at improving workplace writing. In this study, thirty-two students were interviewed at length and described the ways in which they tackled the various group assignments they were given during their secondary school and undergraduate studies.

All the students interviewed were engaged in a final-year Professional Communication Project (PCP), whereby they worked in groups (four to eight per group) attached to a host organisation, carrying out a wide variety of tasks intended to promote the organisation. These tasks required the students to communicate both internally (among themselves and with the host organisation) and externally (with other organisations and the general public); this communication involved the production of a range of texts, including proposals, reports, emails, press releases, flyers, posters and other promotional documents. The idea behind the research was to compare students' approaches and interactions on the PCP with the ways in which they dealt with other group tasks that they had encountered in their studies; typically, these latter task types would be research assignments leading to a report or presentation, or an analytical task of some kind.

The findings from this study suggested that the design of the group tasks did in fact affect student interaction, in that there were notable differences when comparing their approaches to the PCP and to their other group tasks. These differences were seen in a number of areas: the amount of brainstorming that took place before participant roles in the group were allocated; the criteria the participants used for dividing up the tasks; the intensity of editing cycles and the levels of attention to detail; and the causes of conflict and the ways in which participants dealt with this. In general, it was found that the ways in which the students collaborated and interacted on the PCP were more "workplace-like" when compared to their approaches to other academy-based tasks, as explained below.

In the PCP, high levels of brainstorming took place as students worked out how to allocate roles and tasks for the project, whereas in other assignments students reported little or no discussion before dividing up the tasks. The division of labour and the allocation of roles in the PCP were based on the skills and strengths of each group member; in other assignments, the main factors affecting division of labour were concerns for the equitable distribution of the workload and the inclinations of individual group members. As for the actual process of writing, the PCP tended to involve substantial recursive cycles of editing and reviewing; other assignments underwent fewer stages of editing. Finally, when it came to the role of conflict, in the PCP students reported instances of disagreement, saying that these tended to be cognitive rather than emotional; significantly they viewed these positively and as an opportunity for learning. By contrast, students said that in other assignments they tried to avoid conflict. The main issue that led to disagreement was that of workload, and their desire to avoid conflict often led to an imbalance in this regard.

The inference from these findings is that the PCP generated the kinds of interactions that characterise "collaborative work", whereas many of the other assignments that the informants worked on led to "group work", i.e. work that did not require them to interact frequently or meaningfully. The study goes on to try and identify the features of the PCP that engendered collaborative interaction within the student groups. The first point is that there should be a need for a collective approach inherent in the task, a point made by Fredrick (2008). Because this feature was lacking in many of the non-PCP tasks, students were able to divide them up into roughly equal parts and complete these independently, without any need to consult other group members. In the case of the PCP, however, the size and complexity of the projects required the groups to address them collectively and to pool their skills and strengths, such as design, editing and so on; it was also explained by one respondent that "even if you're not required to do some parts, you still need to have a basic understanding of the whole project". If the different elements of a project are connected intertextually this will also necessitate more interaction to achieve consistency and conformity in the various texts that are produced. A set of promotional texts, (for example flyers, posters, press releases and so on), would be expected to have a consistency of vocabulary and style that would require consultation among the writers to ensure that they were delivering the same message in the same manner.

Second, the presence or absence of a creative element in the assigned task was found to be a major influence on the interaction patterns in the student groups. The presence of a creative element led to higher levels of engagement and interaction, which was seen in the PCP groups whose task was to come up with ideas and textual products to help promote their host organisations. Involvement in a creative project and the accompanying sense of achievement served as powerful motivational factors for many of the respondents. The non-PCP tasks, however, rarely provided opportunities for creativity.

A further motivational element lay in whether the task was intended to lead to a real-world outcome, as was the case with the PCP, as opposed to the display of knowledge (most of the non-PCP tasks were limited to this). Further discussion of this distinction can be found in Gimenez (2016), Nathan (2013) and Zhu (2004). Connected with this is the idea that the students should see the task itself as important, which should come from the nature of the task itself, i.e. "from the challenges of creating textual products for authentic purposes and authentic audiences" (Bremner *et al.*, 2014, p. 16).

Much of this section and indeed the whole thorny problem of how we can induct our students into the complexities of collaborative writing in a useful and meaningful way, is concerned with the question of authenticity. Mabrito's (1999) point that it is more or less impossible to duplicate workplace scenarios in academic contexts (see Chapter 1) is well taken, but we should nevertheless make an effort to create an approximation of the dynamics, tensions and constraints of the workplace insofar as we can. Client-oriented projects such as the one discussed here, and considered by Fredrick (2008) and Rentz *et al.* (2009), go a long way towards creating the kind of environment that has workplace-like features and which will engender something resembling real-world collaborative interactions. In this way, students will be able to experience and reflect on the challenges these kinds of scenarios present as they prepare for their entry into the real world of work. Such projects are also motivational in that they appear to the students both valid and purposeful. As Freedman and Adam (1996) explain, "A key criterion of success ... relates to the degree to which the learner sees the task as authentic—that is, one that has consequences in its context" (p. 411).

Conclusion

It has been stressed throughout this book that the elements that contribute to workplace writing are very much interconnected and that successful performance will not be achieved by the management of the mechanics of writing alone. This point is very much evident when it comes to collaborative writing – collaboration involves working with other people and interacting with them in different ways, both spoken and written. Studies of writing in the PR industry, for example, show that writers often need to take on board the perspectives of different internal audiences and these may be divergent (Pander Maat, 2008; Sleurs *et al.*, 2003; Sleurs and Jacobs, 2005), illustrating the kinds of challenge that working together can present. Much interaction in relation to jointly produced texts will involve the management of interpersonal relationships, with all their attendant power issues. As intimated earlier, hierarchy and power are undoubtedly major factors in collaborative writing. By extension, it seems reasonable to suggest that the ability to manage relationships is a necessary component of collaborative writing competence. The question of power and relationships and how these impact on workplace writing are looked at in greater detail in Chapter 6.

Collaboration is a far-reaching element of workplace writing and, as well as being instrumental in the production of texts, it also plays a part in the ways in which newcomers learn to write and in which they are inducted into professional communities of practice. By interacting (i.e. collaborating) with more experienced colleagues, or "old timers", newcomers to a given workplace can develop relevant knowledge and skills. This form of interaction and learning is explained as cognitive apprenticeship by Lave and Wenger (1991) in their work on situated learning and legitimate peripheral participation; the question of learning through participation and interaction is also considered by Rogoff (1991), Freedman and Adam (1996), and Beaufort (2008, p. 230), who makes the point that "Collaborative writing is not just a division of labor; rather it entails interactive cognitive processes among writers, editors and managers". The ways in which new writers learn and are socialised into workplace communities are examined in Chapter 9.

A further consideration that intersects with collaboration is the use of technology and its effects on the ways in which writers can interact to produce texts collaboratively. Kock *et al.* (2001) talk about e-collaboration, which they define as "collaboration among individuals engaged in a common task using electronic technologies" (p. 1). Such collaboration can take different forms and might involve software that enables group decision-making or the actual creation of texts online by geographically dispersed participants using Wikis or Google Docs, for example. The impact of different channels of communication on writing, the ways in which they are used and the reasons for choosing them are the focus of Chapter 7 – the ways in which technologies are used to facilitate collaborative writing will be looked at in that chapter.

In many ways collaboration is one of the more elusive elements of workplace writing performance because of the multiple factors that influence its course, and as a result it poses a greater challenge from a pedagogical perspective than some of the other aspects of workplace writing examined in this book. Despite the efforts of some researchers to pin it down and reduce it to a set of identifiable, manageable and even teachable skills, the reality is that it is a messy, unpredictable business, because so many other contextual elements of workplace activity come into play: other texts, other people, power, accepted ways of doing things, time, the availability of media to communicate and so on. These attempts at creating taxonomies are laudable and certainly have helped in providing a greater understanding of the complex nature of collaborative writing; yet its very complexity and messiness is a problem from a pedagogical perspective, simply because it does not add up to a body of behaviours than can be easily passed on in the classroom. It is something to be experienced and reflected on rather than taught and explained, notwithstanding the substantial gap that exists between the culture and the realities of the classroom and the workplace. Having said that, there are no simple solutions, nor are there any generally agreed ways of narrowing this gap.

Nevertheless, as teachers we need to create tasks and situations that provide students with opportunities to experience and reflect on the kinds of interactions and tensions that they may encounter in the workplace. These situations will not replicate those of the workplace exactly, for the reasons discussed in this chapter, but we can go some way to providing something that approximates to the real world. Such opportunities can offer a number of benefits, such as building interactivity and teamwork, developing negotiation skills (Spilka, 1993), improved decision-making (Hansen, 2006; Storch, 2005) and "understanding about diversity in the workplace, and experience coping with group dynamics" (Ding and Ding, 2008, p. 458). This can be achieved in different ways: my own experience is that something along the lines of the PCP can provide a rich experience, requiring students to engage in a substantial project that entails multiple audiences, both internal and external, and multiple interactions. Not all institutions have access to organisations that can give such opportunities, but there are alternative approaches that can be located in the academy yet which have external audiences (Fredrick, 2008) or more structured tasks of the kind described by Bremner (2010). But collaborative writing should not be ignored – it is a pervasive feature of workplace practice and one that needs to be addressed head on.

6

POWER, POLITENESS AND LANGUAGE

Introduction

The fundamental differences between the academy and the workplace as contexts for writing have been highlighted at various points in this book thus far, and perhaps nowhere are they more evident than in the ways that power is distributed in the respective settings. In the classroom, we tend very often to see homogeneity in age, experience and knowledge, which leads to a context where power, insofar as it is an issue, is for the most part shared equally among students, with only the teacher representing a figure of authority. As for the workplace, power and disparities of power are ubiquitous. Within an organisation we can see differences in areas such as age, experience, knowledge, status, authority and so on, while communication with audiences outside the organisation also involves the handling of power differences, such as those implied in a relationship between buyer and seller, for example. Imbalances of this kind place considerable constraints and expectations on the ways in which people can write in professional settings.

Managing workplace interactions in the context of power relationships, whether internal or external, requires an understanding of the prevailing situation and writer–reader (or speaker–listener) relationship and the subsequent selection of appropriate language to meet one's communicative goals. This chapter discusses the nature of the challenges that this poses and ways of addressing them. It looks at notions of power and politeness and how the relationship between these is manifested in language, considering theories and unresolved issues that have come out of the research that has been conducted in this area.

A central element of managing politeness and relationships more generally is the selection of an appropriate register for communication. Students and novice writers often struggle with this, and this chapter briefly surveys research that has attempted to identify the kinds of problems they experience. The chapter concludes by considering different approaches and tasks that could be deployed to help students handle this particularly testing aspect of workplace writing.

The study of the interrelationship between power, politeness and language has generated a vast body of research and it is necessary to restrict the scope of this chapter, inasmuch as this is possible, to the aspects of this subject that pertain to writing in workplace settings. However, in focusing on writing, I do not wish to underplay the role of speaking, which if anything plays a more substantial role in the management of power relations. It has already been seen in Chapters 4 and 5 that much writing is surrounded by and influenced by intertextual and collaborative talk, and the point was made that one component of successful collaborative writing is the ability to manage relationships, with much of this involving speaking rather than writing. Certainly, a substantial proportion of the research relating to power and politeness is concerned with speaking, but as will be seen, the key issues surrounding this topic largely apply to writing as well. In the light of this, the chapter deals with some of the thinking relating to politeness and spoken discourse before shifting the focus more specifically to writing. To limit the scope yet further, the chapter takes a particular look at the challenges and problems posed by making requests, as these are a common and yet problematic element of workplace writing.

Power and language: the challenges for writers

In line with the theories outlined in Chapter 2, this chapter views the relationship between power and language from a social constructionist perspective, following Holmes and Stubbe (2003): "Language is clearly a crucial means of enacting power, and equally a very important component in the construction of social reality" (p. 3). The chapter is to a considerable extent problematised around the difficulties that student and novice workplace writers experience when trying to frame their writing in the context of the power relationships they have with their intended readers, and it is therefore motivated to some degree by the concomitant pedagogical implications. For this reason, it will focus on aspects of power and the management of relationships through writing that seem most relevant for writers embarking or about to embark on their careers. Holmes and Stubbe explain that power "includes both the ability to control others and the ability to accomplish one's goals" (2003, p. 3), and it is on the latter ability that the emphasis in this chapter lies.

Writing to get things done, to achieve one's goals, is a demanding task for even the most seasoned professional, and it represents a substantial challenge for the newcomer. In the context of power, the challenge for novice writers is heightened by the fact that as a general rule they do not have any power or status within an organisation, and most of their writing will be directed at people who sit further up the hierarchy. As noted in Chapter 1, Bargiela-Chiappini and Harris (1996) make a distinction between inherent status, which "results from holding a powerful position ... acknowledged by all members of the ... community and beyond" and relative status, which is "enjoyed as a result of the power an individual can exercise in an interpersonal relationship" (p. 637). Those who hold inherent status have considerable leeway in terms of the language they can choose when it comes to framing messages. For the novice with no status, however, the choice is more limited, and making the wrong choice can have problematic consequences. One thinks of the students who write to their professors with lines such as "Please feel free to contact me on 44535627 if you have any questions", unaware of how inappropriate this is, given the power relations that usually exist between student and teacher. In the academy, the deployment of phrasing like this can be overlooked, while in the workplace, writing in this way can have more serious reverberations. But in addition to managing writing in power-asymmetrical situations, novices may be required to write persuasive messages to colleagues of similar status, which can also pose its own challenges. The task of the teacher is to make students aware of the ways in which language can be used in situation- and status-appropriate ways to get things done in workplace settings. It is a considerable task.

Politeness theory

At the heart of any contemplation of language and power is the notion of politeness, a much-studied area. As with any phenomenon that has received the attention of numerous researchers, it is has been defined in different ways. For many, e.g. Lakoff (1975), Brown and Levinson (1987), politeness serves as a means of reducing the possibility of conflict, prompting Kasper (1990, p. 194) to suggest that perspectives of this kind see communication "as a fundamentally dangerous and antagonistic endeavor". Other perspectives see politeness more as a form of consideration for others, for example, Watts (2003), who talks of the notion of "mutual cooperation" (p. 17); Sifianou (1992, p. 86) also stresses the mutual element, describing politeness "*as the set of social values which instructs interactants to consider each other by satisfying shared expectations*" (original emphasis). In these definitions, we can see the idea that the conventions of politeness are both understood and expected by all parties, an idea summed up by Bremner: "politeness is about participants in an interaction following the rules and expecting that they will be followed" (2013a, p. 1).

While there have been a number of key studies of the nature of politeness (e.g. Lakoff, 1973; Leech, 1983) no consideration of this topic seems to be possible without looking at the work of Brown and Levinson. Their 1987 book, *Politeness: Some Universals in Language Usage*, originally published as a paper in 1978, is referenced in almost any discussion, and while this has had its critics, their theory remains the touchstone for work in this area. As Harris (2003) suggests, their theory "has attained canonical status" (p. 27).

Like Lakoff (1973) and Leech (1983), Brown and Levinson build on the work of Grice (1975), in particular his "Cooperative Principle". Their aim was to develop "a tool for describing … the quality of social relationships" (1987, p. 55), but also to build a single universal theory that could explain manifestations of politeness across cultures: "We want to account for the observed cross-cultural similarities in the abstract principles which underlie polite usage" (p. 57). Their theory centres around the notion of face, which Goffman explains as "the positive social value a person effectively claims for himself (sic) by the line others assume he (sic) has taken during a particular contact" (1967, p. 5). Developing this idea, Brown and Levinson (1987, p. 61) define face thus:

> the public self-image that every member wants to claim for himself (sic), consisting in two related aspects:
> (a) negative face: the basic claim to territories, personal preserves, rights to non-distraction – i.e. freedom of action and freedom from imposition
> (b) positive face: the positive consistent self-image or 'personality' (crucially including the desire that this self-image be appreciated and approved of) claimed by interactants.

According to the theory, the face wants of an individual can only be satisfied by the actions of others, which means that there should be a mutual interest among these interactants in maintaining one another's face. As mentioned, Brown and Levinson's work is posited on the notion that communication is a threatening business and any act that threatens someone's face is called a "face-threatening act" or FTA. Thus, the task of an interactant is to select an appropriate strategy doing an FTA. These strategies will either be oriented towards the positive face of the hearer (e.g. complimenting, expressing solidarity) or their negative face (e.g. hedges and other softening mechanisms). A further dimension of the model is provided in a set of sociological variables, which serve as criteria for assessing the seriousness of an FTA: the social distance between the speaker and hearer, the relative power relations between them, and the degree of potential imposition on the hearer that is contained in the act. These elements of Brown and Levinson's theory are revisited later in the chapter in the discussion of pedagogical approaches.

A number of doubts have been raised about the possibility of a universally applicable theory, many of them suggesting that politeness is in some ways culturally bound and that the theory does not fully consider Asian ideas of politeness (e.g. Fraser, 2005; Gu, 1990; Ide, 1989; Kong, 1998; Matsumoto, 1988). There have been similar discussions with regard to the nature of face in different cultural contexts (e.g. Cheng, 2003; Haugh, 2004; Yu, 2003), and meanwhile, Spencer-Oatey (2008) has highlighted difficulties in providing a precise definition for this concept.

Politeness and context

Aside from these concerns, one potential problem with a theory that attempts to be universal in its application is that its distance from specific contexts of production reduces its explanatory power for a researcher. Locher (2004) makes the point that politeness "cannot be investigated without looking in detail at the context, the speakers, the situation and the evoked norms" (p. 91). The reality is that authentic exchanges involving the deployment of politeness are located in specific contexts (Meier, 1995); once research takes account of this and comes down to the level of context, the situation demands a consideration of a range of other contextual factors: the sociocultural context, the specific community of practice in which politeness is being done and the workplace culture (Schnurr and Chan, 2009).

There is also the interactional nature of dialogue to consider. As noted, this chapter, and indeed this entire book, is underpinned by a social constructionist view of language in workplace settings, and a number of critics of Brown and Levinson's universal theory of politeness take similarly informed positions. Eelen (2001), for example, presents a revised notion of politeness, which he sees as representing "a turn towards a firmer embedding of politeness within the dynamics of social reality" (2001, p. 257). In keeping with this view, Watts (2003) explains that polite behaviour cannot be evaluated out of context, saying that the behaviour of speakers and hearers during an interaction is open to modification as it progresses. Arundale similarly argues for an interactional view of face, saying that it is "an emergent property of relationships, and therefore a relational phenomenon, as opposed to a social psychological one" (2006, p. 201). Holmes and Stubbe (2003) and Schnurr and Chan (2009) also stress the dynamic and mutually constitutive relationship between doing politeness and the contexts in which this takes place, the latter explaining that "cultural expectations influence interactive norms, and by regularly drawing on these particular norms, members at the same time enact, reinforce and shape culture-specific notions of politeness" (p. 132).

This is not to suggest that Brown and Levinson's politeness theory has no value or utility. While its claims to universality have been subjected to considerable scrutiny – and certainly the work of many of the researchers cited above has placed a question mark above these claims – the theory still serves as a launchpad and point of reference for much politeness-related research. Meanwhile, the calls to recognise the dynamic nature of politeness and to locate politeness-related research in the contexts in which it is enacted, can be seen as offering the opportunity to provide richer accounts of how politeness works than are afforded by Brown and Levinson's model i.e. as ways of building on their work rather than as alternatives. Other theories and models have emerged to explain politeness behaviour, such as rapport management (Spencer-Oatey, 2000) to name one example, although this is primarily concerned with speech. But the robustness of Brown and Levinson's theory as a basic model seems to endure, which is evidenced in the continuing reference to many of its elements in studies of politeness.

Politeness and writing research

It has been pointed out (Yeung, 1997) that Brown and Levinson's (1987) framework has for the most part been applied to the study of spoken interactions. In principle, there is no reason why it cannot be applied to written discourse. One reason that a theory primarily intended to look at spoken discourse can be usefully applied to written discourse is the point made in relation to intertextuality in Chapter 4, and also touched in this chapter, namely, that writing is often a dynamic process and as such can – like speaking – be regarded as an ongoing interaction and dialogue.

Having said that, some concern has been expressed about the extent to which spoken discourse is treated as a contextualised and interactive process in studies of politeness. Bargiela-Chiappini and Harris (1996), for example, stressing the importance of context when studying the politeness phenomena, contrast their use of contextually embedded data for their research with the isolated requests or elicited responses that are used in other studies employing Brown and Levinson's model. Pilegaard (1997) also highlights the need to see politeness "in a dynamic perspective which includes the extralinguistic dimension" (p. 224), and looks for "the coupling of situationality and intertextuality" (p. 242) within Brown and Levinson's conceptual framework. Similarly, I have questioned (Bremner, 2006) whether the dynamics of interaction are being addressed in many studies of requests and politeness, saying that "The gathering of text corpora may capture much of the surrounding textual context, but these are essentially snapshots, the enactment of politeness at a moment in time" (p. 398).

While, as noted, much of the politeness-related research has used spoken data, there have nevertheless been a number of studies of politeness in writing. These have had varied aims. Maier (1992), for example, looked at native and non-native production of requests in business settings; several studies have had a cross-cultural focus (Kong, 1998; Vergaro, 2004; Yeung, 1997; Yli-Jokipii, 1994); Bargiela-Chiappini and Harris (1996) examined the relationship between requests and status in business correspondence, while Mulholland's (1999) study is an early examination of the use of politeness in email. Rogers and Lee-Wong (2003) examined the writing of subordinates reporting to superiors with a view to developing a politeness framework with pedagogical applications, which will be discussed later. A more recent study (AlAfnan, 2014) looks at the use of politeness strategies in a Malaysian context, considering how this relates to the ethnicity of the communicators, power relations and social distance. There is also a growing body of studies that have looked at the enactment of politeness in student-to-faculty email (Biesenbach-Lucas, 2007; Chen, 2006; Economidou-Kogetsidis, 2011) – these will also be looked at in greater detail later in this chapter.

My own work in this area (Bremner, 2006) involved a year-long ethnographic study of writing processes in an institutional context, considering the demands made on writers as they made requests of their colleagues. This study views context not just as a central factor in framing requests, but also as part of an ongoing dynamic (cf. Pilegaard, 1997; Schnurr and Chan, 2009), and the longitudinal nature of the research enables us to see the interactions within the institution under study as part of an ongoing dialogue, rather than as standalone texts. The study also considers the requirement on the part of writers to balance their relational needs with the expectations of the institution, particularly as they are often writing for multiple audiences. (Chapter 3 looks at this in greater detail in the discussion of how writers attempt to exploit genres to achieve their individual objectives, reporting on the findings of Bremner (2012b).) This need for writers to position themselves in relation to their peers and those further up the hierarchy gives rise to a problem explained by Russell (1997, p. 532): "At the level of the individual, people experience double binds, seemingly irreconcilable demands placed upon them by the pull of two competing motives". Furthermore, the linguistic choices the writers make in such situations act as a form of indexicality (Ochs, 1992), thereby defining and reinforcing their identity in the institution. As Russell (1997, p. 532) concludes: "Eventually, individuals' agency or identity may be transformed". In this particular study, perceptions in the community of one of the writers were seen to be very much influenced by the way in which she framed her requests and managed her communication with the target audience.

The study (Bremner, 2006) thus identifies and considers aspects of the context beyond variables of relative power and degree of imposition, namely, the need for writers to take into account the possibility of multiple audiences (see also Skovholt and Svennevig, 2006), the need to position themselves appropriately and the ways in which their writing will define them in the eyes of their colleagues. These considerations, added to the point regarding the interactional nature of face (Arundale, 2006), make for a very complex picture of writing, a picture which has considerable implications for the teaching of strategies intended to make relationships work, in that, as with intertextuality, students need to see their written interactions as ongoing, as dialogues in which positions, and therefore appropriate responses, are in a state of ongoing development.

Politeness and pedagogy

Tone and register

This leads on to the question of appropriate pedagogies. As with many of the other areas addressed in this book, there is a sense of a substantial gap between the findings of a burgeoning body of research into power and politeness, and the offerings of textbooks (for which read business communication textbooks). Although these books have not been subjected to the kind of scrutiny that has been seen in relation to intertextuality and collaboration (Bremner, 2008, 2010), a brief look at three or four books yields no mention of politeness in the index. There are, however, occasional references to "tone", which appears to be the umbrella term used to cover this area of workplace interaction, whether spoken or written. It is worth quoting one book on this topic at some length to give an idea of a typical approach:

> One important aspect of adaptation is *tone*. Conveyed largely by the words in a message, tone reflects how a receiver feels upon reading or hearing a message. Skilled communicators create a positive tone in their messages by using a number of adaptive techniques, some of which are unconscious. These include spotlighting audience benefits, cultivating a "you" attitude, sounding conversational, and using inclusive language.
>
> *(Guffey and Du-Babcock, 2008, p. 33) (Original emphasis)*

As can be seen, this represents very general advice and while it may be applicable in certain situations, this explanation, and indeed many of the prescriptions regarding "tone" in books of this type, do not appear to address in any depth the role of context, which, as discussed, is considered by many as integral to the understanding and production of politeness.

One concept that does take context fully into account, and which is highly pertinent here, is that of register, explained by Halliday and Hasan (1976) as "the linguistic features which are typically associated with a configuration of situational features – with particular values of the field, mode and tenor" (p. 22). In any communication, a writer needs to achieve an appropriate register by making specific lexical and grammatical choices, depending on the situational context, the participants in the exchange and the function of the language in the discourse. If we are to acknowledge the complex and often subtle challenges involved in managing relationships through language, then a toolkit for unpacking communicative situations to help select appropriate language to get things done is needed. An understanding of register and the contextual elements that make it happen would be very helpful in this regard, whereas broad notions such as tone do not really capture the nuances and intricacies of this area of workplace writing. Suffice it to say that the term "register" is not found in the index of any business communication textbooks consulted, with, as noted, only a few references to the notion of tone. It should be pointed out that the term "tone" seems to be generally used by students to refer to language that acknowledges power relationships, expresses respect, deference, politeness and so on.

Internal and external communication

An important distinction that needs to be made in respect of the management of relationships and related pedagogy, is that between internal (or in-house) and external communication. Suchan and Dulek commented some time ago that "conventional pedagogy does not account for in-house communication" (1988, p. 239) and while it has not received as much attention in textbooks and classrooms as external communication, models and tasks in textbooks nowadays appear to be taking greater account of writing for internal audiences. However, there is less evidence that the significant challenges posed by internal communication are being fully considered. Graham (1998, p. 239) talks of "the complex issues affecting in-house writing", while Holmes and Stubbe (2003) articulate more generally the multiple demands associated with the management of relationships, explaining that "Effective management of workplace relationships takes account of the face needs of colleagues, as well as the objectives of the organisation and the individuals involved" (p. 3). Certainly, the findings from my own study (Bremner, 2006) and elaborated upon in a later article (Bremner, 2012b), seem to indicate that internal communication may impact on the writer's identity, relationships and standing within the organisation and therefore merits being approached with considerable care.

While textbook tasks often give student writers the opportunity to consider the ramifications of power relationships, purely in the sense that these are implicit in any communicative situation, this aspect of the writing task is rarely focused on. An explanation for this might lie in an assumption on the part of textbook writers that there is no need for explicit awareness raising or instruction in this area as the primary audiences for business communication textbooks are usually L1 (first language) users of English or high-level L2 (second language) users, who may be sufficiently proficient in the management of register. As someone who has spent the bulk of their teaching career working with L2 writers, I cannot comment with authority on the abilities of L1 students when it comes to writing context- and relationship-appropriate workplace discourse, but my experience of working with even very proficient L2 writers is that they would benefit from a far greater focus on this aspect of workplace writing than is afforded by the activities and tasks found in standard business communication textbooks.

Politeness and requests: writing emails

Although much writing in the workplace requires consideration of power relationships and the need to accommodate these in choice of language, there are certain common functions for which the selection of an appropriate register is essential for successful performance. Perhaps the most common of these is making requests, which has been the focus of numerous studies, with data gathered from both workplace and academic settings. Among the former is the work of Bargiela-Chiappini and Harris (1996), Ho (2011), Kong (2006) and Yeung (1997), while examples of the latter, which largely consist of student-to-teacher emails, include Biesenbach-Lucas (2007), Chen (2006), Duthler (2006), Economidou-Kogetsidis (2011) and Lee (2004). Different theories and frameworks have been deployed to analyse these data, most notably Brown and Levinson's (1987) politeness theory, discussed extensively earlier in the chapter, and Blum-Kulka, House and Kasper's (1989) Cross-Cultural Speech Act Realization Project (CCSARP). The CCSARP coding framework analyses requests in terms of direct and indirect strategies, the ways in which requests are modified by lexical items and syntactic elements, the request perspective and the ways in which these are harnessed towards mitigation of the force of the request. The application of this framework can be seen in Chen (2006) and Biesenbach-Lucas (2007).

When it comes to identifying the nature and causes of the problems that students experience in handling email, studies have for the most part tended to focus on student-to-faculty email, perhaps for reasons relating to ease of data collection. Given the status differences between writer and reader in such situations, this is a very fertile source of data. Examples include Chen (2006), who reports a case study of a Taiwanese student's "struggle for appropriateness" with email communication with professors, Biesenbach-Lucas (2007), who looks at how native and non-native speakers of English formulate low- and high-imposition requests to faculty, and Economidou-Kogetsidis's (2011) examination of the ways in which Greek Cypriot university students make email requests. She identifies problems relating to forms of address and complementary closes, the presence or absence and levels of mitigation, and the degree of directness, as well as a lack of status-congruent language in general (Economidou-Kogetsidis, 2011, 2015).

These findings are echoed in my own experiences of student-to-faculty email, which similarly show inconsistency in levels of formality and directness, suggesting considerable uncertainty on the part of the writers. A number of possible factors may contribute to this situation – as explained, there is little reference to managing register in teaching materials; Biesenbach-Lucas (2007) suggests that students are "simply uncertain about email etiquette due to lack of experience and because typically it is not explicitly taught" (p. 59). Indeed, training in writing emails appears to be often limited to textual organisation, dealing with issues such as direct and indirect approaches, the use of buffers and so on. Moreover, when students write to their instructors, this is of course an opportunity for authentic communication, but they rarely get feedback on their handling of register (Chen, 2006), as faculty are largely concerned with understanding and responding to the message rather than the tone in which it is delivered. As a result, students often persist in adopting certain approaches and registers because they are not given any corrective feedback. In addition to this, the types of communicative goal in student-to-faculty email tend to be limited to a small number of functions, such as setting up meetings, sending in assignments or requesting deadline extensions. Other factors may apply when the writers are not L1 users of English, such as a lack of confidence in handling the language generally and uncertainty about register because of the influences and expectations associated with their cultural background, whereby some groups are comfortable adopting a fairly informal register, while others prefer to deploy a more formal, deferential style. Further possible contributing elements include students' perceptions of the role of email as a channel of communication (for example, whether it is simply an electronic form of memo or a means of delivering a spoken message in electronic form), and the casual attitude of the younger generation towards stylistics (Baron, 2002).

Writing email requests in academic settings

Although requests are a common object of study among researchers interested in how politeness plays out in different contexts, when it comes to student populations, there is little in the way of research looking at how learners manage requests in workplace-like scenarios. Given the dearth of material in textbooks that asks students to focus specifically or in any detail on the issues relating to the management of politeness discussed thus far, instructors often need to fall back on their own resources. The following section looks at initiatives in the classroom that have addressed the function of making requests from a workplace perspective.

An excellent set of activities proposed by Graham (1998) exemplifies the kind of work that can help bring home to student writers the importance of context in linguistic use and the challenges of managing relationships in writing. Students were initially asked to analyse texts which illustrate the relationship between power dynamics and politeness strategies in request memos written to subordinates. This was followed up a task whereby they were to write in the role of manager to their staff about the problematic noise levels in their department. They had to write two versions, accompanied by a rhetorical analysis, with the instructions thus:

> In one memo assume you work in the academy where legitimate rank are somewhat hidden and ambiguous. In the other, assume you work in a company where rank and power are generally recognized and accepted. Both memos will include politeness strategies, although the degree and kind of strategies used will vary.
>
> *(1998, p. 244)*

This highlights ways in which different power hierarchies and relations can influence the kind of language a writer can use.

I have adapted this task for my own students in Hong Kong, requiring them not only to write from the perspective of a manager, but also to attempt an email in which they make requests of their own colleagues, i.e. a situation in which – as is normal in the early stages of one's career – they have none of the "inherent status" (Bargiela-Chiappini and Harris, 1996) that comes with positions of real power. As University President they write to the university community informing them that mobile phones can no longer be used in classrooms or lecture theatres unless authorised by faculty; as a university lecturer they write an email asking their students not to use their mobile phones in class for calls or texting; in the third email they work in an office where the level of phoning and chatting among their colleagues makes it very difficult to concentrate – they need to write their colleagues an email asking them to make less noise.

Interestingly, students tend to perform best on the first task and appear quite comfortable with the impersonal style, largely free of politeness strategies, that seems appropriate for this missive. On the second task they perform reasonably well, although they are less confident as to what register to use; in many cases, they said they drew on their experience of emails from their own professors. However, in the third task, perhaps unsurprisingly, they struggle, the main problem being that they adopt too directive and divisive a style that does not befit their putative status. Their evident difficulty bears out some of the points that emerged from my own research (Bremner, 2006), which as noted highlighted problems that writers had managing their identity and position in relation to their colleagues.

There is little doubt that many students do have trouble trying to achieve an appropriate register when producing workplace texts. Indeed, in a recent study that I conducted (Bremner, 2014c) looking at student performance on internships, host organisations identified register as the most problematic challenge for their interns, who, while competent writers, found considerable difficulty in adjusting their tone when writing for different readers. One employer captured the essence of this problem, saying of one of their interns that she was "very good at two ends, very official writing, or very friendly … (But) it's difficult for her to position herself in between the two ends". Similarly, one of the interns in this study expressed her frustration in trying to manage her emails in general, and the register more specifically: "Which emails must I reply to, which ones can be ignored? Should I use a formal or informal tone when the person starts with an informal tone? Sigh. Business etiquette can sometimes be very tiring".

Given the lack of readily available teaching materials that provide writing practice with a close focus on politeness issues in workplace contexts, I have been carrying out small-scale research to try and identify areas where students are having problems, and in so doing to point towards possible intervention in the classroom. As explained, student-to-faculty emails generally deal with a limited number of functions and in order to gain a fuller understanding of the kinds of problems that they encounter, it is also necessary to look at their performance on more complex tasks with a greater variety of audiences. The study (Bremner, 2015) was conducted with a group of third and fourth year English majors in a Hong Kong university – L2 writers, but with generally high levels of English. They were each given two email writing tasks, to be completed within a specified time, and the resulting output was analysed with a particular focus on register (degree of formality, degree of directness, presence and amount of mitigation, consistency) and use of politeness strategies (Brown and Levinson, 1987). The two writing tasks are presented below.

Task 1
Your manager, Phyllis Wong, has called a meeting at which all staff are expected to be present to discuss staff development across the organization. You are unable to attend as you have other commitments that day. Write to her and explain your situation. You have been with the organization for six months.

Task 2
You have been given the task of organizing an all-day training workshop on marketing techniques for your department. This is a major task that will involve a lot of work. Write to your colleague, Felix Chan, to try and persuade him to help you.

Sharp readers will notice that in these tasks I have veered in the direction of the "scripted context" that I have criticised as being a typical feature of business communication textbooks (see Chapter 4), and that I have also failed to provide other texts for writers to respond to, refer to or draw on, as they might find in a real, intertextually active workplace. It should be stressed that the goal of the exercise was primarily to identify the problems that writing of this nature presents to these students, rather than creating a totally authentic writing experience. At the same time, it was intended that the wording of the rubric would be sufficiently neutral, so that the writers could bring their own voice and thinking to the texts. All student writing here is reported verbatim.

What was evident in this study is that students experienced a range of problems with both email tasks, which were seen in the ways that they read the nature of the situation in terms of its power distribution and in their attempts to produce a register that was appropriate to the respective situations. In the case of the power-asymmetrical task, many writers misread the situation in that their email was predicated on the assumption that the manager would agree to their missing the meeting, often giving the reader little room for manoeuvre. Few writers asked the manager but simply told her that they would miss the meeting; some apologised, while others did not. This misreading may have been a conceptual one and unrelated to the teaching of register for managing power relationships, but what was more noticeable, and perhaps more pertinent to the central issue of workplace writing, was the prevalence of inappropriate, status-incongruent phrasing, which at times came across as quite condescending. This particular problem is illustrated in examples of employee-to-manager discourse such as these:

- *I am writing to regretfully notify you …*
- *Do send me any supplementary material for the meeting.*
- *I will read through the meeting minutes … and would be happy to have further discussion on this topic.*
- *Thank you for your time.*

As for the second task, which involved writing to a colleague of similar status, few of the texts produced came across as persuasive, for a variety of reasons, again relating to reading of the situation and ability to produce an appropriate register. In terms of the situation, few writers seemed to understand or perceive that they were potentially demanding a considerable amount from their colleague, and the weight of the imposition (cf. Brown and Levinson, 1987) was rarely acknowledged. There were also issues with perspective, in that the onus for action was often placed quite heavily on the reader; this often combined with somewhat over-directive language, resulting in the kind of language more usually seen in manager-to-employee discourse, as can be seen in these examples:

- *We are willing to hear your sharing on the topic "Successful Business Communication" for around 15–20 minutes. Please reply me by 15 October so that I could have your name printed on the poster.*
- *Let me know ASAP if you are interested in organizing the workshop as the name list is finalizing soon.*
- *As I need enough time to prepare the materials, please give me a reply by next Friday. If you have any concerns or enquiry, please don't hesitate on contacting me. I look forward to hearing from you.*
- *This training workshop is regarded as an important event in staff development and therefore, your participation matters to us. Thank you for your consideration and I am looking forward to hearing from you.*

In addition to this status-incongruent language, there were also instances of what might be termed "organisational speak" that would be inappropriate in colleague-to-colleague discourse, e.g. "*With an aim to enhance our team's marketing techniques …*" Indeed, at times it was not evident in the choice of language that they were writing to a colleague, and few of the writers drew on the idea that friendship or collegiality might be a resource to exploit, i.e. there was little recourse to the "relative status" that Bargiela-Chiappini and Harris (1996) refer to.

When it came to the use of politeness strategies, it was noticeable that the majority of those deployed were aimed at positive face (*"Knowing you are an expert in this field ..."*) and at times bordered on the sycophantic, as in this example: *"Your experience and contribution are very recognised within the company and we shall feel pleasure to have you, as an excellent model, to share your remarkable marketing insights with our staff."* Meanwhile, negative politeness strategies were largely absent or came in the form of weak indirect requests, with few explicit attempts to reduce the sense of being imposed upon. Only three examples of the latter were identified in the student texts:

- *If you are willing to help me, I can definitely arrange my other work in order to fit your schedule.*
- *I know it's a challenging idea and there's no rush.*
- *So I am wondering if you could help me a little bit on the preparation of the workshop (only some paper work.) Thanks so much! I will buy you lunch.*

A final point of note was the extent to which students deployed formulaic closings that were inappropriate for colleague-to-colleague discourse, as seen in these examples:

- *Should you need further information, please don't hesitate to contact me.*
- *If you have any concerns or enquiry, please don't hesitate on contacting me.*

Combined with more informal language, these made once more for a fairly inconsistent register, which was noticeable in quite a number of the texts.

Email requests: challenges for research and pedagogy

It should be acknowledged that at the time of writing this was a small-scale preliminary study; at this stage, all that can be seen are indications rather than definitive findings, and these are open to interpretation. Nevertheless, a few tendencies were seen to emerge, some of which resonate with the findings in earlier studies (e.g. Biesenbach-Lucas, 2007; Economidou-Kogetsidis, 2011, 2015). The first of these was that students were often inconsistent in their use of register or used language that was inappropriate for the writer-reader relationship, and this was perhaps exacerbated by an over-reliance on formulaic phrasing, especially in closing the message. This is not to suggest that the students were unaware of the importance of finding the right language for the situation. Indeed, there was general acknowledgement among this student population of the need to find the appropriate register – a questionnaire was administered to the group before the tasks and the vast majority agreed that "tone" was a very important feature of email writing; in the study of intertextually linked emails reported in Chapter 4 (Bremner and Costley, 2016), most of the students interviewed also expressed concern about their management of tone. This is similar to other studies (e.g. Biesenbach-Lucas, 2007; Chen, 2006; Danet, 2001) that have indicated that students are aware that stylistic differences are needed to deal with readers in authority when compared to peers.

Alongside their recognition of the need to manage tone in an appropriate manner, the general view from the group who produced these emails was that Task 2 was less challenging because it was a colleague-to-colleague message. This is in keeping with Chen's (2006) contention that "people can write e-mails to peers in any manner they like" (p. 35). However, this study and student performance on the colleague-to-colleague task reported earlier, adapted from Graham (1998), as well as my own research in a university setting (Bremner, 2006) suggest that this type of writing is just as challenging as writing upwards, possibly more so. Further investigation would be necessary to find out exactly why they believe this kind of writing poses fewer challenges.

Overall there was insufficient *demonstration* of understanding of the situation in relation to the audience. Writers seemed to have difficulty in analysing the task from the perspective of the reader in terms of their expectations and likely reaction, and this was often manifested in a lack of acknowledgement of the degree of imposition involved. This may explain the ways in which politeness strategies were used – if a writer did not see the request they were making as a heavy imposition, then they would not see any need to reduce the sense of imposition through the deployment of strategies aimed at negative face. However, an alternative interpretation is that they did recognise that a relatively high degree of imposition was entailed in the request but that they were uncertain as to the type of politeness strategy to call upon.

Making a request threatens a reader's negative face in that it imposes upon them, thus some means of mitigating the force of that imposition would appear to be the logical choice. This is borne out by the underpinnings of Duthler's (2006) study of email and voicemail requests, in which the judges evaluating levels of politeness in the elicited requests "were instructed that the use of positive politeness (expressions of solidarity) was less polite than negative politeness (admissions of impingement)" (2006, p. 517). Yet, as noted, in my own study very few examples of negative politeness strategies were seen. As for the writers who did appear to understand that they were making a difficult request, the implicit acknowledgement of the weight of imposition seemed to drive them in the direction of more formal language, leading them to overlook the possibility of using other mitigating strategies, such as external (concrete reasons and justifications) and internal modifiers (embedding, downtoners, hedges, consultative devices, etc.), which would reduce the threat to negative face. This is largely speculative, however, and warrants much further investigation.

Predicting and accounting for the deployment of politeness strategies in different contexts has produced a variety of findings, not necessarily contradictory, but certainly not consistent with one another. Bargiela-Chiappini and Harris (1996, p. 658), for example, found that "the degree of imposition of the request overrides status considerations as a motivation for linguistic politeness". Yet, it is interesting to note that in Duthler's (2006) study, contrary to his hypothesis, email messages with unimposing requests contained more formal address phrases than imposing requests. As he suggests, "Politeness theorists would expect imposing requests to be accompanied by a higher degree of formality of address phrase" (2006, p. 517). Meanwhile Biesenbach-Lucas (2007) found writers deploying more direct strategies for requests with a lower imposition, but not for highest imposition, which would seem to be more in line with the expectations of these politeness theorists. The findings from the study reported here partially corroborate such theoretical expectations but, ultimately, what emerges is a very mixed – and unclear – picture of language choice and accompanying motive, and this serves as a powerful indication of the need to delve deeper into the reasons why students and writers more generally make particular linguistic choices in situations of this nature. Chen's (2006) study of a Taiwanese student's email interactions with a lecturer is one of the few that attempts to provide insights into the writer's motivations.

It is perhaps not surprising that the findings of research into the relationship between politeness and requests should be so mixed. It should be remembered that there are a number of factors or variables that will affect the choice of language. Blum-Kulka and Olshtain (1984) suggest diversity in speech acts can be the result of intra-cultural and situational variability, cross-cultural variability, and/or individual variability, notions that are articulated in terms of the workplace and communities of practice by Schnurr and Chan (2009). It is worth picking up on the idea of individual variability – in addition to the cultural, contextual and organisational factors, there is also the individual factor to consider in that some writers may perceive certain approaches to requests and other work-related functions to be too direct (or indirect) and may not be comfortable with particular phrasing. Many of the models seen in business communication textbooks, for example, would not be to the taste of all writers because they would project an image or identity that they might not see as representative of themselves as individuals.

One further question to consider is that of why students in my study (Bremner, 2015) made particular choices as to phrasing: whether the inappropriate register they opted for was the outcome of a misreading of the situation or their view of the weight of the imposition, which could have been culturally influenced or simply a personal opinion, or whether, alternatively, they had a complete grasp of the situation and all its nuances but did not possess the linguistic resources to word their emails in a situation- and status-appropriate manner. As Biesenbach-Lucas points out, "students can plan, compose, revise, and edit toward an appropriate and polite email message only if they *have* flexible linguistic means at their disposal and *know* which linguistic structure and politeness devices to use" (original emphasis, p. 74), which of course begs the question of what students could actually be taught in this respect.

Conclusion

Although, as shown in this chapter, there appear to be many questions that remain unanswered in this area of power, politeness and language, this should not discourage teachers from addressing related issues in the classroom. Biesenbach-Lucas (2007) believes that "NNSs [non-native speakers] could benefit from explicit email instruction as well as activities that involve discovery and raising of meta-pragmatic awareness" (p. 75). There is certainly value in looking at how different degrees of formality can be realised linguistically and teaching particular structures: examples might include lexical or syntactic modifiers to add a mitigating effect to an imposition, ways of achieving directness or indirectness in requests, and so on. However, given the weight of contextual factors in any encounter i.e. the fact that each situation has its own particular features, more valuable is to raise awareness of how politeness can play out in different situations. An example can be seen in the analytical task in Economidou-Kogetsidis (2015), in which different realisations of requests made by students to faculty can serve to demonstrate what makes for successful or unsuccessful management of writing in power-asymmetrical relationships.

Students need to be exposed to a wide variety of scenarios and power relationships but also to get a sense of the dynamic nature of doing politeness. Thornbury (2005) provides a very clear illustration of this in a short email chain consisting of three brief messages between an editor and an academic, showing how the register becomes more informal as the relationship evolves (p. 92). Evidence gathered from interviews in the intertextual study reported in Chapter 4 (Bremner and Costley, 2016) suggests that students struggled to find an appropriate register because they had not had enough exposure to this type of writing to be confident in their linguistic choices. More authentic examples of politeness in action are needed to help students understand how relationships can be managed through language. In conjunction with this, the concept of register (Halliday and Hasan, 1976) could usefully play a more prominent role, so that writers could see more clearly the relationship between language and the contextual components of field, tenor and mode.

As for Brown and Levinson (1987), their model needs to be treated with some caution. A theory which lays claim to universal application can imply universal solutions, which is something to be discouraged – contexts are so specific, so laden with cultural and organisational influences, that they demand more localised responses. Nevertheless, the categories and distinctions established by this model can serve as a springboard for discussion of what might be culturally appropriate and of the kinds of politeness strategies that could be used in different situations.

It should be stressed that early career writers will be writing largely from positions without power. This issue is addressed in an excellent study by Rogers and Lee-Wong (2003). Their concern is with writers who on entering the workplace will be expected to report to superiors and the paper homes in on the tension that exists for a writer between satisfying relational needs and organisational obligations, pointing out that "conventional politeness strategies look a bit different when counterbalanced by organizational needs" (2003, p. 396). Rogers and Lee-Wong (2003) have developed a politeness framework that captures the tension between these potentially conflicting needs – relational and organisational – by pairing communicative dimensions for subordinate reporting (deference and confidence; non-imposition and direction; solidarity and individuality) and considering how these can be managed in tandem. Through the lens of this framework they analyse the writing of subordinates as they report to superiors and are able to offer clear paths to pedagogy and further research by means of this approach. A final point is that in many instances newcomers will be required to copy their messages to managers as part of the systems of control that are often seen in organisations. The phenomenon of writing for multiple audiences was touched on earlier (Bremner, 2006; Skovholt and Svennevig, 2006): this is an area that is underinvestigated and is one that should also be considered in the classroom.

The importance and prevalence of power-related issues and the ability to manage these linguistically in professional settings cannot be overstressed. Any consideration of power and politeness and their relationship with workplace writing should be firmly located in the precepts of social constructionism, seeing the selection of appropriate discourse as being linked not only to the context but as part of an ongoing, fluid interaction between participants. As a challenge to the novice writer, the management of language in terms of power relationships is something of a minefield, simply because so many different factors – contextual, cultural, organisational, personal – can affect the choice of language intended to realise an appropriate level of politeness. Fraser and Nolen's remark that "No sentence is inherently polite or impolite" (1981, p. 96) captures something of the uncertainty that bedevils the handling of this area of workplace communication. But this rather stark observation serves as a powerful reminder that there is no room for prescriptivism when it comes to power and language. A heavy diet of exposure, awareness raising and discussion are more likely to lead writers to linguistic choices that meet both the context at hand and their sense of identity as a writer, communicator, organisational member and individual.

7

CHANNELS OF COMMUNICATION

Introduction

It is a truism to point out the dramatic way in which communication has changed over the last twenty years or so, as opportunities opened up by technology in general and the internet more particularly – "the subject of much breathless contemplation" (Goodman and Hirsch, 2014, p. 130) – provide a vast and ever-increasing range of channels with which to communicate. The so-called 'new' technologies are developing at great speed, to the extent that it is not clear at what point any given means of communication might be no longer considered new – at the time of writing, for example, the book *New New Media* (Levinson, 2009) was already in its second edition. Moreover, it is quite probable, given the rapid pace of development in information and communications technology (ICT), that many of the channels and platforms that are currently modish may have fallen out of favour or been superseded by the time this book appears in print. (Note: In this chapter I have used a number of terms to talk about communication that is mediated through electronic channels, and these are intended as interchangeable, rather than representing different, nuanced forms of communication.)

From the perspective of those engaged in workplace writing, the story is much the same, with increasing reliance on digital discourses seen in the workplace and writing more generally (Hafner, forthcoming) deftly summed up by Warschauer, Zhang and Park (2013, p. 825): "there is little serious writing that is not done digitally". Certainly, a huge range of electronic options is at the disposal of the workplace writer that goes beyond well-established channels such as email and instant messaging (IM), and includes a variety of social media, various platforms for the collaborative production of texts, blogs and group decision support systems, to mention but a few.

It would be impossible – and inadvisable – in the space of a few pages to try and cover even a portion of these digital technologies in any detail, and it is not the intention in this chapter to attempt such a feat: there is already a body of work out there that addresses many aspects of this rapidly developing field (e.g. Darics, 2015; Goodman and Hirsch, 2014; Jones and Hafner, 2012). Rather, the aim of the chapter is to look more generally at principles and issues relating to the use of communication channels in workplace writing, both technologically supported and more traditional, but with the primary focus on the former. While acknowledging – as throughout – the strong influence of the organisation on writing practices, the chapter will place greater emphasis on the individual writer within the organisation, given that this book is to a large degree motivated by how we prepare individuals for the demands of the workplace in terms of writing.

There is much talk of affordances and constraints (e.g. Jones and Hafner, 2012) with regard to technology and communication, i.e. the idea on the one hand that technology can offer new ways of mediating a message and, on the other, that ways of communicating can be in some ways limited or constrained by the nature of the medium. A considerable amount of excitement and optimism surrounds the speedy development of digital technologies, and, perhaps unsurprisingly, most of the talk is concerned with what is afforded by electronic media. The possibilities in general terms are well documented; these include fast transmission of information, the capacity to reach large, often widely dispersed audiences, increased opportunities for interaction both with colleagues and the wider public, and the option of asynchronous communication, whereby there is no requirement for writers to be communicating with one another in real time, allowing for the creation of virtual teams of writers collaborating across different geographical and time zones. Alongside these possibilities, electronically mediated communication channels generally offer more efficient means of storing and retrieving information than previously. There is also an increasing number of ways in which messages can be conveyed through multiple semiotic resources in addition to written text (i.e. multimodality), along with the provision of easier access to further texts and information by means of hyperlinks. This is by no means an exhaustive list, but it serves to capture many of the elements of the contemporary workplace that developments in ICT have brought about. For the most part these developments are perceived as positive in their impact on writing in professional settings, but it will be seen in later sections of this chapter that for the individual writer the world opened up by the new technologies brings with it certain expectations and challenges.

The burgeoning array of technologies available provides new opportunities for workplace writers, presenting them with a wide range of media options to choose from to get things done. Goodman and Hirsch (2014), on the basis of their examination of leading practices of corporations in terms of managing their online presence, offer advice which recognises that different options are made possible by different channels because of their particular features: "Do not simply replicate the same content across multiple platforms but design content (including navigation and applications) that take advantage of the unique characteristics of each platform" (p. 133). Advice of this kind leads to the question of why one platform or channel would be seen as preferable to another in a given situation and the extent to which media choice relates to the innate features of a particular platform or communication channel.

Models of technology adoption

Why, then, might writers, or communicators more generally, choose a particular medium to deliver their message? Are there principles or implicit guidelines on which a writer can base their media selection? An early attempt to account for this can be seen in the "Media Richness" model proposed by Daft and Lengel (1984, 1986). This model posits a relationship between the richness of the available media and the ambiguity of the planned message. In the model, channels of communication are considered in terms of the range of communicative cues or "social presence", that they offer (Short, Williams and Christie, 1976). Face-to-face communication, for example, would be seen as particularly rich, in that the available cues could include, in addition to the verbal message, paralinguistic features such as facial expressions, eye contact, touch, tone of voice and so on, and along with these is the possibility of immediate feedback. A notice on a wall, however, would be considered a very lean medium, in that no cues beyond the bald message would be available, nor would there be any immediate opportunity for the reader to respond. As for the notion of ambiguity, this refers to the degree to which a message is open to multiple interpretations and the possibility of differing views on an issue. A reminder about a meeting time and venue, for example, would be a message that was unambiguous in its intent and expected interpretation, while consideration of an organisation's promotional activities for the coming year would invite multiple opinions and interpretations.

The Media Richness model proposes matching the level of ambiguity of a message with a channel that has an appropriate degree of media richness. Thus, an unambiguous message like the meeting reminder could be matched with a relatively lean medium such as a mass email to staff that did not anticipate or invite a response. The discussion of promotional activities, however, with its scope for multiple viewpoints, would be better served by a rich medium that allowed for high levels of interaction, most probably a face-to-face meeting. Effective communication, it is suggested, will be achieved through making appropriate media selection on this basis. There is some support for the model in research, suggesting that managers can be more effective if they follow this approach (e.g. Masnevski and Chudoba, 2000).

While the Media Richness model is intuitively logical and appealing – indeed, why would one choose a rich medium such as face-to-face interaction to remind people about an upcoming meeting? – it offers a fairly simplistic view of media choice. Thurlow, Lengel and Tomic (2004) looking at this and two other models relating to communication and technology (the Social Presence model, the Cuelessness model) dub these "Deficit Approaches", "because they suggest that technologically mediated communication – and especially text-based CMC [computer mediated communication] – *lacks* important qualities of F2F [face-to-face]communication and so will always be inadequate" (original emphasis, p. 48); on this basis the Media Richness model, they argue, privileges spoken interaction over "technologically mediated, *text-based* communication" (ibid., p. 50, original emphasis), an interpretation of the Media Richness model that is perhaps overly protective of computer-mediated communication.

A more important concern relating to the model is that in attempting to match media choice with the characteristics of a channel or platform, it is potentially deterministic in nature, i.e. it predicts that a particular situation will demand a particular medium. Thurlow *et al.* (2004) rightly point out that there will be circumstances when a lean medium for communication might be preferred even if the situation from a media richness perspective suggests a rich channel. This leads to a more significant issue in respect of this theory, namely that it does not take sufficient account of the context in which communication takes place. Context is of course a central factor, in the light of the influences that are likely to be found in any professional or organisational setting, discussed elsewhere in this volume, most notably in Chapter 8.

Other models relating to media choice have been proposed that take more local contextual factors into consideration. The Dual Capacity model (Sitkin, Sutcliffe and Barrios-Choplin, 1992) is one. This suggests that any channel of communication has two types of capacity: its data-carrying capacity is its ability to carry and convey information, while its symbol-carrying capacity allows it to carry information about the message and the writer sending the message, i.e. to convey information about the values of the individual writer or the wider organisational culture that they are operating in. A simple example of this might be seen in the quality of paper chosen by an old established law firm to convey its long presence in the field and thereby to suggest expertise and trustworthiness. As for internal communications, if we consider the example of the meeting reminder, it was suggested that a lean medium such as email might be appropriate to deliver this unambiguous message, but if managers had a preference for face-to-face interaction they might choose to go to offices in person to remind their employees, thereby conveying the value that they placed on this kind of interaction as a hallmark of friendliness and informality, and perhaps information about the organisational culture more generally. The Dual Capacity model, then, adds a dimension to our understanding of why workplace members might choose a particular medium for communication, acknowledging as it does the potential influence of individual preferences and organisational culture.

One other model which gives fuller consideration to the influence of context on media choice is the Social Information Processing model (Fulk, Steinfeld, Schmitz and Power, 1987), which takes account of the ways in which social influence processes impact on the use of media. This builds on the idea proposed by the Media Richness theory that media choice involves making an "objectively rational" choice (Fulk *et al.*, 1987, p. 532), based on an evaluation of the available communication channels and their inherent features, synthesising this perspective with one that sees attitudes to media as partly the outcome of the social context. These attitudes might come about as the result of past experience and knowledge accruing from this, individual differences, or particular information about the social context (Miller, 2015). The model thus takes into account the nature of both the communication media and the social environment in which they are used, and can be seen as a model that fits in with views of workplace communication as being socially constructed. It should be pointed out that there are many other models relating to media choice in addition to those discussed here; these were chosen because they address certain key underlying questions that a writer might want to consider: Will this particular medium allow or enable me to deliver my message in an efficient and effective way? What message in addition to the basic message will I convey about myself and my organisation through my choice of channel? What aspects of the social context will influence my choice of channel?

It should not be thought, however, that media selection lies solely in the hands of the individual writer. As Miller (2015) points out, writers often have little choice about the media they use because of the power of organisational influence, a point captured by Beaufort (2000) with her explanation that the "overarching goals and value assumptions of a community of writers influence the communicative purposes, the modes of communication" (pp. 194–195) and also made by Dias *et al.* (1999) in relation to rhetorical goals more generally. But while the traditions, practices and conventions that have developed within the organisation will have some influence, it can be assumed that decisions in relation to media selection, while not necessarily deterministic, will be based to a considerable extent on the features that are inherent in a given medium. An important rider is that – as with any decision that a writer makes in a workplace setting, whether this relates to media selection or register or any other choice – they will nevertheless need to take into account a range of contextual factors in addition to the characteristics of the medium, and these will include the purpose of the communication, the participants in the process and the nature of relationships with them, issues of power and so on.

The impact of technologies on writing

The next section moves on to look at a different aspect of new technologies for writing in the workplace, namely how developments in this area are affecting writers, writing and texts. In the context of research into the impact of technology on writing in the professions, Beaufort (2008) suggests that two main areas of investigation have emerged: "(a) how technologies affect writers' processes (or don't), and (b) how technologies spawn new genres or new communicative patterns (or don't)" (p. 224). Built into her suggestion is an implied question as to the extent to which technology will impact or – nearly ten years on – has impacted on the processes of writing for writers themselves and on the texts that emerge from these processes. Hafner (forthcoming) provides a possible response to this question, explaining that it is "important to realize that digital discourses are not just digital versions of analogue text types", going on to remind us of the point made in Jones and Hafner (2012), namely, that "digital media provide us with the tools to establish new ways of doing, meaning, relating, being and even thinking" (Hafner, forthcoming).

The two points of investigation raised by Beaufort (2008) are concerned with research, but these can be loosely reframed and envisioned as lines of enquiry from the perspective of the workplace writer. The issues thus addressed here pertain to the question of whether new genres or ways of communicating have emerged as a result of the advances seen in digital technologies, and what effect technologies are having on the ways in which writers construct texts in workplace settings. As explained, this chapter will not attempt a comprehensive examination of digital technologies, but will instead look at a number of areas relating to the use of technology in workplace writing as a means of addressing these questions: the evolution of the promotional email from its earlier incarnation, i.e. the sales promotion letter; the role that IM has taken on in workplaces; the communicative opportunities made possible by multimodality; interactive engagement with the public through social media platforms; and challenges relating to the management of collaborative writing in virtual space.

Promotional emails

Promotional emails, i.e. what most of us would consider as spam, are a well-established feature of the marketing landscape, having largely superseded the unsolicited promotional letter (analysed in an influential study by Bhatia (1993) and discussed in Chapter 3). Promotional email has been the focus of a number of research studies (e.g. Barron, 2006; Cheung, 2008, 2010) and what appears to emerge from these is the sense that the technologies have not so much "spawned" a new genre (cf. Beaufort, 2008), as allowed an established genre to evolve along the same essential lines, taking on features that are afforded by its new electronic medium. As explained in Chapter 3 in the discussion of genres, purpose plays a highly influential part in shaping a text, and this influence is evident in the findings from these various studies. Barron (2006), for instance, found the texts analysed in her study to contain moves related to their promotional goals, sharing some with Bhatia's (1993) analysis, and displaying others which could be seen as the outcome of the mode in which they appeared. Examples of the latter included "Capture attention", a move intended to get the reader to open the email, and "Give a polite way-out", which gives the reader the opportunity to unsubscribe. Cheung (2008) also noted features in the electronic texts in her study that she attributes to the influence of new media and reaches a similar conclusion to that of Barron (2006), saying that her "results seem to confirm a genre-based hypothesis which predicts that texts written for similar communicative purpose will display similarities in discourse structure" (2008, p. 182).

Research of my own (Bremner, 2013b) also looked at unsolicited promotional emails, in this case a corpus of 80 business development emails sent to the marketing manager of a major British organisation, considering the extent to which these emails observed the move structure of a sales promotion letter as identified by Bhatia (1993) and at how marketing specialists attempted to exploit the capabilities of the electronic medium. In common with the studies reported already, this study found that while the move structure of this genre has remained relatively stable, ways of crafting individual moves were seen to be more varied than in sales promotion letters, as writers exploited the medium to try and realise particular moves in a more creative way. This was seen in, for example, the imaginative use of subject lines (*Apologies in advance; Don't overdo it on the social media; When's best for you XXX?; Fingers crossed*), which relates to the need to capture the attention of the reader (Barron, 2006) such that they will open the email rather than simply delete it. These were followed up by a variety of lead-in strategies designed to hold the reader's attention if they have taken the plunge and opened the email, and included informal, chatty openings, as seen here:

> *There are never enough hours in the day so do excuse the email at this late hour, but I've been meaning to email to see how things are going and would love the opportunity to meet/talk to see how we could work together and now seemed as good a time as any!*

Another example, shown below, displays a more targeted focus, with a link to a microsite specially created for the reader:

> *I've had little joy trying to reach you by 'phone, so thought it might be more interesting to make a microsite based around us, our work and our relevance to the XXX brand. It's available at: http://ddd.co.uk/karen-smith*

This example shows the writer making use of the technology through the provision of hyperlinks, a strategy that was more widely evident in the variety of ways in which the email writers attempted to establish their credentials, as they provided links to apps, animations and even to an article written by their managing director. Similarly, several ways of soliciting response were seen that took advantage of the medium: these went beyond straightforward links to their website, and included invitations to like them on Facebook, to connect on LinkedIn, to register for an event and to click onto a link to set up a meeting directly with the writer.

Other features of these emails that were in evidence included a considerable degree of personalisation, a high incidence of informal language (*Hope all is good; But hey ...; Bye for now*), and also the occasional use of humour, something not often seen in more traditional sales promotion letters. Much of this suggests that in texts with this promotional goal in mind, the electronic medium, with its heightened opportunities for interactivity, leads writers to adopt a more informal register to achieve a closer sense of interpersonal communication. The perception that electronic media allow for more informal registers than print media will be revisited later in the chapter.

What we see in these various studies is a promotional genre that retains many of its obligatory moves because of the expectations that are associated with its purposes, but, as Cheung explains, "it seems that the ritual of the sales discourse can be challenged by taking into account the impact of new media on the communication of persuasive messages in this information age" (2008, p. 184). Hafner's point that "digital discourses are not just digital versions of analogue text types" (forthcoming) is pertinent here in that the discourse that results from the genre being placed in a new – in this case electronic – environment is indeed more than just a digital version of the analogue: it is a discourse that has taken advantage of what the new medium has to offer, particularly in terms of "dynamism and interactivity" (Cheung, 2008, p. 184). At the same time, it would be difficult to argue that what we are seeing is a different genre: although the electronic medium seems to allow new ways of realising individual moves, the genre in this case, while evolving, remains fundamentally the same in terms of its move structure. The point was made in Chapter 3 that successful exploitation of a genre requires an understanding of how that genre works, and the ability to work within that basic genre structure. The same caveat applies here – the electronic medium in which these promotional emails are constructed allows for new ways of realising elements of the basic genre in creative and innovative ways, but writers should be careful of how they go about this, in that they may appear to have opted out of the genre if they diverge too dramatically from the conventional script.

Instant messaging and web-chat

The next section considers a situation where a new technology, in this case IM, is having an impact on processes of writing. While at one time IM was considered largely as a channel for interactional communication (Bax, 2011; Thurlow and Poff, 2009), it has taken on increasing importance as a channel for transactional communication in a number of business settings, according to Markman (2015), who reports a variety of uses for this medium, including asking and answering questions, exchanging information and discussing other task-related issues. Darics (2014) talks of "the novel communication situation that IM represents" (p. 339), looking at the discourse produced by a virtual work team, but it is its use as a channel for web-chat in contact centres (Lockwood, 2017) that this chapter turns in order to examine the ways in which IM has been exploited in the contemporary workplace, and to convey a sense of the demands that this can make on a writer.

The phenomenon of web-chat, defined as a "synchronous exchange by generating written text on phones and computers for customer service" (Lockwood, 2017, p. 27), represents a shift in the way in which customer support is provided by organisations which take advantage of Business Process Outsourcing (BPO). Whereas this support has traditionally been provided through contact by phone with call centres, increasingly customers are using text messaging to access this kind of service, getting in touch with what are now more commonly known as contact centres, which provide voice, email and web-chat mediated support. For the most part, web-chat mediated customer support is outsourced to countries such as India and the Philippines, which have huge BPO industries.

Web-chat makes considerable demands on the agents who provide this customer service, as they are usually under pressure to meet goals set by their employers, which relate among other things to the length of each call and their ability to resolve problems quickly. The fact that they may be expected to handle multiple calls concurrently adds extra pressure, which can be further increased if, as seen in the setting investigated by Lockwood (ibid.), there is a stipulation that periods of "dead air", when there is no active communication between agent and customer, should last no longer than thirty seconds.

But one of the biggest challenges for these agents relates to the kinds of discourse they need to produce to satisfy the various stakeholders involved in this form of customer service. IM has been seen to use language that displays features of spoken discourse: Thurlow and Poff (2009) point to what they call paralinguistic restitution, that is, the use of symbols and language to replace actions, gestures and so on that in face-to-face communication would be achieved through body language, tone of voice and other cues, and to the phonological approximation found in messages whereby spelling moves closer to colloquial speech (e.g. "gonna" and "cos"), while Bax (2011) mentions the use of odd abbreviations, symbols and exaggerated punctuation as giving IM the flavour of colloquial language. However, while this would be suitable for informal interactional purposes, it would less likely be seen as appropriate in a transactional customer service scenario. Indeed, Lockwood (2017, p. 28) explains that "most outsourced contact centres appear to discourage the use of social media strategies when web-chatting with customers", conjecturing that this may be in the interests of projecting an appropriately professional image. But at the same time these centres, understandably given their broader function, place considerable value on relationship building, which typically requires more interactional styles of discourse. An interesting finding reported by Lockwood (ibid.), from her extensive research relating to call and contact centres, is the perception that best practices include an expectation that chat agents should "'direct the written communication flow in the typical pattern of spoken interaction including greeting, customer resolution or sale and closing in direct rapid responses'" (p. 28). This situation can be further complicated by the mandated use of templates as part of the web-chat interaction, similar to verbatim scripts that are commonly prescribed in telephone-mediated customer service encounters. It is beyond the scope of this chapter to consider the advisability of such templates, from the perspective of both agent and customer, although some research (e.g. Forey and Lockwood, 2007) has suggested that these and other forms of prescriptiveness in relation to these service encounters can be counterproductive in respect of good communication.

What emerges from Lockwood's research is a powerful illustration of the demands such work places on writers in these centres, which takes us back to Beaufort's (2008) question as to how technologies might affect writers' processes. It seems that the agents in these web-chat scenarios are having to manage a highly complex set of discourses: interactional in that they need to fulfil relational needs in respect of the customer, and transactional in that they have certain goals to meet, usually within stipulated timeframes. This requires the writers to make appropriate choices in terms of register. The application of Hallidayan notions of field, tenor and mode go some way to helping account for the contextual information that might inform such choices, but added to this will be the extra pressure in terms of prescriptions and proscriptions that are underpinned by the needs of the organisation that these agents work for.

The implications from the perspective of the applied linguist are interesting, in that notions of what can be considered spoken or written discourse may need revisiting. In effect, the writers are being asked to produce a form of interactional written discourse. According to Darics (2014), IM brings together elements of both spoken and written language, the former "in that it is spontaneous, often unedited, responsive, and informal", whereas in the case of the latter the "transcript is permanent and searchable, and the communication lacks the nonverbal cues of the traditional audiovisual sense" (p. 339). The unplanned nature of spoken discourse and all the demands it makes on the writer or texter are captured in her summary, but in her characterisation of the written element she raises an issue that has practical rather than theoretical implications for those tasked with customer service, namely, the fact that their performance is potentially subject to scrutiny by employers looking to ensure that performance standards are met. In effect, this adds a third element, that of accountability, to the task for these writers: they need to build relationships, meet the goals of the customers, and as noted, be seen to be following the prescriptions of the organisation.

The question of accountability is not new – people working by telephone in the customer service industry regularly have their calls monitored and recorded for quality assurance purposes, just as emails sent on behalf of an organisation can be checked or monitored. The extra dimension in this situation is that writers are having to make decisions and produce appropriate discourse in written form in real time, knowing that the kinds of repair strategies that are common in spoken discourse are not so easy to deploy once the initial text has in effect gone on record, and possibly been made permanent. IM perhaps adds to the pressure in that the nature of the medium brings with it the expectation on the part of the reader (i.e. the customer) of a quick response, an expectation in effect endorsed by organisations with their thirty-second response rule in relation to "dead air".

Email and instant messaging

In the light of the foregoing discussion, not only of the use of IM for web-chat, but also of the relationship between media selection and the characteristics of a particular channel, it is perhaps worth comparing IM and email, and considering the question of what causes a writer to choose email as a communicative medium over IM or vice versa.

In the case of email as a medium for workplace communication, there has been a perception (e.g. Darics, 2015) that as a platform it allows for a more informal register, i.e. something approximating more closely to spoken language, than that seen in the media it has largely superseded, namely letters and memos. But while there may be a general tendency in this direction, we can still see a considerable amount of variation in the register of emails, depending on the situation for which they are written (Lenassi, 2015). At one end of the spectrum we can find very formally crafted messages, for example, an internal directive initiated from the higher reaches of an institution, or an external email aimed at making an initial contact with a potential client; at the other, if we look at the kinds of exchanges reported by Warren (2013) in his analysis of emails, we find instances of brief informal interactions that to a large extent resemble spoken discourse. This suggests that email can be a vehicle for a variety of purposes and interactional styles. Similarly, IM, as noted (Markman, 2015), can be harnessed to a range of workplace transactions in addition to serving interactional needs, and thus can work as a platform for varying levels of formality depending on the interactants and their communicative purposes.

The two channels, then, have the capacity to mediate discourse using varied registers, and indeed are seen to do so, but perhaps the most salient difference lies in perceptions of the synchronicity of these two different media. Darics (2014) suggests they have been traditionally viewed as different in that email has been regarded as asynchronous and IM as synchronous, although she notes that what she calls "the clear divide" between the two "has become blurred in recent years" (p. 341). While email and IM can theoretically function both as synchronous and asynchronous media, it is perhaps the sense of expectation attached to these that makes a reader or writer feel they need to respond more promptly to a text message than they would to an email. When it comes to email, Skovholt and Svennevig (2013) suggest that "the asynchronicity of email interaction influences participants' expectations of responses", going on to say that in email interaction, "traditional adjacency pairs are modified and adapted to fit the asynchronous context" (p. 599). In the context of IM, Darics (2014) explains that chronemic, or time-related cues such as silence or immediacy of response, play an important part in communication processes, and that "they are essential for the participants to orientate themselves in interpreting messages (or the lack of messages)" (p. 340). Presence information, i.e. the knowledge as to whether a potential interlocutor is available, can serve as an extra paralinguistic cue, to which communicators can assign meaning. It is interesting to note that presence awareness systems are built into most IM platforms (Darics, 2014; Markman, 2015), giving writers or texters a further layer of information that needs to be fed into their decision-making processes regarding when and how to communicate. In essence, this is another challenge for the writer that comes about because of the characteristics of a particular technology.

The general sense with regard to these two different media, then, is that there is a higher expectation of a prompt response with IM, but this is by no means a clear-cut distinction. In Darics' (2014) study, it was found that the participants used IM as both a synchronous and an asynchronous medium; she points to a number of factors that might influence the ways in which IM is used in respect of time-related expectations, including hierarchical relations, length of team membership, personal variables such as gender, and how urgent the issue is, as having "a considerable effect on what is considered acceptable, normative, or as a flouting of the norm" (p. 353). With email, meanwhile, according to Skovholt and Svennevig (2013), "(T) here is great variation in patterns of response that are not normatively regulated", as well as "great idiosyncratic variation, symptomatic of a system of interaction that is not (yet) strongly codified" (p. 599). What this suggests is an arena of communication where there are no clear guidelines, rather a range of contextual factors that seem to play a part in media choice and how the medium in question is exploited. It is a case of developments in technology offering new ways of communicating, but as shown with these media, particularly IM, these new opportunities bring with them new demands.

Technology and writing: opportunities and challenges

It can be seen, then, from the extensive discussion of IM, that as a developing technology it offers new ways of communicating, but at the same time exposes the writer to a world of greater complexity. The tension between the affordances of new technologies and the challenges they pose is further addressed in the final section of this chapter, looking in brief at issues relating to multimodality, the managing of corporate image through social media platforms, and the handling of collaborative writing in virtual space.

Multimodality

An area that has been opened up considerably by developments in technology, and which poses its own challenges, is that of multimodality. The need – and the ability – to repackage information for different purposes and audiences has been mentioned in the context of the PR industry (see Chapter 2), where it was seen that writers were reworking and recontextualising information in both written and spoken form to achieve their particular goals. In this regard, Iedema (2003) discusses the notion of "resemiotization", which "is about how meaning making shifts from context to context, from practice to practice, or from one stage of a practice to the next" (p. 41). Multimodality involves managing a variety of semiotic resources, such as image, colours, page layouts and so on, and as Iedema (ibid.) explains, moves the ways in which meaning is represented away from language to the deployment of these other modes. It is easy to see how the affordances of technology open up a wealth of new paths for writers to communicate through multimodal means, and by way of illustration Iedema (ibid.) notes changes in the ways that bureaucratic and corporate organisations are adopting multimodal approaches to representing themselves to the world.

It is beyond the scope of this chapter to address the huge body of research relating to multimodality, and I shall restrict myself to two points in relation to this, both of which pertain to the ramifications multimodality has for the workplace writer. The first of these is that embracing multimodality entails working with a much wider range of semiotic resources than are afforded by text alone. Iedema (2003, p. 38), drawing on the work of Eco (1990) characterises these as "more disparate, non-linear, non-hierarchical, more freely combinative, circular and serialized kinds of representation" when compared to the "logic of linear progression and causal or temporal contiguity such as associated with language and linguistic expression". It would be possible to infer a degree of chaos in this characterisation, but that is not the case. While multimodality opens up myriad creative possibilities for achieving a particular communicative goal, the ways in which these are managed have their conventions. Essentially, the writer (and this of course extends the notion of writing quite considerably) has in effect to learn a new language, the language of space and image and so on. The second point can be found in Kress and van Leeuwen's (1996, p. 35) explanation of semiotic modes as being "shaped by both the intrinsic characteristics and potentialities of the medium and by the requirements, histories and values of societies and their cultures". As can be seen from this, there is an implied reminder that in selecting and exploiting a particular medium, writers always need to bear in mind the practices, conventions, expectations and constraints that have developed in the contexts they find themselves in.

Management of corporate image

Developments have also been seen in the ways in which organisations manage their corporate image by means of social media platforms, once again exemplifying the opportunities afforded by technology but also pointing to new challenges for writers. Creelman (2015, p. 161) captures the essence of what is happening in this area:

> These social media platforms have become the digital marketplace where the give-and-take of conversation, at its best, takes on a cooperative aspect, as companies collaborate with their customers and clients to sustain, mitigate, and, in some cases, repair their relationships with customers through digital online conversations.

The activities seen on social media platforms can be regarded as a new and increasingly important way of communicating with customers, leading to "what might be seen as a change of paradigm in corporate communication" (Lillqvist and Louhiala-Salminen, 2014, p. 4). It is important to note that this is no longer one-way communication, but a dialogic event. Creelman (2015), for example, describes the use of corporate blogs as social media marketing tools, explaining that these serve as a two-way asynchronous form of communication, which gives customers the opportunity to voice their opinions about products and services. Like other electronic channels, social media platforms such as blogging, Facebook and Twitter lead to a "dialogic conversational style" (Creelman, 2015, p. 161). Lillqvist and Louhiala-Salminen (2014, p. 22) also observe that "a more personalized communication style than that found in traditional corporate communication" is afforded by the interactive nature of Facebook when used by organisations for their impression management. This dialogic turn brought about through the use of social media is further indication that discourse in many electronic channels is moving towards a more informal and interactive style.

However, as organisations venture into these new electronic spaces to project and manage their images, they also encounter elements of the unknown. One of these is that they no longer have a clear idea of their audience. If we consider the PR industry, in which mediated communication has more or less come to be the norm (Jackson, 2007), we see that press releases, once targeted at journalists with a view to getting coverage, are now placed on corporate websites and therefore available to much larger sections of the public. Writers who are steeped in the principles of preparing texts for specific audiences are thus faced with new challenges as they move away from one-to-one texts to texts that are attempting to meet the needs of wider, unknown audiences. Essentially, they can no longer be sure who will read what they write. A second issue is related to the proliferation of different means for consumers to communicate about and with organisations, such as blogs of various kinds, Twitter, or fan pages initiated from the community rather than the organisation. Darics (2015) explains that these represent a decentralisation of the "previously centralized channels of marketing, PR and corporate communication", and as such can be seen as "channels that reach beyond the control of organizations" (p. 2). Once again, we see great possibilities opening up with the development of new ways for organisations to interact with their clients, but alongside these we see new demands for the writer: the need to communicate with an often faceless audience, and to engage in an ongoing dialogue with their customers on a public forum that can be subject to considerable scrutiny. And as we are reminded by Lillqvist and Louhiala-Salminen (2014, p. 23): "corporate representatives must always be mindful of the impressions they are giving their wider audience".

Collaborating in virtual space

The theme that has run quite strongly through this section of the chapter, namely, that with new opportunities come new challenges, can be iterated for a final time in the context of collaborative writing in virtual space. The advent of wikis and other e-collaboration (Kock *et al.*, 2001) platforms that enable virtual teams or groups to construct texts together are a very welcome development, in that they help "to facilitate work flow between participants in the networked enterprise" (Goodman and Hirsch, 2014, p. 136). There is huge variety of software available for professionals to collaborate in virtual, distributed settings, and which allow for document authoring and sharing, ranging from the simple combination of the affordances of word processing and email as seen in Townley and Jones's (2016) study of the drafting of contractual documents, to more sophisticated packages. A detailed examination of the many CMC technologies that are used in workplaces to facilitate collaboration can be seen in Hewett and Robidoux (2010), with an interesting added element to this article being that it was collaboratively written using wikis and Google Docs. In the light of the proliferation of such CMC technologies, there is a need for research that will "enable us to expand our notions of collaboration and the writing process in general" (Jones, 2007, p. 292), and to investigate ways of helping students adjust to the possibility of working in environments where virtual collaboration is common. While research has been conducted on this latter topic (e.g. Buechler, 2010; Eastman and Swift, 2002; Rehling, 2005), developments in technology are of course ongoing and rapid, prompting Paretti, McNair and Holloway-Attaway (2007, p. 328) to suggest that "such transformations ... require concomitant transformations in our educational practices".

But wherever collaboration takes place, whether in an office or in virtual space, it is still an interactive process that requires the ability to manage relationships with colleagues, i.e. to consider the kinds of factors discussed in Chapters 5 and 6. Adding comments to a Word document or suggesting changes by means of groupware, or any other intervention relating to a collaboratively constructed document, still require a sensitivity to the other participants involved. The additional challenge is that what might be handled with relative ease in a face-to-face situation can be more difficult to deal with when mediated in virtual space, given the reduced levels of "social presence" (Short *et al.*, 1976) that are found in many electronic media. Once again it is a case of a new technology throwing up a new challenge.

Conclusion

When Computer Assisted Language Learning (CALL) emerged as a new force to reckon with for language teaching, the familiar question relating to new technologies raised its head, namely, whether people were doing old things with new technology, or whether the technology enabled them to do new things because of its particular affordances. In the case of some of the early CALL software there was little doubt that the former was taking place, as cloze exercises and sentence matching tasks made their way onto the computer screen in the same formats as they had enjoyed in textbooks.

If we pose the same question in respect of communication technology, we can see a number of different developments, ranged along a continuum – from doing old things with new technology to doing new things with it. There are some instances where the technology facilitates in simple ways some of the tasks we need to perform as writers, such as the editing work reported in Townley and Jones (2016); there are other cases where the text is essentially the same in its intent and schematic structure, as seen in the case of promotional emails, but where writers are able to achieve their goals in different and more creative ways because of the possibilities afforded by the medium. And then there are instances where it seems that new possibilities are opening, bringing with them new challenges for writers, most powerfully seen in the ways in which IM has developed as a tool in the workplace.

Technology as a resource for writing in the workplace is undoubtedly a good thing, but as seen, it brings its own challenges and expectations, whether "the pressure of continuous availability" (Bargiela-Chiappini, 2015, p. ix) associated with IM, or the demands of handling a social media presence in the glare of public attention. Furthermore, it should not be assumed that all of these features afforded by technology are necessarily beneficial or advantageous for everyone. While they may be seen from a management perspective as making for swift and efficient communication, and also as providing a means of overseeing communication activity in the organisation, from the perspective of the employee they may be viewed differently. It has been observed that workplace documentation, notably in the form of organisationally prescribed templates, can serve as a form of control (Winsor, 1999). The ubiquity of technology in communication practices in contemporary workplace settings allows for increased management monitoring of employee activity, seen, for example, in the accountability that goes with emails circulated among workgroups (Gimenez, 2006), the records of activity left by IM (Darics, 2014), or the common practice of requiring employees to copy management into emails sent both internally and externally (Bremner, 2006, 2012b; Skovholt and Svennevig, 2006), discussed in Chapter 6. Never has it been so easy to monitor the work of individual writers.

Surveying the changes in the workplace brought about by rapidly changing technology, Rogers (2006) reminds us that "some things do not change. Age-old communication problems persist" (p. 250), and it is important to bear this in mind in summing up: essentially all of the considerations that are addressed in the different chapters of this volume apply to the handling of new communication technologies, i.e. the ways of doing things that are sanctioned by the professional community, questions of purpose and audience, the need to draw on different texts as writers create new ones, the ability to manage collaborative relationships, issues of power, the considerable influence of the individual organisation manifest in its culture and practices, and the fact that it is only in the workplace itself that full knowledge of the organisation-specific expectations, conventions and practices can be acquired. Technology does not trump these considerations – it makes things possible, but it should not determine our choices. It is a question not simply of what is afforded by technology, but of what is allowed and expected in relation to the local context. Thus, as with the other areas dealt with in this book, when, as teachers, we address the role and management of new technologies for workplace writing, raising awareness and fostering adaptability among our students should be a central goal.

Finally, what comes across very clearly as we consider the impact of technology on workplace writing is that we cannot afford to take a narrow view of writing. In this chapter, we are not only concerned with what is beyond the text, but with what the text is, whether it is written discourse, spoken discourse, or the use of image and space, and what this means for the workplace writer.

8

ORGANISATIONAL CULTURE

Introduction

Every organisation has its own culture, or as Pacanowsky and O'Donnell-Trujillo (1983) explain, "its own way of doing what it does and its own way of talking about what it is doing" (p. 128). An organisation's culture is the reflection of an accretion of values and beliefs about how things should be done, and can be seen in a variety of indicators, from physical features such as office furniture and clothing, to communication practices such as decision-making and water-cooler encounters. Morgan (1986) takes a fairly explicit view of this aspect of the workplace, describing culture as "the underlying values, beliefs and principles that serve as a foundation for the organization's management system as well as the set of management practices and behaviors that both exemplify and reinforce those basic principles" (p. 2). The culture will have an influence on the ways in which the organisation's members interact and communicate, and by extension on the ways in which writing is enacted and the forms that it will take. This chapter examines the factors that help shape and express the culture of an organisation, and discusses the importance of understanding this aspect of the workplace, arguing that the ability to read the culture of an organisation is not only a necessary skill for successful assimilation but also a contributor to success as a writer.

While the notions of organisational culture and discourse community have some elements in common and to some extent overlap, they are in many ways distinct, and this chapter sets out by explaining those distinctions. It goes on to look at definitions and views of organisational culture in the context of the workplace, considering both prescriptive and descriptive approaches and their implications. Approaches to the measurement and understanding of organisational culture are reported from the literature. The next part of the chapter is concerned with the artefacts and behaviours that are the indicators of a culture with the potential for revealing organisational values and influences; an important element of this discussion is the relationship between different management philosophies and the prevailing culture. If, as will be demonstrated, an organisation's culture and values can be interpreted through its artefacts and behaviours, then it follows that an ability to read these is a skill that should be fostered in students who are about to enter the workplace. The final sections of the chapter discuss this topic from a pedagogical perspective, looking in particular at an assignment designed to help develop in students an awareness of organisational culture and its implications.

Organisational culture and discourse community

As noted, the notions of discourse community (addressed in Chapter 2) and organisational culture overlap somewhat, but it is important to show the ways in which they differ, and in doing this to make clear the focus of this chapter. In Chapter 2, I looked at the relationship between genres and discourse communities, arguing that it is through the study of genres and the practices that typically surround their construction that we can learn about the communities that produce them, thereby providing useful information for those wishing to enter those communities. The related phenomenon of organisational culture also reflects and influences the ways in which people communicate in different workplaces, yet these two concepts can be distinguished from one another in a number of ways.

How can the differences between them be characterised? In a sense the two are quite different in that one – the discourse community – is a group of people, and therefore in some ways a physical entity, while the other – organisational culture – is intangible, even though it is located in specific contexts. Having said that, when considering discourse communities, researchers are more likely to conceive of them as theoretical groups, rather than visualising actual assemblies of like-minded people communicating with a shared jargon. Organisational culture too, like any culture, while it plays out in the everyday, is not a physical thing that can be latched onto, rather something that emanates in an abstract way from the contexts that construct it. Thus, it seems reasonable for the purposes of comparison to regard them as concepts rather than concrete entities.

To some extent the difference between them is a question of the specificity of the context under consideration: banking, for example, could be considered a discourse community in that members of the profession share similar goals and largely perform their work in the same way, using the same shared genres to do this, such as bank statements, letters of credit and so on. The fact that a proportion of a bank's work is likely to be spent dealing with other banks lends strength to this idea of a broadly conceived discourse community of bankers. However, not all banks share the same organisational culture, for a number of reasons: there will of course be differences that can be ascribed to the nature of their activity – whether they are an investment bank or a high-street bank, for example – but there will be other differences that are the result of their history, their client base, their ambitions and the values that are associated with these. A British merchant bank with 300 years of history and tradition will have a different culture from a New York investment bank, for example, just as a retail bank in Hong Kong will have a different culture from its counterpart on a high street in England.

To take a different professional setting, we could look at the airline industry, which again has its own genres, whether they are safety instructions, interactions between flight attendants and passengers, websites, loyalty programmes and so on. But different airlines, depending on their values, the business model they are pursuing, the types of customer they want to attract, the prices they charge for their tickets, the image they want to project, will be using these basic genres in different ways. Everyone's experience of particular airlines is somewhat different, so I will not cite specific examples here, but most people would probably agree that the experience of travelling on a well-funded national airline is different from that of using a budget airline. Thus, employees of these airlines could be considered members of the same discourse community, but they would be experiencing a different organisational culture depending on which airline they worked for.

As explained in Chapter 2, at the heart of any examination of genre and discourse community is the assumption that underlies social constructionism, namely, that there is a strong mutually constitutive relationship between the two. It should be stressed that the relationship between organisation and culture is similarly reciprocal – just as organisational practices help form the culture of the organisation, so that culture influences the practices found there (see Miller, 2015; Morgan, 2006; Schnurr, 2013). In the field of organisational communication, the view that organisations are socially constructed is captured by the concept of communicative constitution of organisation (CCO), which sees communication as a constitutive process. By this token, the artefacts and behaviours that are seen in an organisation are indicators of the culture, and a reading of these will provide insights into how the culture works. Alongside this it is generally held that learning the culture is an important element of the process of being socialised into an organisation (Kramer, 2010; Mumby, 2013); a similar scenario is also seen in the relationship between genre and community, with the idea that an understanding of genre conventions will help us learn about the norms and ideologies of the community, leading to participation in the community's activities (Berkenkotter and Huckin, 1993).

This leads onto the question of what we look at to understand the nature of community or culture respectively. It was explained in Chapter 2 that attempts to uncover how a discourse community functions centre around language and its construction, thus researchers will study genres and their discoursal features, and increasingly the processes that help create these genres, to answer the question of how and why texts are written in particular ways. In the case of organisational culture, although the context of investigation is often more tightly defined, the question is more broadly conceived, asking how and why people behave the way they do in this particular organisation. In framing the question more broadly, researchers will look at a wider range of indicators, both tangible and intangible, to try and understand what is going on; language can be included in these investigations, but it is just one of many factors that is considered.

In asking different questions, and looking at different aspects of the workplace, research will of course yield up different information: in the case of discourse community this information relates largely to language and how it is used, while in the case of organisational culture it relates to a broader set of elements, which might include organisational values, management beliefs and so on. This has implications from a pedagogical standpoint in terms of what can be learnt or understood, and how this can be usefully passed on to students.

An understanding of both discourse community practices and organisational culture is important for someone about to enter the workplace. Consider the student who wants to become an investment banker: on the one hand, they need to understand the genres that are used by the banking community to do their work, but if they have a particular bank in mind, an understanding of the culture of their targeted employer is also very valuable. Goldman Sachs, to take a somewhat extreme example, has a very distinctive culture that any aspiring employee would do well to try and understand before applying. Considerations of this nature are also relevant for people looking at transitioning from one organisation to another within a community of which they are an established member. This can be seen in the case of universities, for example: faculty working in business communication, English language teaching, discourse studies and so on may have a clear idea of how they fit into a particular discourse community, with its conferences and journals and related gatekeeping procedures, but as they move from one department to another, possibly to another country, they will often encounter a set of expectations quite different from those they have become accustomed to, a group of people who tell them that "This is the way we do things here"; in other words, they will need to understand and adjust to another organisational culture.

To sum up from the investigator's standpoint, which is the most relevant for this chapter, the differences between the notions of discourse community and organisational culture lie ultimately in what manifestations we are looking for as researchers or potential members and why we are looking for these: we ask different questions, use different data to answer them, identify different phenomena, learn different things, and make different use of the findings. An important question from the perspective of this book is in what form these findings can be passed on to students: it may be that the degree of specificity of the investigation has implications for how we as teachers deal with this information as we prepare our students for the workplace. This question will be revisited in the concluding sections of the chapter, by which time it is hoped that the value of making a distinction between the concepts of organisational culture and discourse community, and of treating them separately, will have been made clear.

Finally, although this section has sought to show ways in which the two notions are distinct, it should be emphasised that communication, whether written or spoken, is an object of study in the investigation of both of these; however, whereas it is the central point of interest in discourse communities, it is one of just a number of indicators that are studied in investigations of organisational culture.

Organisational culture: definitions and approaches

Approaches to describing and understanding organisational culture have come from a number of directions, each with their own different underpinnings and motivations. This section will briefly look at the most common of these approaches, and the ways in which they are applied, before focusing on the definition of organisational culture that is most relevant to this book and which I believe serves the aim of helping students in their transition to the workplace most effectively.

Miller (2015) makes a distinction between looking at culture as "something that an organization *has*" and as "something that an organization *is*" (p. 71) (Original emphasis), these two positions leading respectively to prescriptive and descriptive approaches to understanding organisational culture. Taking a prescriptive approach is predicated on the idea that "successful companies can be identified in terms of their cultures" (Miller, 2015, p. 72), with the underlying assumption that if you can point to the features of a culture that make that particular organisation successful, then it may be possible to apply these in other contexts with similar success. Two books, published in the early 1980s, were instrumental in this thinking: *Corporate Cultures: The Rites and Rituals of Corporate Life* (Deal and Kennedy, 1982) and *In Search of Excellence: Lessons from America's Best-Run Companies* (Peters and Waterman, 1982). The title of the latter in particular is suggestive of the motivations behind this approach to understanding culture. However, Miller sees shortcomings in this approach to organisational culture in that it implies a single route to success, and she points out that what may work in one company may not work in another. She also has concerns about treating culture as something an organisation *has*: "The objectification of culture is risky because when we objectify culture, we de-emphasize the complex processes through which organizational culture is created and sustained" (Miller, 2015, p. 74). This second point will be picked up again later in the chapter.

As mentioned, there are a number of ways in which to approach organisational culture, and one idea that has attracted many researchers is the notion that culture is in some way measurable. This notion is often motivated by management concerns, with the implicit expectation that an understanding of what is going on in an organisation might provide insights into ways of improving things there. Indeed, Dev (2013) articulates the potential value of such a perspective: "Productive cultural change will take place if leaders analyse the organization's existing culture prudently, and assess it against the cultural attributes required to achieve strategic objectives" (p. 4). She goes on to explain the perceived need to measure culture, citing what she calls "one of the golden rules of business management: 'If you cannot measure something you cannot manage it'" (pp. 5–6).

Much of the work involving the measurement of organisational culture has led to the generating of dimensions to account for behaviour in workplaces and the design of survey questionnaires to gauge employee perceptions of what is going on. The work of Hofstede and his colleagues (1990, 1997) is an often-cited example of such an approach. He (1997, pp. 182–183) contends that "shared perceptions of

daily practices should be considered to be the core of an organization's culture",
and with this in mind used a sixty-one-item survey, asking respondents to indicate
the extent to which they agreed with a series of statements relating to their organisation. From this his team was able to generate a set of dimensions of organisational
culture, which were used as the basis for a comparison of twenty different organisational units.

Other examples of survey questionnaire work – to name two recent studies
among many – include that of Marchand, Haines and Dextras-Gauthier (2013),
who used O'Reilly *et al.*'s (1991) Organizational Culture Profile instrument to
examine the association between different organisational culture types and aspects
of occupational health such as psychological stress, depression and well-being.
Meanwhile Zhu and Engels (2014), in the context of higher education, looked
at the relationship between organisational culture and organisational innovations,
using the Organizational Cultural Environment Survey (Zhu *et al.*, 2011), drawing
on the literature and their previous studies to generate their dimensions of culture.
It should be pointed out that more than ten years ago Van den Berg and Wilderom
(2004) recognised the challenges for comparative research posed by the proliferation of studies in this area, prompting them, on the basis of a literature review and
empirical studies, to propose a definition and a set of dimensions to try and increase
comparability. However, thus far, the uniformity of approach that has been largely
enjoyed, say, in the case of the study of language learning strategies, with the use of
Rebecca Oxford's (1990) *Strategy Inventory for Language Learning*, has not been seen
to the same extent in the measurement of organisational cultures.

While questionnaire surveys are a helpful instrument for researchers seeking to
identify relationships and associations with other workplace phenomena, there are
some potentially problematic issues – in addition to that of comparability – relating
to this particular analytical approach. Hopkins (2006) points out that questionnaire
surveys look at employees' perceptions of what is happening in an organisation
rather than what is actually happening there, and that these may not be the same,
also suggesting that they provide "a relatively superficial description" (p. 6). Miller's
(2015) point regarding the fact that the objectification of culture overlooks the
ways in which cultures are created and sustained, is also very pertinent here in that
as a snapshot of employee perceptions, surveys do not take account of organisational culture as a developing phenomenon.

This takes us back to the question of why people examine organisational culture
in the first place: managers, researchers and aspiring participants in an organisation
will all have different motives in seeking to understand this aspect of workplaces.
Managers, as observed earlier (Dev, 2013), may be considering the influence of
the prevailing culture on their organisation's ability to move in a particular direction, and their investigations are often motivated by a desire for change; in other
words, they see culture as something that can be managed (Miller, 2015). Meanwhile it can be seen as reasonable for researchers to want to make comparisons
among organisations, but in seeking and abstracting commonalities or differences
in terms of cultural dimensions, they are to some extent moving away from a view

of organisations as distinct entities with their own particular cultures. As for the individual wishing to understand the practices that can be seen in the organisation that they have just joined, a more context-specific picture is necessary, especially bearing in mind the point expressed at the beginning of this chapter, namely, that every organisation has its own way of doing things.

It is the motivations of the individual in studying organisational culture that are most pertinent for this chapter, and the role that learning the culture of an organisation plays in assimilation and socialisation (Mumby, 2013). Kramer (2010) goes as far as proposing that "A general understanding of an organization's culture is often indicative of successful transition from newcomer to full member" (p. 98), while Schnurr (2013, p. 60) stresses the importance of looking at "the specific norms that characterise a workplace in order to understand and make sense of people's behaviour", suggesting that the workplace culture provides a framework for interpreting this behaviour. For the newcomer to a workplace, access to these norms and to this understanding will not be achieved with an instrument used for identifying and measuring dimensions shared with other organisations, but will more likely be gained through a close examination of what is going on there: and it is to the highly influential work of Edgar Schein on organisational culture that this chapter now turns, as this provides a useful lens through which organisations can be viewed.

Schein's model of organisational culture

Schein's approach to understanding organisational culture is concerned with what an organisation is rather than what it has, i.e. it is descriptive rather than prescriptive. He (1987, p. 262) defines the culture of a social group as:

> a pattern of basic assumptions that a given group has invented, discovered or developed in learning to cope with problems of external adaptation and internal integration, and that have worked well enough to be considered valid, and, therefore, to be taught to new members as the correct way to perceive, think and feel in relation to those problems.

This captures both the essence of organisational culture and its value to learners in that it is seen as something that can be taught to new members to enable them to assimilate into their target organisation.

Before addressing the question of how cultures can be examined through the lens offered by Schein, it is necessary to point out the challenges that the complex nature of organisational cultures poses for those attempting to read and understand them. Miller (2015) has synthesised much of the scholarship in this area and highlights four aspects of culture that have emerged from descriptive perspectives, namely, that organisational cultures are complicated, are emergent, are not unitary and are often ambiguous (2015, pp. 74–78).

The first point relates to the multiplicity of indicators of a culture: while the study of discourse communities and genres centres around language and the processes surrounding its construction, in the case of culture, analysts look at a vast range of artefacts and behaviours, both tangible and intangible, to try and understand what is going on. As for the second point, this is tied up with social constructionist notions mentioned above that cultures – and texts – are created through the interactions of members of an organisation or community, or as Morgan (2006, p. 136) puts it, an "ongoing, proactive process of reality construction". (This issue is discussed in greater detail in Chapter 2.) The non-unitary nature of cultures presents a further challenge, in that it is unlikely that any organisation can be characterised as having a single culture, rather it will be made up of a number of sub-cultures. These sub-cultures can be configured in different ways. Louis (1985) talks of "vertical slices", which could be represented by departments or divisions, and "horizontal slices", which might be represented by different hierarchical levels. In a university, for example, one would expect a different culture to prevail in a Department of Engineering when compared to a Department of History ("vertical slice"), while the culture of the senior management team will be markedly different from that of the team responsible for the security of the university ("horizontal slice"). Schnurr (2013) also talks about the idea of "occupational culture", the concept coming from Hofstede (2001), whereby members identify with a type of occupation more than a specific employer. Even within an occupation or discipline one can see different sub-cultures – this often plays out within the discipline of English when one compares what is seen in an academic department with what happens in an English language centre: each unit is driven by different expectations, plays a different role, is made up of teachers who are qualified to different levels, and as a unit may be seen as nearer to or further from the margins of what the university sees as important. Finally, Miller (2015) points to the ambiguity that attends attempts to interpret organisational cultures, explaining that the various manifestations of the culture may be difficult to read, a situation compounded by the changing nature of organisations. Added to this is the possibility that organisational members themselves may find it difficult to articulate their understanding of the culture because so much of the relevant knowledge is tacit (Ledwell-Brown, 2000).

Given these observations and caveats regarding the nature of organisational culture it is perhaps not surprising that a number of research perspectives have emerged to approach its potential messiness. One of the most thoughtful attempts to address this can be seen in the work of Martin (1992), who describes three perspectives: the integration perspective, the differentiation perspective, and the fragmentation perspective. Under the integration perspective, organisational cultures are seen as homogeneous, and researchers focus on similarities of perception, ignoring deviations from organisation-wide consensus, but thereby running the risk of overlooking sites of conflict. Meanwhile, the differentiation perspective challenges the idea of homogeneity, suggesting that organisations are constituted by sub-cultures, looking at how these are interrelated and how they make for a culture that is potentially contradictory rather than integrated. As for the fragmentation perspective, this does not see organisations as coherent, but focuses on ambiguity, accepting that their cultures will lead to multiple interpretations that are unlikely to result in a clear picture of what is going on.

The utility of this model can be seen in Mills and Hoeber's (2013) study of a community sports organisation, in which they show how Martin's (1992) perspectives can be applied to an investigation of its culture. They examined members' perceptions of the artefacts in a local figure skating club to see the extent to which these were shared or contested, concluding that "participants perceived the artifacts in integrated, differentiated, and fragmented ways, which challenges the assumption that everyone will experience the environment in a similar, positive fashion" (p. 493). While Martin's (1992) work offers a model that is perhaps more appropriate for researchers rather than individuals trying to make sense of their work environment, it nevertheless reinforces the points summarised by Miller (2015) relating to the somewhat elusive nature of organisational cultures.

Examining an organisation's culture

How do we learn about organisational cultures through Schein's model? The model consists of three elements, namely, artefacts, values and assumptions, and the relationship among these is often represented as an "onion" of concentric layers, with artefacts, as the visible manifestations of an organisation's culture' on the outer layer, values in the middle layer, and assumptions in the innermost part of this arrangement.

Artefacts can consist of both objects and behaviours. Examples of these might include physical elements such as architecture, office layout, furniture, uniforms or other clothing; written documents such as signs on the wall, rules and regulations, manuals, emails; spoken interactions including modes of address, organisational stories, meetings, also considering the channels of communication that are favoured for these interactions; rites and rituals (particular ways of observing and celebrating that are enshrined in the organisation's practices); and representations in the public domain, such as websites and job advertisements. These examples are only a small selection of the kinds of artefacts that can be observed in an organisation.

It is through the examination of these surface elements of an organisation that we can gain insights into the values and assumptions that exist within its culture. Values are what an organisation is purportedly attempting to achieve, and can be articulated publicly or can be evidenced in visible behaviour. Examples of values might include innovation, customer satisfaction, environmental awareness, safety and so on. As for the assumptions within an organisation, these are "the emergent understandings that are created by group members as they interact with each other" (Schein, 1992, p. 9). They are for the most part unconsciously held and unarticulated, and represent the deepest elements of an organisation's culture, as is implied by the arrangement of the "cultural onion".

The idea behind this, then, is that through examination of the surface elements of a culture, one can gain a sense of the values that exist within the organisation, and possibly go beyond those to the basic assumptions that underpin its modus operandi and vivendi. An examination of this kind demands a combination of methodological and investigative tools, that might include looking at the physical environment, the analysis of documentation and ethnographic observation. Moreover, a central element of any exploration of an organisation's culture should be interviews with its members, if we accept a view of organisational culture as "shared perceptions of organisational practices" (Van den Berg and Wilderom, 2004, p. 572; see also Dev, 2013; Hofstede, 1997), since it is through these members that we can gain access to a sense of what these practices and associated values are. We should nevertheless bear in mind, as pointed out in relation to questionnaire surveys (Hopkins, 2006), that employee perceptions may not be the same as what is actually going on in an organisation.

One example of a study which draws on multiple data to analyse an organisation – in this case a large pharmaceutical company – is that of Ledwell-Brown (2000), in which she hoped to show "how the overall values and attitudes of the organization translate into specific expectations of writers" (pp. 200–201). The study looked at two divisions within the organisation (marketing and management information systems) and involved analysis of interviews, company texts and recorded observations. She found that although there were some differences in emphasis relating to desired outcomes and prescriptions for writing, the two divisions held many attitudes to writing in common, and concluded overall that "the managers' responses reflect the goals and values of their particular division and the organization as a whole" (2000, p. 217). The study is a very insightful – and very rare – example of research that has specifically investigated the relationship between organisational culture and writing practices.

Management beliefs and organisational culture

If we are to undertake an examination of a particular culture, how are we to interpret the artefacts that we find in the organisation? Morgan's characterisation of organisational culture as "the underlying values, beliefs and principles that serve as a foundation for the organization's management system" (1986, p. 2) is pertinent here, and for a principled and systematic way of analysing the relationship between organisational culture and management beliefs, I am indebted to the work of Katherine Miller and her excellent book *Organizational Communication: Approaches and Processes* (2015), now in its seventh edition. In this she explains three approaches to organisational communication that can be seen as prescriptive in that they are underpinned by beliefs about how communication and other functions should operate in a workplace, namely, classical, human relations and human resources approaches. These approaches represent views of how organisations should be managed that developed during the last century, but as Miller points out, they should not be seen as "dead" subjects. As continuing influences on workplace communication and practices more generally, they represent a powerful lens through which we can view organisational culture. A brief account of each approach is included here.

Classical approaches, influenced by the thinking of Henri Fayol, Max Weber and Frederick Taylor, are associated with the conception of an organisation as a machine, with the corollary that its employees are parts of that machine. Accompanying this metaphor of organisation as machine, we see the notions of specialisation, standardisation, replaceability and predictability – each worker, or part of the machine, is expected to perform a particular function in a planned, standardised and therefore predictable way; if they are not up to the task they can be replaced. Decision-making is the prerogative of management, and the role of the manager in a classically influenced organisation will be to organise their employees (or machine parts) in the most efficient way. Such a view of the workforce has a potentially dehumanising effect, in keeping with the machine metaphor.

The evolution of human relations approaches is in part attributed to the Hawthorne studies that were conducted in the 1920s and 1930s, in which it was found that the social and emotional needs of workers were a factor in their performance in the workplace. The work of Abraham Maslow and Douglas McGregor is very influential in this approach, in that both recognise that employees have a need for attention, social interaction and a sense of individual achievement. In the human relations approach, it is believed that the satisfaction of employee needs such as that of affiliation, and "higher order" needs such as those of esteem and self-actualisation (Maslow, 1943), can lead to higher productivity. This represents a considerable shift away from the classical approach, in that workers are now looked upon as individuals with feelings rather than parts of a machine, and the metaphor that is often associated with the human relations approach is that of the family.

The human resources approach, which draws on the work of Robert Blake and Jane Mouton, and Rensis Likert, among others, is predicated on the belief, as partially implied by the label, that employees are able to make valuable cognitive contributions to the running of an organisation. In doing this they will not only help to maximise the productivity of the organisation, but will be able to satisfy their own needs as individuals by contributing and having this recognised. In this way, human resources approaches can be seen as building on the motivations of both classical and human resources approaches, but with the emphasis being placed on the notion that employees should be valued as sources of ideas that can help the organisation.

These brief, somewhat crude summaries of the three different approaches are intended to give a general idea of the beliefs and motivations associated with each. It should be pointed out too that they are not mutually exclusive approaches to managing an organisation: it is not that common for a single approach to be embraced in its entirety, to the exclusion of the others, rather organisations tend to display combinations of influences from these three prescriptive approaches to a greater or lesser degree. The reason for providing these potted accounts of the three approaches is that they offer a useful framework in which to examine organisational artefacts and values as featured in Schein's (1992) model, and to thereby try and make sense of an organisational culture.

In terms of communication, the practices seen in an organisation can be potential indicators of management beliefs. The idea of "participatory mechanisms" (Bhatia, 2004) that are seen in workplaces was introduced in Chapter 1. This pertains to who can contribute, and about what, in a particular organisation, and this can be indicative of the kinds of influence that prevail there. Miller (2015), drawing on the typology of Farace, Monge and Russell (1977), explains that three broad types of communicative content can be found in organisations: task-related communication, maintenance communication and innovation communication. It is easy to see how these could relate to the three different prescriptive approaches. In a classically influenced organisation, where the workers' role is to function as part of the machine, it would be expected that the bulk of communication would revolve around getting the job done, hence a focus on task. A human relations approach, which believes that worker satisfaction can be achieved through affiliation needs, would favour maintenance communication in addition to task-related communication. Meanwhile managers influenced by the human resources approach, with its emphasis on the cognitive contributions of employees, would encourage innovation communication.

Miller (2015) goes on to look at other aspects of the communication process that can be associated with or indicative of a particular influence, namely, the direction of communication flow, the selected channel of communication, with its attendant potential for feedback and paralinguistic cues, and the style of communication in terms of levels of formality. These, in combination with other artefacts observed in the workplace, can help build up an idea of the prevailing influences, as can seen in the admittedly unnuanced scenarios outlined below. For example, an organisation which has an organogram displaying a vertical hierarchy, modes of address based on rank, uniforms to denote status and role, and an abundance of written rules and regulations, would suggest strong classical influences. On the other hand, an organisation where a flatter hierarchy is seen, where interactions are on an informal first-name basis, and which has a strong employee involvement in decision-making, would suggest that human resources influences are present.

In investigating an organisational culture, it is necessary to look at visible artefacts as a collectivity to build up a picture of the prevailing management influences and values, and each observed element should be interpreted within the context of the larger picture that is being assembled, as there is not necessarily a one-to-one relationship between artefacts and management influences. If the analyst noted, for example, an open-plan office arrangement, this could be open to a number of interpretations: it might have been set up for monitoring purposes, so that managers could see that employees are performing their assigned tasks; it could be intended to provide opportunities for employees to interact and develop social relationships, thereby satisfying affiliation needs; or it could operate as a space in which employees can share ideas. However, once this particular office arrangement was placed alongside the other artefacts assembled by the analyst, it would become much easier to work out what was intended in setting up the office in this way.

Organisational culture and pedagogy

Learning about an organisation's culture, as noted, is an important part of the processes of assimilation and socialisation (Kramer, 2010; Mumby, 2013), and the application of Schein's (1987, 1992) model to the analysis of a culture would appear to provide a useful way into it, particularly from the perspective of a newcomer who wishes to assimilate into that culture. If they are able to read the signs, they will be better able to participate on terms appropriate to that organisation. From the pedagogical perspective, however, learning about organisational cultures while still in the academy presents a particular challenge, because of the inevitable distance between the classroom and the workplace. So, what can be done to help students in this regard? Barclay and York (1996), for example, contend that students find discussions of organisational culture "confusing if the concepts are not related concretely to their own experience" (p. 125). The challenge, then, is to somehow bring organisational cultures closer to the classroom.

Organisational culture, while recognised as an important influence on workplace discourse (Schnurr, 2013), is not usually considered in relation to language pedagogy. In educational contexts, it turns up as a concept in management textbooks, although according to Barnes and Smith (2013), "Little is done to educate and inform the student with regard to discovering and defining an organisation's culture" (p. 45). To remedy this situation, they have developed a multimethod cultural analysis project in which groups of students are required to gain access to an organisation and analyse its culture, using investigative instruments including interview protocols, organisational culture surveys, and what they call "organisational unobtrusive observations" (p. 50), which in effect involve looking at the artefacts on the outer layer of Schein's onion. The project receives positive feedback from students, although we are not given any sense of the quality of the work produced. The creators of the project conclude that it enables students to "experience and discover the subtleties and nuances of organisational culture" (Barnes and Smith, 2013, p. 52).

My own work in this area (Bremner, 2013c) involves an assignment that is aimed at linking organisational culture in a more targeted manner to communication practices. This is the capstone project for *Organisational Culture and Communication*, an undergraduate course for English majors in a Hong Kong university, which offers a theoretical approach to understanding workplace culture while at the same time drawing on students' existing work experience. The main assignment requires students to work in groups to conduct an in-depth analysis of an organisational culture, and to demonstrate how specific communication processes reflect the prevailing culture.

To do the assignment, as with the project reported by Barnes and Smith (2013), access to a workplace is required. The vast majority of those taking my course have work experience or are doing part-time jobs, and it is these workplaces that they use as the sites for their research, rather than attempting access to organisations with which they have no work connection. Focusing on the outer and middle layers of Schein's (1992) model, they describe in detail the physical artefacts and behaviours they observe, and use these to explain values and management influences; this is complemented by interviews with employees and by their own experiences of working in the organisation where possible. They then focus on a central communication process within the organisation, such as assimilation, decision-making, conflict management or any other they choose, and demonstrate how this process reflects the organisational culture. This is a crucial component of the assignment in that it is the point where they often identify what they believe to be mismatches between their reading of the culture and the ways in which their chosen communication process appears to be enacted. It is at this juncture that they need either to recalibrate their understanding of the culture and its communication processes or to follow up on the possibility that the organisation is not practising what it preaches. This is an opportunity, which many groups take, to pursue a more critical line in their analysis.

Refined over some years, the assignment has enabled students to experience a number of epiphanies and to offer shrewd insights into the organisations where they work or have worked. The main component of the assignment is a final report that pulls their observations and analysis together within the theoretical framework offered by Schein's description of organisational culture and the three prescriptive management influences (classical, human relations, human resources). I have included a few extracts from student work over recent years to illustrate what I believe to be the value of this assignment. All student comments are reported verbatim.

The first example is Hong Kong Disneyland (HKDL). The students' analysis juxtaposes claims made by the organisation with their own comments, revealing a certain scepticism about the public face of HKDL. In response to HKDL's description of itself as "A magical world which is full of happiness, energy and fun", they counter "*To the customers, probably, yes*". They are similarly dismissive of the suggestion that "Employees will have the opportunity to join a cast of dreamers and doers, committed to creating magic for our guests and working as a big family", saying that there is "*No space for creativity … Anyone can do the same job … Personal features are being hidden under the uniform …*" Their analysis points to an organisation strongly influenced by classical approaches: they describe training for newcomers at Disney University, "*where they explain the restrictions on employees e.g. hair style (girls will tie hair up, boys can only have short hair which cannot reach their shoulders; no dyeing hair is allowed so that a sense of unity is created)*" and "*the way to speak when they are on stage (when the cartoon characters are resting in the backstage, tell the customers that the princess is resting in the castle)*". They conclude that "*HKDL requires manpower but not aptitude and creativity*", and the idea expressed by the organisation that "We are a big family" is dismissed thus: "*this is the public face … It seems that there is another story in reality*". Earlier, I suggested that it is not common for an organisation to embrace one management approach in its entirety, but student analysis of the culture of HKDL offers a persuasive account, drawing on their reading of its artefacts, of an organisation heavily and almost exclusively influenced by classical approaches.

A second example, this time looking at an organisation that provides check-in services for airlines at Hong Kong Airport, provides an illustration whereby students not only question some of the organisation's claims about its values, but also revisit some of their initial interpretations of the artefacts. For example, they note the use of first names as the normal form of address, saying, "*Initially we saw this as evidence of human relations influences, but later …*", going on to say that, "*Informal address is used not because the organization wants to satisfy the affiliation needs of employees, but merely because it is important to show a friendly image to customers as it is a service-providing company*". They doubt the value of training, explaining that it is a short process, which "*shows that the organization has little intention of investing in the individual development of workers*". As for teamwork, which is claimed as a value by the organisation, "*we disagree … we cannot see any convincing evidence to prove it … communication between team members is very limited*". They also explain that "*task-based communication is the dominating one, as supervisors pass down information in the form of instructions, employees just follow*" concluding that what they see is "*just a kind of subordination of individual interest to general interest*".

The final example is a powerful illustration of the need to look closely at the artefacts in the context of the picture that emerges. These data come from the analysis of a tutorial college where two of the group were working, which is referred to here as "Springtime College". The students struggled to reconcile the claim of the college that "Springtime teachers are young, fun, creative and motivated individuals", which was accompanied by advertising providing a similar message, with the interviews and observations they experienced. In the interview, they explain, applicants are required to give a ten-minute teaching presentation to the Director, who "*will give them feedback and provide suggestions to them if they are not doing something that the Director is looking for*". As for the teaching observation, "*they have a formal meeting about how the Student Teachers can improve their teaching and remind them about the Springtime way of teaching*". For much of the process of examining the college, they assumed that the organisation was influenced by human relations approaches, but closer analysis led them to say: "*We believe we have been deceived by the artifacts*", and they went on to conclude that "*the happy and friendly working environment as a family shown in the artifacts is an illusion as it is controlled and instructed by the Director to make parents and students happy*".

The value of this assignment, I believe, is that it enables students to take a principled analytical approach to understanding an organisational culture in order to try and understand why things are done in particular ways. Very often this will require them to take a critical stance, and to question the significance of or the motives for different practices that they see in the organisation, such as training, mentoring, fostering teamwork and so on. They are also encouraged to look closely at the surface appearance of a culture and the underlying reality, particularly in respect of the public claims that an organisation makes about itself when compared to how employees are managed.

For students, the process of analysing an organisational culture, and relating theory to real world practice and personal experience, can serve as a valuable preparation for their entrance to the workplace on graduation. There is some evidence of the value of this in my own research. In a study of an intern's reflective journal as she socialised into the practices of a Hong Kong PR company (Bremner, 2012a), she acknowledges that one of the contributory factors to her socialisation was her ability, as a graduate of the course *Organisational Culture and Communication*, to notice and interpret certain artefacts that helped her understand the practices of the organisation. In the early stages of her socialisation, she makes frequent references to the culture of the company, and talks specifically about artefacts, mentioning examples she has observed, such as a division of labour and a flat structure. With reference to role played by the course in her socialisation, she said that "observing how people work and interact, and relating their behavior to concepts from the course, was a 'very important factor'" (Bremner, 2012a, p. 21). Overall, it is suggested, this approach to unpacking organisational cultures not only allows students to make sense of workplace experiences they have had thus far, but it also provides reflective tools to help them make sense of future work environments, so that they can understand the various communication practices they encounter and what they signify, and can adapt accordingly.

Conclusion

At the beginning of this chapter the differences between the notions of discourse community and organisational culture were considered, and it was suggested that the degree of specificity which attaches to these two concepts could have implications for how they are dealt with in the academy. The question, then, is whether organisational culture can be considered in the same way as discourse community from a pedagogical perspective. To some extent they pose a similar challenge, in that we cannot fully take on the discourses of a community unless or until we are a member, just as we cannot engage with a culture fully unless we are a part of it. But in the case of discourse communities, there is a certain amount of preparation that can be made in advance of the workplace, in that the discourses of different communities can be taught – up to a point – in the academy. However, as iterated throughout this chapter, organisational cultures are specific to their particular work settings, and we cannot induct students into these in advance. What we can do in the case of organisational culture is give students an awareness of how it can impact on the practices found in the organisation, and provide them with a critical toolkit for reading the culture which will help them as they make their transition into the workplace.

Finally, it should be acknowledged that this chapter has dealt less specifically with writing than many of the others. Having said that, organisational culture will have an influence on writing in multiple ways: the "sedimented practices" (Berkenkotter, 2001, p. 338) that help shape the templates and other documents produced in the organisation; the norms for collaboration; the choices of channel for communication, both internal and external; the formality of register; the ways of opening and closing emails. In every organisation, there are accepted ways of doing things, which have evolved over time, and which reflect the organisation's values in some way, and newcomers need to learn how things are done, to understand and to assimilate into practices that go beyond disciplinary communities, beyond professional communities, to the norms that characterise individual organisations.

9

SOCIALISATION PROCESSES

Introduction

The chapters leading up to Chapter 9 have – I hope – given a sense of the complexities of workplace writing. The particular nature of discourse communities and organisational cultures, the instrumental purposes associated with workplace genres, the interactions with texts and colleagues, and considerations of register and media selection, as discussed in those chapters, all add up to a context that is very rich, and one which requires consideration of a highly diverse set of factors on the part of the writer. This chapter revisits these and the differences between the academy and the workplace as explained in Chapter 1, and considers the key question of how – and where – the written discourses that are needed to perform in workplace contexts can be acquired.

The chapter begins by explaining the nature of language socialisation, a process that is very much linked to social constructionist views of language and context. It goes on to discuss ways in which the academy and the workplace differ from one another as contexts for learning, with two studies chosen to illustrate these differences, showing how context can influence the shape of written products, and highlighting in particular the issues of aim and audience that relate to the respective settings. This leads to a consideration of the power of the workplace as a context for learning, looking at the idea of the community of practice (Lave and Wenger, 1991; Wenger, 1998) and theories of situated learning. Two key perspectives are outlined and explained in this regard, namely, "guided participation" (Rogoff, 1991) and "legitimate peripheral participation" (Lave and Wenger, 1991), followed by an examination of Freedman and Adam's (1996) adaptation of these specifically to writing processes in university and professional settings, with their notions of "facilitated performance" and "attenuated authentic participation". In their study, they highlight many of the situated features of university and workplace settings, and their impact on writing, that make attempts to aid students in their transition from one context to the other so problematic. While much of the research relating to socialising into workplace writing remains somewhat pessimistic about the role that the academy can play in this process, there are nevertheless a number of perspectives and studies that suggest possible ways to address the acknowledged gap between the two contexts, and these are considered in the concluding sections of the chapter.

Language socialisation

The processes of acquiring the written and spoken discourses of a particular workplace, considered a central element of becoming an accepted member of the community (Li, 2000), are seen as processes of socialisation, explained by Bazerman (1994) as "learning the orientations and resources and practices that allow one to interact within a group" (p. 29). It should be stressed that language learning is a central and integral feature of the socialisation process, and "goes hand in hand with learning to operate within a particular society" (Vickers, 2007, p. 622). Looking at language in conjunction with the ability to function in a particular community leads to the more specific notion of language socialisation, the simultaneous acquisition of both linguistic and sociocultural knowledge (Ochs, 1993), a perspective that is informed by anthropology, sociology, (socio)linguistics and education (Duff, 2010), and one which "sees development as culturally situated, as mediated, and as replete with social, cultural, and political meanings in addition to propositional or ideational meanings carried or *indexed* by various linguistic, textual, and paralinguistic forms" (original emphasis, ibid., p. 172). In other words, language socialisation goes beyond the mere acquisition of language, extending to the norms, values and practices that are embodied in the relevant communities. A central point in relation to language socialisation, indeed, its "core theoretical premise ... is that language is learned through interactions with others who are more proficient in the language and its cultural practices" (ibid., p. 172). This issue will be revisited shortly in the discussion of theories of situated learning.

This chapter comes with a number of caveats. It was noted in Chapter 2, in the discussion of discourse communities, that we should shy away from the notion that there is one monolithic community discourse that needs to be mastered. As Ochs (1999, p. 231) suggests, "we have tended to overemphasize the unique communicative configurations of particular communities and underspecify overarching, possible universal, communicative and social practices that may facilitate socialization into multiple communities and transnational life worlds". Essentially, workplaces have become very complex environments as a result of globalisation, the ongoing development of communication technologies and the migration of workers (Duff, 2008; Roberts, 2010), leading to the "development of new literacies, new measures of sociolinguistic control, and new expectations about language learning and use" (Duff, 2008, p. 268).

It is not a case, then, of being socialised into a single community, but of "multiple local communities" (Roberts, 2010, p. 214) depending on the particular organisation and the role that the newcomer is expected to play there. By way of illustration, Beaufort (1997), in her study of a non-profit organisation, describes the overlapping nature of different communities, and talks of the need on the part of writers to engage across such communities. Meanwhile the subject of Li's (2000) study of socialisation is seen, on the one hand, to engage with an international community of practice in the form of her discipline, and, on the other hand, with a local community of practice, in the form of her department.

Moreover, the process of socialisation should not be seen as one-way traffic (Ochs, 1999; Roberts, 2010): language socialisation, as explained, is an interactive phenomenon involving exchanges between newcomers and more experienced practitioners, which should allow for the possibility of change in both directions. More than this, we do not want to encourage scenarios whereby newcomers are passively absorbed into a dominant culture. In Chapter 8 we saw the importance of helping students develop a critical stance towards what they see in terms of organisational culture; similarly, students or newcomers should not see it as given that they should unquestioningly take on the practices and ideologies of whichever communities they enter. A fuller discussion in the context of language socialisation of the complex nature of the contemporary workplace and the attendant challenges can be found in Duff (2008) and Roberts (2010).

The second point to bear in mind in this chapter is connected to the roles of both speaking and writing in relation to socialisation processes. While the focus of this book is writing, it has been seen throughout, particularly in the discussions of intertextuality and collaboration, that writing and speaking in workplace settings are very much intertwined, and that the management of writing is both achieved through speaking and through the incorporation of speech into written text. Given that processes of language socialisation involve interaction between newcomers and old-timers, as already observed, any discussion of socialisation processes will necessarily include a consideration of the role of speaking, but the focus here will be on how socialisation is or can be realised in writing.

Finally, it should be acknowledged once more that while the academy and the workplace do represent different contexts, for all the reasons outlined in Chapter 1, and revisited at various points throughout this volume, they are not totally distinct from each other. Roberts (2010, p. 211) makes the point that there is an overlap between education and work, that they "are no longer patrolled by time", while Duff (2008, p. 257) notes that "the distinction between (higher) education and work is becoming increasingly blurred" by practices such as internships, on- and off-site training and other initiatives. This is reflected in the diversity of research that has considered workplace socialisation processes. Some studies, for example, have considered the impact of academy-based simulations (Freedman *et al.*, 1994), others have as their subjects interns taking professionally oriented writing courses in conjunction with their internship (Anson and Forsberg, 1990; Freedman and Adam, 1996; Galtens, 2000; Le Maistre and Paré, 2004; Paré, 2000; Smart and Brown, 2006), while others have provided in-depth accounts of writers being socialised into specific workplaces (Artemeva, 2005, 2009; Beaufort, 1998,

1999, 2000; Winsor, 1996, 1999). But comparison between the two contexts is inescapable, given that the mission of students and instructors alike is to enable transition from one context to the other, and the discussion surrounding the differences between the two contexts serves as a useful prism through which the problems attending socialisation processes can be viewed.

The academy and the workplace as contexts for learning

The differences between the academy and the workplace in terms of goals, activities, people and so on, are explained at some length in Chapter 1. Of most relevance for this chapter are the "radical differences" (Freedman and Adam, 1996) between the two as contexts for learning. These differences can be accounted for in theories of social constructionism: if we see genres and social contexts as being mutually constitutive, as intrinsically interlinked (see Chapter 2 for a discussion of this), and if we see language socialisation as the simultaneous acquisition of both linguistic and sociocultural knowledge (Ochs, 1993), then it is difficult to avoid the conclusion that such a view "invites a focus on writing as an activity inseparable from the contexts in which it takes place" (Schneider and Andre, 2005, pp. 197–198). This of course begs the question of whether workplace writing can be learnt in academic settings.

Two studies are outlined here as a partial response to that question, and have been chosen to illustrate crucial factors that differentiate the contexts from one another. The first of these is the work of Freedman, Adam and Smart (1994), who capture the essence of the issue, describing an attempt to bring the classroom and the workplace nearer to one another for the purposes of writing pedagogy, but that in fact culminates in a demonstration of the power of the prevailing institutional context. In this study, they examine student writing in financial case studies designed to elicit workplace discourse, finding that despite this attempted simulation, the "university classroom setting fundamentally shaped and constrained the writing" (p. 202). This was evidenced in different elements of the process, including the social roles taken by instructors and students, the motives for writing, the reading practices and the ways in which collaborative writing processes played out. In analysing their findings, they note "the degree to which school writing is and must remain radically different from workplace writing" (pp. 220–221), with the somewhat bleak corollary that what is needed to achieve genre knowledge can only be achieved "through immersion in workplace contexts" (p. 222).

In their study, the roles of aim and readership in the writing process emerge as very powerful influences on the students' texts, and a distinction is drawn between praxis-oriented and epistemic goals (Freedman *et al.*, 1994), the former entailing real-world consequences and the latter the demonstration of knowledge for evaluation by a limited readership. The fact that students are writing for a university professor for evaluation purposes is a dominant influence on their written output, compounded by the possibility that much of the information may already be known to the reader.

These factors of aim and readership also come through very strongly in the second illustrative study, that of Hafner (2013), who examines the issue of professional expertise in the context of law. Hafner's research is concerned with the transfer of skills addressed in law school to the real world of legal practice, in this case considering two genres – on the one hand, the legal problem question that is addressed in the academy and, on the other, the barrister's opinion. Hafner (2013, pp. 132–133) explains that "The values that underpin these two genres are in some sense shared, as part of the shared disciplinary culture of the law", but goes on to show that the ways in which the two genres are realised reveal different approaches on the part of the novice lawyers and their expert counterparts that can be attributed to the contexts in which they are operating. Specifically, the study examines the ways in which writers make intertextual appeals to authority, finding that when compared to the expert barristers, "novice lawyers tend to take a more 'academic' approach to their writing, overemphasizing the analysis of law and underemphasizing the practical analysis of facts" (p. 131). These differences, as with the study outlined earlier, are ascribed to the epistemic and praxis-oriented goals (cf. Freedman *et al.*, 1994) that are found in the respective contexts of writing, and once again highlight the challenges that are faced by instructors preparing their students to transition into the world of work.

These are but two studies that illustrate the differences between the academy and the workplace as contexts for learning; many other studies that also grapple with this issue (e.g. Anson and Forsberg, 1990; Beaufort, 1999; Dias and Paré, 2000; Freedman and Adam, 1996, 2000; Vickers, 2007), raise similar questions about the difficulties of teaching workplace genres in classroom contexts. From the foregoing discussion, it would be easy to gain the impression that the classroom-workplace divide is insurmountable, and that the gloomy prognoses of Freedman *et al.* (1994) and others hold sway, a sentiment captured deftly by Knoblauch (1989, p. 257): "workplace practices are embedded in additional layers of social reality and cannot be understood – or learned – apart from them". Indeed, Knoblauch goes further in suggesting that an argument which emphasises the continually evolving and socially contextualised nature of language "has potential to call into serious doubt the very idea of professional writing curricula" (p. 257), recalling Mawer's (1999) observation about the workplace itself in effect becoming the curriculum, mentioned in Chapter 2. In highlighting this divide, the research described here implicitly speaks to the power of the workplace as a context for learning; the next section considers this power, partly to provide further insights into why the workplace is seen as so central to learning, but also to help cast light onto what can be achieved in terms of pedagogical interventions outside the workplace.

Situated learning

To understand the central role of the workplace in the acquisition of workplace genres, one has to look at theories of situated learning, a process in which knowledge is co-constructed in communities of practice by means of interactions between newcomers and more experienced practitioners. The concept of community of practice was mentioned in Chapter 2, with Kwan's (2014, p. 446) observation that it can be seen as "shorthand for (a) social theory of learning", developed by Lave and Wenger (1991) and further developed by Wenger (1998). A community of practice is defined by the practice in which the relevant group is engaged, and this has three dimensions: a jointly pursued enterprise, mutual engagement and interaction, and a shared repertoire of knowledge, history, language, artefacts, ways of communicating and so on (Wenger, 1998). It is to such communities of practice that newcomers aspire to belong, and according to the theory this is achieved through participation in the activities of the community, a notion that lends strength to the view that genre knowledge can only be acquired through engagement with genres in their socially constructed environment (Freedman *et al.*, 1994; Knoblauch, 1989).

Two major analytical perspectives have been developed with regard to situated learning: Lave and Wenger's (1991) "legitimate peripheral participation", in which newcomers learn about the practices of the community through engagement in simple, low-stakes (i.e. peripheral) tasks, gradually moving from the periphery to the centre; and Rogoff's (1991) "guided participation", whereby novices are helped to achieve tasks through assistance from people equipped with the relevant experience, with an emphasis on an active role for the learner. Both of these perspectives are linked philosophically to Vygotsky's (1978) "zone of proximal development", a zone in which the learner operates – and learns – alongside an experienced practitioner. While in both cases learning takes place as a result of doing rather than receiving knowledge, a key difference is that guided participation has learning as the goal of its activities, whereas in legitimate peripheral participation learning is incidental and comes through participating in communities of practice.

In a significant study, Freedman and Adam (1996) build on these ideas, transposing the two frameworks for learning to the classroom-workplace writing arena. They propose the concepts of "facilitated performance" and "attenuated authentic participation". The first of these is based on Rogoff's guided participation, and provides a theoretical framework to explain how students learn discipline-specific writing in the classroom, with the associated activity being "undertaken primarily for the learner" (1996, p. 403). "Attenuated authentic participation", however, is a workplace-based scenario whereby learners are given tasks within their ability which "engage(d) them in processes that ultimately enable(d) fuller participation" (1996, p. 412), following the principles of Lave and Wenger's (1991) notion of legitimate peripheral participation. The two concepts proposed by Freedman and Adam (1996) mirror the frameworks they have drawn on in that in the university context ("facilitated performance") the collaborative activity between guide and learner is focused on learning, whereas in the workplace ("attenuated authentic participation") the interactions are aimed at getting the task completed.

Their study compares the writing of novices in the workplace – in this case graduate students engaged in full-time internships – with students learning new genres in the academy. While the learning which takes place in both scenarios is the outcome of collaboration and social engagement, they observe differences in several respects: the kinds of interaction and collaboration seen between workplace mentor and learner compared to those that obtain among students; the "improvisatory" nature of workplace tasks, which are not seen in a planned university curriculum; task authenticity; the variety of roles played by participants; the focus on task outcomes as opposed to student learning, and the attendant feedback on performance and criteria for success (Freedman and Adam, 1996).

Two important related points emerge from this study. The first is that the classroom context is a relatively controlled learning environment, with "carefully orchestrated processes of collaborative performance between the course instructor and students" (Freedman and Adam, 1996, p. 403), when compared to the less predictable, messy nature of the workplace. The second is that students expect to learn in the academy, and have a schema for how this usually takes place; when they reach the workplace, however, their expectations may be quite different, and it is seen in the study that some of the participants overlooked learning opportunities in their new setting "because they are used to the way they learned in the old setting" (1996, p. 416). Thus, the two contexts are not only distinct in their aims, audiences and the ways in which writing processes play out, but as settings for learning they come with different expectations on the part of the learner, leading Freedman and Adam to conclude that students entering the workplace "not only need to learn new genres of discourse but they also need to learn new ways to learn such genres" (1996, p. 424).

If I have gone into Freedman and Adam's (1996) work in considerable depth it is because I believe that it has gone to the heart of the challenge for those seeking to resolve the tension between the academy and the workplace: the two settings are unavoidably different as contexts for learning, but in explaining these through their frameworks adapted from the work of Rogoff (1991) and Lave and Wenger (1991), and identifying key differences between the contexts, and in reaching their particular conclusion, Freedman and Adam have not only thrown light on this issue but have also provided a stimulus for thinking about possible ways of addressing it. These will be discussed later in the chapter.

The issue of transferability

If we accept the view – and much of the research cited and discussed here supports this – that knowledge of workplace writing rests firmly in its contexts, then this has considerable implications for pedagogic practice, and leads to the question of what can or should be taught in classroom contexts. This is closely linked to notions of transferability and the question of whether there exists a body of "general" knowledge and skills that can be applied across different contexts, as opposed to skills that can only be acquired in the specialised target context. As Smart (2000, p. 246) explains, "the conundrum of where the local ends and the general begins is a vital concern for all who teach in academic and professional settings". This question has been much discussed in general terms (Brown, Collins and Duguid, 1989; Carter,

1990; Perkins and Salomon, 1989; Smagorinsky and Smith, 1992), in the context of EAP – English for Academic Purposes (Meyer, 1996; Hyland, 2002), and in relation to workplace writing (Artemeva, 2005, 2009, 2011; Beaufort, 1998; Brent, 2011; Smart, 2000; Smart and Brown, 2002, 2006).

In respect of writing, the existence of both general problem-solving skills and context-specific knowledge are acknowledged (e.g. Beaufort, 2000); Carter (1990) proposes a "pluralistic theory of expertise" whereby there is a difference between "domain-specific knowledge and skills and general, transferable rhetorical ability" (Smart, 2000, p. 245). Yet there are also many ardent advocates for the power of context. Hyland (2002), for example, as noted in Chapter 2, is concerned with the issue of specificity, and he rejects the notion of a common teachable core of knowledge, contending that "By incorporating meaning into the common core ... we are led to the notion of specific varieties, and to the inescapable consequence that learning should take place within these varieties" (2002, p. 389). Parks (2001) offers similar views on the value of specific contexts for learning, while Smart (2000) concludes that "writing expertise is *not* easily transferable from one domain of discourse to another, even by highly skilled professionals working within a single occupational setting" (original emphasis, p. 245). He does, however, qualify this with the caveat that we should not arrive at the conclusion whereby "we assume writing expertise to be an *entirely* local matter" (original emphasis, ibid., p. 245), and he offers some support for Carter's (1990) theory of expertise.

Artemeva (2005, 2009), on the other hand, while acknowledging the research that questions the portability into the workplace of genres taught in professional writing classes (Anson and Forsberg, 1990; Dias and Paré, 2000; Freedman and Adam, 2000), contends that it may be possible to teach domain-specific communication separately from the local context and proposes this as one of several "genre knowledge ingredients" that include both formal education and workplace experiences. Further evidence in her work of the possibility of learning transfer is reported in Artemeva and Fox (2014), describing Artemeva's (2011) study of an engineering student in which "some actions that she had performed consciously in the classroom, dropped to the level of more or less automatic operations in the workplace" (2014, p. 465).

Brent (2011) looks at what he calls "the uncomfortable relationship between writing studies and the concept of learning transfer" (p. 1), and visits many of the issues discussed previously within the context of a framework of rhetorical genre studies, activity theory and situated learning as proposed by Artemeva (2009). In bringing together transfer theory in its various forms and the thinking from workplace - writing studies on the question of where the relevant skills might be taught and acquired, he offers a more optimistic picture of the challenges facing pedagogy than is often implied by the hard-line views of situated knowledge that have been reported in this chapter.

It can be seen that for the most part, researchers question whether specific knowledge can be taught outside its natural habitat and made ready for transfer. Indeed, there is a sizeable constituency in workplace writing research circles who see the highly situated nature of writing as a considerable obstacle to students' acquiring professional discourses outside the relevant community – this of course is totally consistent with the precepts of social constructionism. These notions of situated learning may lead us towards the idea that the gains from engaging students in workplace-like activity while they are still in the academy may be limited, but this is not a reason for us to avoid the issue, and there is moreover a danger in accepting this view of downplaying the role that the academy can play. There is still much that can be done in university contexts (Dias *et al.*, 1999; Galtens, 2000, Schneider and Andre, 2005) and a trawl through the various studies discussed offers a number of possibilities.

As noted, one conclusion from Freedman and Adam's (1996) study was that students entering the workplace "need to learn new ways to learn" (p. 424). An important question, then, is what these students can bring from their experiences in the academy that can help them in their new learning processes in their new environment. It is not a case of taking specific knowledge from one context to the next, as has been explained, but of taking an awareness and understanding that things will be different, and of acquiring a set of tools and strategies that will help in unpacking those new environments. This perspective is seen in Chapter 3 – in the discussion of genres and genre knowledge it is not proposed that students will take a set of genres that they have mastered into their future workplace, rather the ability to analyse the genres that they find there.

The process of sensitising students to different features of the workplace as a context for writing, and the transformation of their learning and understanding into tools in the new learning context, can be usefully viewed through the lens of activity theory. As noted earlier, this theory has been deployed by Artemeva (2009) as part of an integrated framework for investigating the transition from school to work, a framework also employed by Brent (2011) in his consideration of the possible marriage of writing studies and transfer theory. The principles of the approach, derived from the work of Vygotsky (1978), Engeström (1987) and Russell (1997), are seen in a number of studies relating to socialisation processes (Artemeva, 2005, 2009; Berkenkotter, 2001; Bremner, 2012a; Le Maistre and Paré, 2004; Parks, 2001; Smart, 2006). Russell (1997, p. 510) describes an activity system as "any ongoing, object-directed, historically conditioned, dialectically structured, tool-mediated interaction". Examples he suggests of such systems include a family, a school or a discipline. In its simplest form, an activity system consists of three elements: the subject, the tools or mediating artefacts and the object. The interplay of these three can be seen through analysis of the systems of activity that they constitute. The theory brings to the fore the interconnected nature of the processes found in a given system, whether it is the academy or the workplace, and also helps us view and understand the interaction between the individual (the subject) and the context.

Russell (1997) describes it as a theory that "treats context not as a set of variables but as an ongoing, dynamic accomplishment of people acting together with shared tools, including—most powerfully—writing" (pp. 508–509). Central to this theory is the idea that the cultural tools of a community can evolve and be modified as its members go about the business of constructing knowledge, and that "professional organizations advance in their work by building achieved knowledge into their tools, which are then in turn used to engender new knowledge" (Smart, 2006, p. 107).

At any one time, we are likely to be participants in a number of different activity systems, mostly moving from one to the other with relative ease. But in the case of the academy and the workplace, as discussed, this is not necessarily a smooth journey, and in the context of activity theory, the work of Le Maistre and Paré (2004) is particularly illuminating. They give a sense of the way that an activity system in the academy differs from that seen in a workplace, but crucially they show that as a student migrates from one system to the next, what constitutes the object in one system (the academy) can subsequently become a tool in the new system (the workplace). In other words, when the student assumes the subject role of practitioner in the workplace, the objects that they have achieved in the academy, such as rules and theories, now become tools or "mediational means" (ibid., p. 45) in the workplace activity system. In this way, the theory helps to cast light on the ways in which the academy might assist in the socialisation process, by helping identify objects (goals) in the academy that can become tools in the workplace, part of a process "whereby the focus of learning becomes the means of practice" (ibid., p. 45).

The next section considers viewpoints and suggestions that can be considered from the perspective explained by Le Maistre and Paré (2004), and goes on to look at the challenge of bringing students closer to the reality of the workplace. It then looks in some detail at one of my own studies which draws on activity theory, and which highlights some of the key issues relating to socialisation and the acquisition of workplace writing as discussed in this chapter.

Towards possible pedagogies

Among the various approaches proposed for the teaching of professional written communication, many are focused on raising rhetorical awareness and are premised on the assumption that this could aid transfer across contexts, a view that can be accommodated within the thinking of Le Maistre and Paré (2004). Flower (1989) suggests teaching rhetorical strategies, "both general ones and those which underlie the conventions of different kinds of discourse" (p. 33), and helping students to "develop a meta-awareness of their own strategic process" (p. 34). Beaufort (1998) develops this idea, discussing the role of metacognition in the learning process; she advocates active awareness raising, explaining that if knowledge of how to accomplish a writing task "is tacit or unconscious, it is harder to harness that knowledge in new and unfamiliar writing situations than if metacognitive thinking has made that knowledge conscious and accessible to the writer" (p. 182).

A second point of pedagogical focus relates to the notion of community and its relationship with situated learning. A number of studies propose the creation or provision of environments which have their own discourses and patterns of interaction (e.g. Bremner, 2010; Dias *et al.*, 1999; Doheny-Farina, 1986; Meyer,

1996); handled thoughtfully, such approaches, which "capitalize on social motives for writing" (Beaufort, 2000, p. 218) can highlight for students the socially influenced nature of writing goals and interactions, as well as giving them a sense of membership. Other researchers acknowledge the interactive nature of workplace contexts and stress the need for students to have opportunities to learn how to interact (Couture and Rymer, 1989) and to acquire the interpersonal skills needed for collaboration (Bremner, 2010; Bremner et al., 2014; Gollin, 1999; Schneider and Andre, 2005), including the ability to work cooperatively and to critique each other (Dias et al., 1999). In this regard, Beaufort also suggests that teachers should "embrace collaborative rather than competitive models" (2000, p. 218). Providing students with opportunities to play multiple roles in whatever communities they are working is also recommended (Dias et al., 1999). Beaufort visits this issue too, asking "If writing is a social act, what social roles aid writers in new forms of writing?" (2000, p. 186).

These suggestions largely centre around providing contexts that reproduce or approximate in some way to conditions found in real workplaces. There are, however, many ways in which we can move nearer to that reality, and these are seen in initiatives that require students to engage with organisations in different ways, whether through having workplace audiences for their academy-based writing, through carrying out projects on behalf of organisations (e.g. Bremner et al., 2014 – see Chapter 5), or working directly for them as interns. Dias et al. (1999) propose a continuum along which learning experiences are positioned in terms of their proximity to the workplace, from facilitated performance (learning in university), to attenuated authentic participation, explained as "closely supervised learning opportunities that students and newcomers experience when they first enter the workplace" (p. 188), to legitimate peripheral participation, which is "near professional practice … during apprenticeship' (p. 188). This reflects the gradual shift that takes place as newcomers are socialised, and demonstrates, for them, "the extent to which learning is contextual and contingent" (p. 202).

By taking learners along this continuum we are moving them from controlled to less controlled learning environments, and as Dias et al. (1999) point out, in this journey out of the classroom towards professional practice, "the moments and sites of learning become less clearly defined" (p. 202). Language socialisation is made up of both formal and informal learning (Roberts, 2010), and Beaufort notes the absence of "clear structures or paths for mentoring, scaffolding, or progressive skill development in these informal learning situations" (2000, p. 216). This seems to be an inevitable consequence of moving learners away from the academy, but the upside of this loosening of control is that learning opportunities will be more located in target situations and communities.

Socialising into a workplace: a case study

In this section, I discuss a research study relating to the challenges that have been presented earlier (Bremner, 2012a), which focused on the experiences of an intern in a Hong Kong PR company (PRHK) as she was socialised into its practices, examining, on the one hand, the evidence that this socialisation was actually taking place and, on the other, the factors which contributed to her socialisation. (Elements of this study are discussed in Chapter 8 in relation to the topic of organisational culture.) The study is based on the daily journal written by the subject, Sammi, over the three months that she spent as an intern in the organisation. The journal served as a detailed record of the activities she engaged in there, and also showed the ways in which her writing developed over the three months. Language socialisation, as explained earlier, is the simultaneous acquisition of both linguistic and sociocultural knowledge (Ochs, 1993), and research in this area requires evidence of learning both in terms of cognition and social interaction (Roberts, 2010). In the case of Sammi this came through very clearly: her engagement with the activities of the PR company deepened, and she became closely involved with processes of press release writing and media pitching to the point where she was taking a significant role in their production. At the same time, the way she wrote about her work evolved, going through three overlapping stages, explained in the study as "outsider discourse", "transitional discourse" and "insider discourse", and reaching a point where she was producing "discourse resembling that of PR practitioners" (Bremner, 2012a, p. 7).

Sammi's experience is positioned quite far along Dias *et al.*'s (1999) continuum, located as it is in an actual workplace, and displays many of the features that are found in their concept of attenuated authentic participation. The study reveals the power of the workplace as a context for learning, as it was clear from Sammi's account that her actual participation in the activities of the company was a central factor in her socialisation and her acquisition of particular genres. Nevertheless, the study also provides evidence of the academy having a role in her development and socialisation, in that she was able to apply ideas and thinking from her university studies to her new working environment. This was mentioned in Chapter 8, where it was explained that a course Sammi took, called *Organisational Culture and Communication* as part of her BA degree, provided her with a set of tools that she could use to try and make sense of new organisational cultures. Here we see in action the idea stemming from activity theory that the object in the academy (understanding how organisational cultures are reflected through their artefacts) can become a tool to be applied in the new system, i.e. the workplace.

Two or three specific examples serve to illustrate the point that her ability to notice and interpret certain artefacts was a contributory factor to her growing understanding of workplace practices in the PR organisation and thereby to her socialisation. More or less from the beginning of her internship she is calling upon concepts from her studies: comments such as "I've also sort of observed PRHK's office artifacts" on Day 2, and "This is the meeting 'rule' and 'culture' at Tom's office" on Day 4 (Bremner, 2012a, p. 25) are indicative of her approach to the new workplace. A more specific instance of the object of learning being transformed can be seen in her Day 5 comment: "It takes me sometime to fully socialize into the company. The socialization technique I mostly use is explicit questioning, since this is the quickest way to get the 'answer'" (ibid., p. 25). In this instance, she is referring to the taxonomy of newcomer information-seeking tactics proposed by Miller and Jablin (1991), which were addressed in the course mentioned. Sammi's observations and her attempts to link these to her studies were also supplemented by her willingness to reflect on what she was seeing and doing. This is a practice to be encouraged among learners, as the ability "to construct and apply localized theories in the course of professional practice" (Smart and Brown, 2006, p. 246) is the hallmark of the successful reflective practitioner (Schön, 1983).

Sammi's actual participation in the activities of the organisation – learning by doing – was a major factor in facilitating her socialisation, but this was also complemented by the input she received from her co-workers, which came in the form of direct instruction, advice, feedback and encouragement, and the value she saw in this support comes through very strongly in her journal. The kinds of help she received from her colleagues served as a form of scaffolding, resembling practices seen in situated learning models (Lave and Wenger, 1991; Rogoff, 1991) and reported as an important factor in the socialisation process by Parks (2001) and Vickers (2007). Not only this, she was being inducted through tasks which gradually became more complex and challenging, again adhering to principles proposed by situated learning theories.

It is worth pointing out that in the process of Sammi's socialisation into the work of the organisation, the levels of support that she received were not only directed at getting the job done, as is typically seen in legitimate peripheral participation, but also at helping her learn, a central element in guided participation models; the organisation had a history of taking on interns and took seriously the business of inducting them. In other words, she was engaged in interactions that had "both learning and task completion as the aim" (Bremner, 2012a, p. 27). This kind of active investment on the part of colleagues is a very desirable scenario, and also raises the question of the role workplaces themselves should play in the active socialisation of newcomers, a point to be addressed more fully in the concluding section of this chapter.

To sum up, it was evident that Sammi's actual participation in the work of the PR company was the central contributor to her socialisation, and she also benefitted from the fact that her colleagues were actively helping her to develop and learn. But the ways in which she brought to bear elements of her schooling on her new situation (cf. Le Maistre and Paré, 2004) were also influential, leading to the conclusion that:

> if students are provided with opportunities while still in the academy to observe and reflect on a range of workplace cultures, and are given the appropriate tools with which to do this, this will help them to play an active part in their own socialization when they enter the world of work.
>
> *(Bremner, 2012a, p. 29)*

A final observation in respect of this study is that it highlights the role and influence of writing itself. Sammi was heavily involved in – and was learning from – the production of press releases and related documents, and this regular and often intensive writing activity helped to ease her path into the PR community. Writing is, as Bremner observes, "simultaneously a means to and an object of learning and in this way plays a powerful role in the process of socialization" (2012a, p. 8).

Conclusion

In this chapter, I have paid what I believe to be justifiable homage to a number of studies that have captured the challenges involved in helping learners socialise into workplace writing, and which illustrate very keenly the distinction between the classroom and the workplace as contexts for writing and learning to write. It is clear from the foregoing discussion that as educators, we have to acknowledge the workplace as the most powerful element in the learning process, but at the same time we should recognise that there are tools we can equip our students with that will enable them to take advantage in a more informed way of the opportunities afforded by the workplace.

I do not wish to imply that the academy must, in deference to the workplace, make do with whatever activities they can devise that approximate in some way to workplace practice. On the contrary, I believe that the academy has a very important role to play in preparing students for their professional lives, and that we would be doing them a disservice if we did not address various fundamental areas that might help in their understanding of issues relating to discourse communities, genre knowledge, organisational culture and the other concerns examined in this book. Raising awareness of these issues can be achieved in a variety of ways, through analysis of a wide range of genres (See Chapter 3), through the provision of environments with their own discourses and opportunities to interact and collaborate, through case studies, which can help to illuminate "the ways of thinking and knowing valued by disciplines and encouraged by the rhetorical practices of those disciplines" (Dias et al., 1999, p. 201), or by means of the kinds of course described in Chapter 8 (Bremner, 2012a), which can equip students with analytical tools that they can apply in their new work environments. These are but a few examples of what can be done.

Many of these activities will, for logistical reasons, be completely located in the academy, but this does not have to be seen as an insurmountable problem – in recognising the differences between the workplace and the academy we should not assume that they are completely distinct from one another. The principles that apply to genre, aim and audience, for example, can be illustrated and explored within academic contexts, and yet still be seen as applicable to workplace contexts. At the same time, we should not be leery of bringing workplace elements into the classroom (Brent, 2011); indeed, these can function as pointers to the differences between practices in the respective contexts. The central role for pedagogy, in my view, is to engender understanding and awareness of what it takes to be a writer in a workplace setting, and in doing this we should be looking at both commonalities in terms of writing demands in the two settings as well as differences – an understanding of both should serve the student well as they move from one context to the other.

Having said that, we still need to recognise the limitations of the classroom: as Freedman *et al.* (1994) explain, on leaving university, students "may have acquired … the intellectual stance, the ideology, and the values necessary for their professional lives" (p. 221), but they will still need to learn how to participate in their new communities. Similarly, we as educators need "to remain critical in (our) expectations of what can and cannot be transferred from the classroom to workplace contexts" (Artemeva and Fox, 2014, p. 475). It was interesting to note, for example, that Sammi, the subject of my socialisation study (Bremner, 2012a) thought that the discourse-related courses she had taken at university had not been very useful, saying that "the study of discourse was 'too theoretical' and that 'you don't have time to apply those things in the workplace'" (p. 26). Certainly, there is much research to be done in this area.

For much of this chapter I have used the term "tools" to describe what it is we should be aiming to equip our students with as they head into their target workplaces, and would like to qualify this by emphasising that these should not be seen as rigid instruments, rather as ways of thinking and reflecting that can be brought to bear on new environments. As explained in the opening section of the chapter, workplace communities should not be seen as containers of monolithic discourses, but as overlapping with other communities and as entities undergoing constant change (Duff, 2008). As Roberts (2010, p. 220) points out, "the communicative environment rarely remains stable", and for this reason the ability to adapt is paramount. Just as we want our students to be able to perform particular tasks effectively when they enter the workplace, we also want them to understand the parameters and constraints within which they can work. Learning to reflect and to adapt, rather than learning a static body of knowledge that is enshrined in model texts, however faithfully they may reflect the zeitgeist of a particular organisation, should be the goal.

When discussing the role of the academy in preparing students for the workplace in the light of the deeply situated nature of workplace writing, it is also worth considering where the responsibility for this preparation lies. The theoretical stance that emphasises the socially contextualised nature of language would leave this task to the workplace itself (Knoblauch, 1989; Mawer, 1999), lending force to the concerns voiced by Kent (1993), who sees a possible corollary of such views as being "that writing instruction is a misnomer, for no body of knowledge in the area of writing exists to be taught" (p. 91). Certainly, there is much support in theoretical views of situated learning to back this position, but if we bring this discussion down to a practical level, and consider the workplace as a set of organisations that have expectations of the graduates they hire, a very different scenario can be seen.

My own experience in Hong Kong is that the expectations on the part of employers are high: the common view is that students should already know how to write professionally, and blame for newcomers' perceived deficiencies in this respect is often laid firmly at the door of the academy. In the light of all that has been discussed here in relation to the power of the workplace as a context for learning, this seems an unreasonable position. What this seems to imply is an unwillingness on the part of these organisations to take an active role in inducting their graduate entrants. Not every newcomer will be as fortunate as Sammi (Bremner, 2012a), whose colleagues played such a vigorous role in helping her socialise into her organisation, and a potential lack of engagement on the part of employers provides all the more reason for the academy to involve itself in preparing students for the demands of workplace writing.

The other implication of this attitude is that employers have a somewhat blinkered view of what can and should be done by universities, and also a limited understanding of the role they themselves can play in socialisation processes. This argues for trying to build closer relationships between universities and employers so that each can understand more about the possible roles they can play in preparing and inducting fresh graduates. These relationships would also have the potential for opening up opportunities for students to engage in learning activities that are located closer to the realities of the workplace, such as internships or professional communication projects of the kind described in Chapter 5. The value of these cannot be underestimated, as can be seen in the fairly unequivocal view expressed by the PR practitioner in Bhatia and Bremner (2014): "When I'm trying to hire people ... I don't think I would hire anyone who didn't have an internship or two" (p. 566).

A final point in respect of responsibility is that it is not only the academy and the workplace that need to take an active role in the induction of newcomers – the most powerful and influential actors in this process will be the students themselves. As Belcher (1994, p. 24) explains: "An apprentice's willingness to identify with, be changed by, and contribute to the evolution of a community may determine his/her membership in it". This willingness was certainly in evidence in the study described (Bremner, 2012a), as it was clear that Sammi benefitted considerably from the efforts that she herself made to understand her work environment.

As seen in the discussion of discourse communities and English for Specific Purposes (ESP) in Chapter 2, Hyland (2002) revisits Spack's (1988) question regarding specificity in relation to disciplinary discourses, asking how far we should go now; in the context of workplace writing it should be taken as given that we need to get as close to the workplace as possible. The question then is "How far *can* we go? and the continuum proposed by Dias *et al.* (1999) indicates the route and the direction we should be moving in. Following Hyland's exhortation, we should go as far as we can, and it is a question of working out what is feasible for students who are located outside the workplace, and what sort of access they can be given to real world organisations.

10

WORKPLACE WRITING AND PEDAGOGY

Concluding thoughts

Introduction

In Chapter 1, it is explained that this volume is based on two premises: the idea that we need to look beyond the text to understand the complexities involved in workplace writing, and the sense that textbooks and pedagogy more generally addressing this particular type of writing tend to overlook these complexities. This chapter revisits those premises, first summing up the extensive range of factors that surround and contribute to processes of text construction in workplace settings and the resulting texts, and second looking at the ways in which workplace writing is approached in textbooks.

From the foregoing chapters it can be seen that writing in workplace contexts is surrounded and shaped by the wide variety of factors that are found there. These include the textual resources that writers draw on to create new texts, the channels available to mediate them, and the collaborative processes that are involved in producing them, as well as context-specific practices that may be explicitly prescribed or overtly encouraged, or that may be more implicitly built into the everyday running of an organisation. Not only this, workplace writing is a dynamic process in that texts are responses to other texts, and writers are in effect engaging in dialogues – of varying lengths – with other writers. It should also be emphasised that an integral feature of these writing-related practices, particularly the collaborative aspect, is that workplace writing involves other people, and thus necessitates an ability to work with these people, handling power relationships and other issues that relate to day-to-day interactions. This leads on to the central point – and one which has been reiterated throughout – that writing is very much tied up with the communities in which it takes place, and that every community and every organisation has its own way of doing things, its own way of thinking about things and its own way of writing.

This implies a close relationship between texts and context, but it should be remembered that is not simply a case of the context – professional or organisational – having a one-way influence on the shape of texts, rather that the relationship is a dynamic, mutually constitutive one in the sense that not only are texts the outcome of the activities of the community, but they also serve the needs of the community, and in doing so contribute to its development. Essentially writing is very much located in its context, begging the question of how in our activities with students we can narrow the gap between the context of the academy and that of the workplace.

Certainly, we have seen the profound differences between these two contexts, discussed at considerable length in Chapters 1 and 9, and we have seen a number of researchers suggest that the two are problematically distant from one another when it comes to pedagogy, a view captured by Mabrito (1999) with his comment that "We will never be able to exactly duplicate in our classrooms many of the constraints and pressures that writers experience in the workplace" (p. 105), and echoed by a host of other researchers. However, throughout the book I have stressed that the gap and its attendant challenges are not insurmountably problematic, and that we should look at ways of getting students ready for the workplace, rather than attempting to create the workplace in the classroom.

Textbooks and workplace writing

This brings us to the role of pedagogy, and in particular the role of textbooks in preparing writers for entry into the workplace. There is a wide selection of textbooks available that deal with aspects of workplace writing but, as noted in Chapter 1, the majority of these are more specifically focused on writing and speaking in business contexts, usually containing the term "business communication" in the title. The market for such books is considerable, and is for the most part located in North America, although they are also used in universities elsewhere, for example, in Hong Kong, other parts of South East Asia and in the Arabian Gulf, where they might be adopted for English courses for business students or for language students taking courses with a workplace focus.

It is probably fair to say that even though some instructors are more comfortable working without textbooks, and are happy to rely on their own ideas and materials or those of their colleagues, textbooks nevertheless represent an important resource for many of those involved in teaching workplace writing. This is particularly true for the considerable number of instructors who are not native speakers of English, and who do not have direct experience of writing in a professional setting. For this reason, it is worth examining the role of such books and considering the extent to which they acknowledge or address the complexities of writing as enumerated in this book.

My own research in this regard, looking at how business communication textbooks deal with intertextuality and collaboration, discussed in Chapters 4 and 5 respectively, shows how scantily these particular phenomena, which are integral to workplace writing, are treated. At best there is acknowledgement of the existence of other texts, or the practice of collaborative writing, but these are not addressed in any meaningful way, and nor are students afforded any opportunities to understand or experience these in the tasks and activities that are provided in the books, leading to the observation that "Such an approach is akin to explaining a grammatical structure without giving any opportunities for communicative practice" (Bremner, 2010, p. 130). In many respects, textbooks can be seen as falling considerably short when it comes to conveying a sense of the reality of workplace, let alone providing activities that might lead in that direction.

A further aspect of business communication textbooks that merits investigation is the often narrow range of workplace activity that is afforded by the world of business and its attendant forces, and that is typically considered by these books in their coverage of spoken and written communication. A recent study I carried out (Bremner, 2014d), motivated by questions relating to the focus of books of this nature, examined four prominent business communication textbooks to gauge the extent to which they could be seen to help develop critical awareness in students. Bearing in mind the "instrumentalist logic and decisively non-reflective view of language that characterizes the business domain" (Weninger and Kan, 2012, p. 66), the study looked at the degree to which business is foregrounded in these books, at the discourse used to exemplify language points and situations, as well as other issues such as the individuals who are held up as "heroes", the kinds of texts and situations used to exemplify good practice and the tasks that students are given. Further questions included whether notions of power and of language as constitutive of social relations, i.e. issues raised by proponents of Critical Language Awareness (e.g., Fairclough, 1992) and discussed in Chapter 6, are evident or absent, and whether the books contained tasks that focus on critical thinking.

One could justifiably ask why business communication textbooks shouldn't focus on business, and indeed there is no reason why they shouldn't. However, these books serve as one of the few resources available that address workplace communication, and at the same time it is expected that not all students will enter profit-focused enterprises. The books were thus considered from the perspective of learners seeking advice and tasks that addressed workplace writing in general, and not just activities underpinned by the thinking and discourse of the world of business. More importantly, though, as has been explained at various points in this volume, there is a need to foster critical and reflective approaches to the workplace in our teaching, and it was therefore considered of value to see the extent to which commercially available materials are able to help in this regard. It is not my intention to go into great detail here, but some general points relating to this investigation are outlined.

The study showed considerable variation among the four books analysed: they sit on a continuum, at one end focused on business, money and the profit motive, at the other on language, and this is reflected in the extent to which business (as opposed to more general workplace activity) is foregrounded, the types of organisation and job that are mentioned, and the discourse used to illustrate language points and situations. Having said that, certain themes common to all the books emerged from the study. To some extent the approach to language and communication in workplaces is infused by what Wee (2003) calls "linguistic instrumentalism", explained as "a view of language that justifies its existence in a community in terms of its usefulness in achieving specific utilitarian goals" (p. 211). Also noticeable is the "commodification" (Fairclough, 1992) of certain elements of the workplace, as seen in the extracts presented below:

- "As many companies have discovered, valuing diversity is good business" (Locker and Kaczmarek, 2014, p. 39).
- "Adopting ethical communication practices helps a firm in crisis overcome short-term losses and maintain its market position" (Guffey and Du-Babcock, 2008, p. 427).
- "Remember, the real expense of a meeting is the lost productivity of all the people attending" (Guffey and Du-Babcock, 2008, p. 310).
- "Writing costs money. Besides the cost of paper, computers and software, there is the major expense: employees' time" (Locker and Kaczmarek, 2014, p. 8).
- "Effective communication provides ... better financial results and higher returns for investors" (Bovee and Thill, 2012, p. 4).

Comments of this nature, along with various other findings (the "heroes" upheld as illustrations of good practice; a number of the tasks) led to the conclusion that the books in the study all seem to embrace the capitalist enterprise to some degree, which as conceded, is not unreasonable in the light of their aim as vehicles for teaching the principles of business communication as they conceive it. However, there are a number of areas where they present perhaps oversimplified versions of workplace practice: none of the books seems to consider the socially constructed nature of communication and its ramifications, nor the power relations that can be seen in the workplace. Issues surrounding the relationship between language and power are generally presented as a series of disembodied skills and examples. Emphasis is on the choice of language (formal/informal), with no real discussion of how linguistic choices index the writer or speaker, or how they help shape relationships, meaning that there is little attempt to foster awareness of the issues involved. Indeed, this claim can be levelled at the materials more generally, in that they are largely bereft of sociolinguistic focus, and skills are presented without much if any context.

There is also an element of the prescriptive in some of the books, one of the more striking examples seen here (Locker and Kacmarek, 2014, p. 282):

> If the style (the company prefers) doesn't seem reasonable ... you have several choices.
>
> **Use the techniques in this module.** Sometimes seeing good writing changes people's minds about the style they prefer.

Help your boss learn about writing. Show him or her this book or the research cited in the notes to demonstrate how a clear, crisp style makes documents easier to read.

(original emphasis)

Prescriptivism in the teaching of workplace writing is something to be avoided, for two reasons. The first relates to the point that workplace communication is very much tied up with its community and context, and that any piece of writing needs to be crafted in relation to that specific context, one which cannot necessarily be anticipated in a textbook. The second reason concerns the potential constraints that prescriptive approaches can place on learners and the language they use: if books and teachers are in the business of developing uniform communication skills in the global marketplace, this can have the effect of making "every language into a vehicle for the affirmation of similar values and beliefs, and for the enactment by speakers of similar social identities and roles" (Cameron, 2002, pp. 69–70), which have been characterised as those of privileged white North Americans (Pan, Scollon and Scollon, 2002).

The world which these books offer, then, with its focus on business practices, may not necessarily account for the ways of thinking, acting and communicating that new entrants to the workplace will encounter, given the variety of professions and organisations that they are likely to join. More importantly, the books are neither critical in themselves, offering largely unreflecting and unquestioning views of business practice, nor do they foster critical thinking or awareness. Weninger and Kan (2013) contend that "A more critical approach to language and language learning is needed that raises students' awareness of the social embedding of discourse practices" (p. 59), and this point is entirely consonant with the views presented in this book, namely that learners need to reflect in an active way on how language works in different situations, and on how this can be applied in situations to come.

As seen in this volume, there is ample evidence in research to support the notion that workplace writing is indeed a complex affair. At the same time, one could argue that these complexities are intuitively evident, i.e. that most people are aware that workplace writing is different from academic writing or informal letter writing or other forms of writing, that it involves other people, that organisations are not endlessly creating new texts without reference to other documents or previous texts. But if this is so obvious, why is it that textbooks seem to draw back from activities that take this into account?

Perhaps part of the answer to this lies in the market. In writing books of this nature, authors and publishers are presumably faced with the challenge of providing materials that are ostensibly appropriate to a variety of contexts, and in so doing they hope to appeal to a diverse audience of would-be writers. This seems to be a reasonable goal. What appears to happen, however, is a kind of homogenisation of the workplace, a reductive approach that treats texts as standalone entities, created without reference to specific contexts, and therefore without reference to the realities of workplace writing as explained in the preceding chapters. The logic behind such an approach is understandable if one accepts the idea that there is such a thing as a report or adjustment letter or other workplace text type that is universally applicable and transportable. (This, of course, is a questionable position in the light of the thinking underpinning this volume.) But by removing the context and the complexity from their model texts, these books run the risk of oversimplifying the nature of workplace writing and of misleading the learner, and ultimately, thereby, of doing the learner a disservice.

This is not to suggest that business communication textbooks serve no purpose, rather that they should be handled with care. Of course, many of the general principles that apply to writing in business contexts are relevant to other workplace contexts. The books do provide general pointers with regard to a variety of text types, both spoken and written, and some insights into various practices that can be seen in business or workplace contexts, but in large part – and this is the key point – they fail to acknowledge the central thesis of this book, namely that we need to look beyond the text to offer students an understanding of what it takes to be a successful writer, and that we need to provide them with activities which will help them develop an awareness of the issues involved. The challenge for textbook writers, on the basis of this argument, is to consider what can be done in textbooks that will take the learner closer to the realities of the workplace as outlined in this book, but at the same time without being too specific, that is to say, while retaining a broad appeal and application across a wide enough range of contexts so as to be marketable.

What teachers can do

This brings us to the final part of this chapter, and indeed this book. If we cannot rely on textbooks, what is it that we should be doing as teachers? Revisiting the various chapters in this volume, each with its different – although, as noted, often overlapping – focus, we can build up a picture of what is required to become a competent and successful workplace writer.

First, there is the need to engage with multiple communities – not just the immediate community that a writer is fully part of – and along with this the ability to interact with both specialists and non-specialists, i.e. the ability to repackage information to meet the needs of different audiences. Recognition of this need has given rise to the kinds of pedagogical activity reported by Hafner (2014). He describes a course in which science students are required to communicate to a non-specialist audience by means of a popular genre, in this case a scientific documentary, but also to present the same information in the more academic genre of the lab report.

In relation to genre, it was seen that genre knowledge is a wide-ranging affair, but central to an understanding of genre is that there are basic principles and patterns associated with the purposes of different genre types; these should not be seen as prescriptive, but they nevertheless represent boundaries within which a writer can operate. The ability to be creative, innovative or to exercise "private intentions" (Bhatia, 1995) as a writer can only be exercised if the writer has knowledge of the genre frameworks they are operating in and an understanding of how resources can be exploited to achieve particular ends within those frameworks. A key competency, then, is the ability to analyse genres and identify the parameters within which writing can take place.

When it comes to the act of writing itself, the central issue for writers to appreciate is that writing is a rich, contextualised process, involving other texts and other people. As Kwan (2014) explains in respect of collaborative writing, students "need to be sensitised to the negotiations and contestations that characterise such joint writing practices" (p. 455). These elements of the writing process should not be seen as a challenge or obstacle, but as a set of potential resources – few of us relish the prospect of having to create an entirely new text out of nowhere, without earlier practices or other texts to refer to, and without the support, visible or less visible, of other colleagues. Fortunately, for the most part, we do not have to, as resources in the form of other texts and other people are usually and necessarily available for us to draw upon. Key to success in this aspect of writing is the awareness that these resources can and should be taken advantage of, and an understanding of how this can be achieved efficiently and acceptably. Awareness also plays a role in the management of power relations in both external and internal communication. As for the management of texts through different media, above all this requires an ability to recognise and take advantage of the possibilities of the media available and to make appropriate choices with regard to their use. As noted earlier, the ability to rework and repackage information for different audiences, i.e. the multiple communities that writers may expect to engage with, is a central element of managing writing, and this is particularly the case when it comes to media selection.

Finally, there is the need for writers to interpret the environments in which writing takes place, whether it is the professional community or the specific organisation, each of which will have their own conventions and expectations, spoken or unspoken. Reading these environments involves an ability to analyse the artefacts that belong to these communities and cultures, in the form of their genres, their ways of interacting and the components of the setting, both concrete (e.g. dress codes, office arrangements) and intangible (e.g. rites and rituals). Acquiring the tools to understand and engage with these is a vital stage on the road to membership of communities and organisations, which is, after all, the central goal of the aspiring workplace writer.

Ideally, we would like, where possible, to enable students to engage in activities that to some degree replicate the kinds of activities they will experience in the workplace, to go as far along the road towards reality as is feasible (cf. Dias *et al.*, 1999; Hyland, 2002). But at the same time, it has to be recognised, as stressed throughout, that we can only take our students so far. Thus, where this is not possible, we need to make our students aware of the complexities and challenges involved in workplace writing, and to provide them with the tools and critical skills needed to make sense of the new environments they will encounter in their working lives as writers. In sum, our task lies first in making students aware of the complexities of what they will encounter when they reach the workplace, and second in preparing them for these as best we can.

The most obvious way in which to acquaint learners with the realities of the workplace is to set up activities whereby there is actual engagement with workplace organisations. Activities of this nature have been alluded to at various points in this book: internships represent perhaps the closest type of interaction with real work-places, while projects which are carried out on behalf of organisations also bring students close to the workplace. In my own university, all final-year students are required, usually in groups of four or five, to engage in year-long projects (described in Chapter 5) in which they undertake promotional or fund-raising tasks on behalf of a host organisation. The projects can be quite complex, and generally involve extensive internal and external communication, along with the production of a variety of texts, ranging from posters and flyers to brochures and websites. The value of these projects is considerable, in that they give students a substantial taste of the challenges and tensions involved in carrying out tasks with real-world consequences and communicating with real-world audiences. Other types of engagement with the workplace might involve different forms of investigation of a particular setting; an example of this was reported in Chapter 8, a task in which learners undertook an analysis of the culture of an organisation along with a central communication process such as decision-making or assimilation.

Activities that allow for engagement with real workplaces will not be the only form of learning opportunity. In the classroom itself, if our goal is to develop in our students an awareness of the richness of workplace writing, we need to provide activities that will help them understand and experience something of this richness. Moving away from the notion of texts as isolated events without context is an important element of any approach that attempts to provide this kind of exposure and experience, and an example of such an activity can be seen in the intertextual writing tasks described in Chapter 4. Tasks of this kind should above all be seen as something that students can experience and reflect upon, so that they can develop awareness and skills that can be applied in new settings.

They will learn that the academy and the workplace are very different when it comes to writing, but they also need to appreciate that every workplace they enter will be different and that they will need to readjust as they migrate from one work setting to another. These differences, as explained in Chapter 9, are unavoidable, but should not be seen as insurmountable obstacles, rather as a springboard for reflection and understanding. Students should be prepared for difference, and be equipped to deal with it.

The likelihood of someone entering and remaining in a single workplace throughout their working life is slim. Much more likely, as we enter the age of what has been referred to as the "precariat" (Standing, 2011), a state characterised by a lack of job security and unpredictable working lives, is that people will move from job to job more frequently, or be obliged to take on more than one job at any one time. In each instance, they will need to learn about their new work environments and to learn the values of their new community. If this is the case, then there is a strong need to develop writers who are versatile and adaptable, and equipped with tools, skills and above all the awareness that will help them acculturate into the different organisations with which they engage.

REFERENCES

AlAfnan, M. (2014). Politeness in business writing: The effects of ethnicity and relating factors on email communication. *Open Journal of Modern Linguistics, 4*, 275–289.

Al-Ali, M. N. (2004). How to get yourself on the door of a job: A cross-cultural contrastive study of Arabic and English job application letters. *Journal of Multilingual and Multicultural Development, 25*(1), 1–23.

Al-Ali, M. N. (2006). Genre-pragmatic strategies in English letter-of-application writing of Jordanian Arabic-English bilinguals. *International Journal of Bilingual Education and Bilingualism, 9*(1), 119–139.

Angouri, J. and Harwood, N. (2008). This is too formal for us … A case study of variation in the written products of a multinational consortium. *Journal of Business and Technical Communication, 22*(1), 38–64.

Anson, C. and Forsberg, L. (1990). Moving beyond the academic community: Transitional stages in professional writing. *Written Communication, 7*(2), 200–231.

Artemeva, N. (2005). A time to speak, a time to act: A rhetorical genre analysis of a novice engineer's calculated risk taking. *Journal of Business and Technical Communication, 19*(4), 389–421.

Artemeva, N. (2009). Stories of becoming: A study of novice engineers learning genres of their profession. In C. Bazerman, A. Bonini and D. Figuieredo (Eds.), *Genre in a Changing World: Perspectives on Writing* (pp. 158–178). Fort Collins, CO: The WAC Clearinghouse and Parlor Press.

Artemeva, N. (2011). "An engrained part of my career": The formation of a knowledge worker in the dual space of engineering knowledge and rhetorical process. *Writing in Knowledge Societies*, 321–350.

Artemeva, N. and Fox, J. (2014). The formation of a professional communicator: A socio-rhetorical approach. In V. Bhatia and S. Bremner (Eds.), *The Routledge Handbook of Language and Professional Communication* (pp. 461–485). London: Routledge.

Arundale, R. (2006). Face as relational and interactional: A communication framework for research on face, facework, and politeness. *Journal of Politeness Research, 2*, 193–216.

Babcock, R. and Du-Babcock, B. (2001). Language-based communication zones in international business communication. *The Journal of Business Communication, 38*(4), 372–412.

Baker, T. (1991). Collaborating the course: Organized flexibility in professional writing. *Journal of Business and Technical Communication, 5*(3), 275–284.

Bakhtin, M. (1986). *Speech Genres and Other Late Essays*, ed. by Caryl Emerson and Michael Holquist, trans. by Vern W. McGee. Austin: University of Texas Press.

Barber, C. (1962). Some measurable characteristics of modern scientific prose. In *Contributions to English Syntax and Phonology*, Almquist & Wiksell, Stockholm. Reprinted in J. Swales (Ed.) (1985), *Episodes in ESP*. Hemel Hempstead: Prentice Hall.

Barclay, L. and York, K. (1996). The scavenger hunt exercise: Symbols of organizational culture. *Journal of Management Education, 20*(1), 125–128.

Bargiela-Chiappini, F. (2015). Introduction. In E. Darics (Ed.), *Digital Business Discourse*. Basingstoke: Palgrave Macmillan.

Bargiela-Chiappini, F., Bülow-Møller, A. M., Nickerson, C., Poncini, G. and Zhu, Y. (2003). Five perspectives on intercultural business communication. *Business Communication Quarterly, 66*(3), 73–96.

Bargiela-Chiappini, F. and Harris, S. (1996). Requests and status in business correspondence. *Journal of Pragmatics, 26*(5), 635–662.

Barnes, K. and Smith, G. (2013). Beyond the textbook: An approach to facilitating student understanding of organizational culture in organizations. *Organization Management Journal, 10*(1), 45–65.

Baron, N. (2002). Who sets e-mail style? Prescriptivism, coping strategies, and democratizing communication access. *The Information Society, 18*, 403–413.

Barron, A. (2006). Understanding spam: A macro-textual analysis. *Journal of Pragmatics, 38*(6), 880–904.

Bartholomae, D. (1985). Inventing the university. In M. Rose (Ed.), *When a Writer Can't Write: Studies in Writer's Block and Other Composing-Process Problems* (pp. 134–165). New York: Guilford.

Barton, D. (2007). *Literacy: An Introduction to the Ecology of Language*. Oxford: Blackwell.

Bax, S. (2011). *Discourse and Genre: Analysing Language in Context*. London: Palgrave Macmillan.

Bazerman, C. (1988). *Shaping Written Knowledge*. Madison, WI: University of Wisconsin Press.

Bazerman, C. (1994). Systems of genres and the enactment of social intentions. In A. Freedman and P. Medway (Eds.), *Genre and the New Rhetoric* (pp. 79–104). London: Taylor & Francis.

Bazerman, C. (1998). Introduction. In J. Swales (Ed.), *Other Floors, Other Voices: A Textography of a Small University Building*. Mahwah, NJ: Lawrence Erlbaum Associates.

Bazerman, C. (2004). Intertextuality: How texts rely on other texts. In C. Bazerman and P. Prior (Eds.), *What Writing Does and How It Does It: An Introduction to Analyzing Texts and Textual Practices* (pp. 83–96). Mahwah, NJ: Lawrence Erlbaum.

Bazerman, C. and Paradis, J. (Eds.) (1991). *Textual Dynamics and the Professions: Historical and Contemporary Writing in Professional Communities*. Madison, WI: University of Wisconsin Press.

Beaufort, A. (1997). Operationalizing the concept of discourse community: A case study of one institutional site of composing. *Research in the Teaching of English, 31*(4), 486–529.

Beaufort, A. (1998). Transferring writing knowledge to the workplace: Are we on track? In M. Garay and S. Bernhardt (Eds.), *Expanding Literacies: English Teaching and the New Workplace* (pp. 179–199). Albany, NY: State University of New York Press.

Beaufort, A. (1999). *Writing in the Real World: Making the Transition from School to Work*. New York, NY: Teachers College Press.

Beaufort, A. (2000). Learning the trade: A social apprenticeship model for gaining writing expertise. *Written Communication, 17*(2), 185–223.

Beaufort, A. (2008). Writing in the professions. In C. Bazerman (Ed.), *Handbook of Research on Writing: History, Society, School, Individual, Text* (pp. 221–235). New York, NY: Lawrence Erlbaum Associates.

Bekins, L. and Merriam, S. (2004). Consulting and collaborative writing connections. *Academic Exchange Quarterly, 8*(3), 233–237.

Belcher, D. (1994). The apprenticeship approach to advanced academic literacy: Graduate students and their mentors. *English for Specific Purposes, 13*(1), 23–34.

Bell, A. (1991). *The Language of News Media*. Oxford: Blackwell.

Berkenkotter, C. (2001). Genre systems at work: DSM-IV and rhetorical recontextualization in psychotherapy paperwork. *Written Communication, 18*(3), 326–349.

Berkenkotter, C. and Huckin, T. (1993). Rethinking genre from a sociocognitive perspective. *Written Communication, 10*(4), 475–509.

Bex, T. (1996). *Variety in Written English. Texts in Society: Societies in Text*. London: Routledge.

Bhatia, A. (2012). The Corporate Social Responsibility report: The hybridization of a genre. *IEEE Transactions on Professional Communication, 55*(3), 221–238.

Bhatia, V. (1993). *Analysing Genre: English Use in Professional Settings*. London: Longman.

Bhatia, V. (1995). Genre-mixing in professional communication: The case of "private intentions" v. "socially recognised purposes". In P. Bruthiaux, T. Boswood and B. Du-Babcock (Eds.), *Explorations in English for Professional Communication (pp. 1–19)*. Hong Kong: City University of Hong Kong.

Bhatia, V. (1999). Integrating products, processes, purposes and participants in professional writing. In C. N. Candlin and K. Hyland (Eds.), *Writing: Texts, Processes, and Practices (pp. 21–39)*. London: Longman.

Bhatia, V. (2004). *Worlds of Written Discourse: A Genre-Based View*. London: Continuum.

Bhatia, V. (2008). Genre analysis, ESP and professional practice. *English for Specific Purposes, 27*(2), 161–174.

Bhatia, V. (2010). Interdiscursivity in professional communication. *Discourse & Communication, 4*(1), 32–50.

Bhatia, V. and Bremner, S. (2012). English for business communication. *Language Teaching, 45*(4), 410–445.

Bhatia, V. and Bremner, S. (2014). *The Routledge Handbook of Language and Professional Communication*. London: Routledge.

Biesenbach-Lucas, S. (2007). Students writing emails to faculty: An examination of e-politeness among native and non-native speakers of English. *Language Learning & Technology, 11*(2), 59–81.

Bishop, W. and Ostrom, H. (Eds.) (1997). *Genre and Writing: Issues, Arguments, Alternatives*. Portsmouth: Boynton/Cook Publishers, Inc.

Bloor, M. (1998). English for Specific Purposes: The preservation of the species. *English for Specific Purposes, 17*(1), 47–66.

Blum-Kulka, S. and Olshtain, E. (1984). Requests and apologies: A cross-cultural study of speech act realization patterns CCSARP. *Applied Linguistics, 5*, 196–213.

Blum-Kulka, S., House, J. and Kasper, G. (Eds.), (1989). *Cross-Cultural Pragmatics: Requests and Apologies*. Norwood, NJ: Ablex.

Blyler, N. and Thralls, C. (Eds.) (1993). *Professional Communication: The Social Perspective*. Newbury Park, CA: Sage Publications.

Bolton, M. K. (1999). The role of coaching in student teams: A "just-in-time" approach to learning. *Journal of Management Education, 23*, 233–250.

Bovee, C. and Thill, J. (2012). *Business Communication Essentials*. Upper Saddle River, NJ: Pearson Prentice Hall.

Bremner, S. (2006). Politeness, power, and activity systems: Written requests and multiple audiences in an institutional setting. *Written Communication, 23*(4), 397–423.

Bremner, S. (2008). Intertextuality and business communication textbooks: Why students need more textual support. *English for Specific Purposes, 27*(3), 306–321.

Bremner, S. (2010). Collaborative writing: Bridging the gap between the textbook and the workplace. *English for Specific Purposes, 29*(2), 121–132.

Bremner, S. (2012a). Socialization and the acquisition of professional discourse: A case study in the PR industry. *Written Communication, 29*(1), 7–32.

Bremner, S. (2012b). Working with genre systems: Accommodating multiple interests in the construction of organisational texts. In P. Gillaerts, E. de Groot, S. Dieltjens, P. Heynderickx and G. Jacobs (Eds.), *Researching Discourse in Business Genres: Cases and Corpora (pp. 53–70).* Linguistic Insights series. Bern: Peter Lang.

Bremner, S. (2013a). Politeness and face research. In C. Chapelle (Ed.), *The Encyclopedia of Applied Linguistics.* Oxford: Wiley-Blackwell.

Bremner, S. (2013b). Exploiting promotional genres: A study of business development emails. Paper presented at *19th European Symposium on Languages for Special Purposes,* Vienna, Austria.

Bremner, S. (2013c). Making sense of workplace experiences: Student perspectives on organizational culture. Paper presented at the *78th Convention of the Association of Business Communication,* New Orleans, USA.

Bremner, S. (2014a). Genres and processes in the PR industry: Behind the scenes with an intern writer. *International Journal of Business Communication, 51*(3), 259–278.

Bremner, S. (2014b). Collaborative writing: Challenges for research and teaching. In V. Bhatia and S. Bremner (Eds.), *The Handbook of Language and Professional Communication* (pp. 486–500). London: Routledge.

Bremner, S. (2014c). Preparing students for the world of work: A study of the internship experience in Hong Kong. Paper presented at the *Asian Convention of the Association for Business Communication,* Shanghai, China.

Bremner, S. (2014d). Critical wastelands: Business communications textbooks and the capitalist enterprise. Paper presented at the *5th CADAAD Conference (Critical Approaches to Discourse Analysis Across Disciplines),* Budapest, Hungary.

Bremner, S. (2015). Shifting registers: Management of social and power relationships in email. Paper presented at the *80th Convention of the Association for Business Communication,* Seattle, USA.

Bremner, S. and Costley, T. (2016). Bringing reality to the classroom: Exercises in intertextuality. Paper presented at the *12th Association for Business Communication Conference of the Europe, Africa and Middle East region,* Cape Town, South Africa.

Bremner, S. and Phung, B. (2015). Learning from the experts: An analysis of writers' self-presentation on LinkedIn. *IEEE Transactions on Professional Communication 58*(4), 367–380.

Bremner, S., Peirson-Smith, A., Jones, R. and Bhatia, V. (2014). Task design and interaction in collaborative writing: The students' story. *Business and Professional Communication Quarterly, 77*(2), 150–168.

Brent, D. (2011). Transfer, transformation, and rhetorical knowledge: Insights from transfer theory. *Journal of Business and Technical Communication, 25*(4), 396–420.

Brown, J., Collins, A. and Duguid, P. (1989). Situated cognition and the culture of learning. *Educational Researcher, 18,* 32–42.

Brown. P. and Levinson, S. (1987). *Politeness: Some Universals in Language Usage.* London: Cambridge University Press.

Bruffee, K. (1986). Social construction, language and the authority of knowledge: A bibliographical essay. *College English, 48,* 773–790.

Buechler, S. (2010). Using Web 2.0 to collaborate. *Business Communication Quarterly*, *73*(4), 439–443.

Burnett, R. (1993). Conflict in collaborative decision-making. In N. Blyler and C. Thralls (Eds.), *Professional Communication: The Social Perspective* (pp. 145–163). Newbury Park, CA: Sage.

Burnett, R. (1996). "Some people weren't able to contribute anything but their technical knowledge": The anatomy of a dysfunctional team. In A. Duin and C. Hansen (Eds.), *Non-academic Writing: Social Theory and Technology* (pp. 123–156). Mahwah, NJ: Lawrence Erlbaum.

Burnett, R. (2001). *Technical communication*. Fort Worth, TX: Harcourt Brace.

Cameron, D. (2002). Globalization and the teaching of "communication skills". In D. Block and D. Cameron (Eds.), *Globalization and Language Teaching* (pp. 67–82). London: Routledge.

Candlin, C. N. and Maley, Y. (1997). Intertextuality and interdiscursivity in the discourse of alternative dispute resolution. In B. Gunnarsson, P. Linell and B. Nordberg (Eds.), *The Construction of Professional Discourse* (pp. 201–222). London: Routledge.

Carter, M. (1990). The idea of expertise: An exploration of cognitive and social dimensions of writing. *College Composition and Communication*, *41*(3), 265–286.

Catenaccio, P. (2008). Press releases as a hybrid genre: Addressing the informative/promotional conundrum. *Pragmatics*, *18*, 9–31.

Chen, C. (2001). Making e-mail requests to professors: Taiwanese vs. American students. Paper presented at the Annual Meeting of the American Association for Applied Linguistics, St. Louis, USA.

Chen, C. (2006). The development of e-mail literacy: From writing to peers to writing to authority figures. *Language Learning & Technology*, *10*(2), 35–55.

Chen, G., Donahue, L. and Klimoski, R. (2004). Training undergraduates to work in organizational teams. *Academy of Management Learning and Education*, *3*(1), 27–40.

Cheng, W. (2003). *Intercultural Conversation*. Amsterdam: Benjamins.

Cheng, W. and Mok, E. (2008). Discourse processes and products: Land surveyors in Hong Kong. *English for Specific Purposes*, *27*(1), 57–73.

Cheung, M. (2008). 'Click here': The impact of new media on the encoding of persuasive messages in direct marketing. *Discourse Studies*, *10*(2), 161–189.

Cheung, M. (2010). The globalization and localization of persuasive marketing communication: A cross-linguistic socio-cultural analysis. *Journal of Pragmatics*, *42*(2), 354–376.

Colen, K. and Petelin, R. (2004). Challenges in collaborative writing in the contemporary corporation. *Corporate Communications*, *9*(2), 136–145.

Connor, U., Davis, K. and De Rycker, T. (1995). Correctness and clarity in applying for overseas jobs: A cross-cultural analysis of US and Flemish applications. *Text-Interdisciplinary Journal for the Study of Discourse*, *15*(4), 457–476.

Couture, B. and Rymer, J. (Eds.) (1989). *Interactive Writing on the Job: Definitions and Implications of Collaboration*. Urbana, IL: NTCE and ABC.

Creelman, V. (2015). Sheer outrage: Negotiating customer dissatisfaction and interaction in the blogosphere. In E. Darics (Ed.), *Digital Business Discourse* (pp. 160–185). Basingstoke: Palgrave Macmillan.

Cross, G. (1993). The interrelation of genre, context, and process in the collaborative writing of two corporate documents. In R. Spilka (Ed.), *Writing in the Workplace: New Research Perspectives* (pp. 141–152). Carbondale, IL: Southern Illinois Press.

Cross, G. (1994). *Collaboration and Conflict: A Contextual Exploration of Group Writing and Positive Emphasis*. Cresskill, NJ: Hampton.

Cross, G. (2000). Collective form: An exploration of large-group writing. 1998 Outstanding Researcher Lecture. *Journal of Business Communication*, *37*(1), 77–100.

Cross, G. (2001). *Forming the Collective Mind: A Contextual Exploration of Large-Scale Collaborative Writing in Industry.* Cresskill, NJ: Hampton.

Cross, G. (2011). *Envisioning Collaboration: Group Verbal-Visual Composing in a System of Creativity.* Amityville, NY: Baywood Publishing Company, Inc.

Daft, R. and Lengel, R. (1984). Information richness: A new approach to managerial information processing and organizational design. In B. Staw and L. Cummins (Eds.), *Research in Organizational Behavior,* Vol. 6 (pp. 191–233). Greenwich, CT: JAI Press.

Daft, R. and Lengel, R. (1986). Organizational requirements, media richness and structural design. *Management Science, 32,* 554–571.

Danet, B. (2001). *Cyberplay: Communicating Online.* Oxford: Berg Publishing.

Darics, E. (2014). The blurring boundaries between synchronicity and asynchronicity: New communicative situations in work-related instant messaging. *International Journal of Business Communication, 51*(4), 337–358.

Darics, E. (Ed.) (2015). *Digital Business Discourse.* Basingstoke: Palgrave Macmillan.

Dautermann, J. (1993). Negotiating meaning in a hospital discourse community. In R. Spilka, (Ed.), *Writing in the Workplace: New Research Perspectives* (pp. 98–110). Carbondale, IL: Southern Illinois University Press.

Deal, T. and Kennedy, A. (1982). *Corporate Cultures: The Rites and Rituals of Corporate Life.* Reading, MT: Addison-Wesley.

Debs, M. (1991). Recent research on collaborative writing in industry. *Technical Communication,* Fourth quarter, 476–484.

Dev, S. (2013). Assessing and understanding organizational culture: Various views and theories. *Indian Streams Research Journal, 3*(5), 1.

Devitt, A. (1991). Intertextuality in tax accounting: Generic, referential, and functional. In C. Bazerman and J. Paradis (Eds.), *Textual Dynamics of the Professions: Historical and Contemporary Studies of Writing in Professional Communities* (pp. 336–357). Madison: University of Wisconsin Press.

Devitt, A. (2004). *Writing Genres.* Carbondale, IL: Southern Illinois University Press.

Devitt, A., Bawarshi, A. and Reiff, M. (2003). Materiality and genre in the study of discourse communities. *College English, 65*(5), 541–558.

Dias, P. and Paré, A. (Eds.) (2000). *Transitions: Writing in Academic and Workplace Settings.* Cresskill, NJ: Hampton Press Inc.

Dias, P., Freedman, A., Medway. P. and Paré. A. (1999). *Worlds Apart: Acting and Writing in Academic and Workplace Contexts.* Mahwah, NJ: Erlbaum.

Ding, H. and Ding, X. (2008). Project management, critical praxis, and process-oriented approach to teamwork. *Business Communication Quarterly, 71,* 456–471.

Doheny-Farina, S. (1986). Writing in an emerging organization: An ethnographic study. *Written Communication, 3*(2), 158–185.

Dourish, P. and Bellotti, V. (1992). Awareness and coordination in shared workspaces. Paper presented at the International Conference on Computer Supported Cooperative Work.

Dovey, T. (2006). What purposes, specifically? Re-thinking purposes and specificity in the context of the "new vocationalism". *English for Specific Purposes, 25*(4), 387–402.

Du-Babcock, B. and Babcock, R. D. (1996). Patterns of expatriate-local personnel communication in multinational corporations. *The Journal of Business Communication, 33*(2), 141–164.

Dudley-Evans, T. and Henderson, W. (1990). The language of economics: The analysis of economics discourse. *ELT Documents 134.* London: Modern English Publications in association with the British Council.

Dudley-Evans, T. and Henderson, W. (1993). The development of the economics article: 1891 to 1980. *Finlance, XII,* 159–180.

Duff, P. (2008). Language socialization, higher education and work. In P. Duff and N. Hornburger (Eds.), *Encyclopedia of Language and Education*, Vol. *8* (pp. 257–270). New York, NY: Springer.

Duff, P. (2010). Language socialization into academic discourse communities. *Annual Review of Applied Linguistics, 30*, 169–192.

Duthler, K. (2006). The politeness of requests made via email and voicemail. Support for the hyperpersonal model. *Journal of Computer-Mediated Communication, 11*(2), 500–521.

Eastman, J. and Swift, C. (2002). Enhancing collaborative learning: Discussion boards and chat rooms as project communication tools. *Business Communication Quarterly, 65*(3), 29–41.

Eco, U. (1990). *The Limits of Interpretation.* Bloomington, IN: Indiana University Press.

Economidou-Kogetsidis, M. (2011). "Please answer me as soon as possible": Pragmatic failure in non-native speakers' e-mail requests to faculty. *Journal of Pragmatics, 43*(13), 3193–3215.

Economidou-Kogetsidis, M. (2015). Teaching email politeness in the EFL/ESL classroom. *ELT Journal, 69*(4), 415–424.

Ede, L. and Lunsford, A. (1990). *Singular Texts/Plural Authors: Perspectives on Collaborative Learning.* Carbondale, IL: Southern Illinois University Press.

Eelen, G. (2001). *A Critique of Politeness Theories.* Manchester: St. Jerome Publishing.

Engeström, Y. (1987). *Learning by Expanding: An Activity-Theoretical Approach to Developmental Research.* Helsinki, Finland: Orienta-Konsultit Oy.

Evans, S. (2010). Business as usual: The use of English in the professional world in Hong Kong. *English for Specific Purposes, 29*(3), 153–167.

Evans, S. (2012). Designing email tasks for the Business English classroom: Implications from a study of Hong Kong's key industries. *English for Specific Purposes, 31*(3), 202–212.

Faigley, L. and Miller, T. (1982). What we learn from writing on the job. *College English, 44*(6), 557–569.

Fairclough, N. (1992). *Discourse and Social Change.* Cambridge: Polity Press.

Farace, R., Monge, P. and Russell, H. (1977). *Communicating and Organizing.* Reading, MA: Addison-Wesley.

Flower, L. (1989). Rhetorical problem solving: Cognition and professional writing. In M. Kogen (Ed.), *Writing in the Business Professions* (pp. 3–36). Urbana, IL: National Council of Teachers of English.

Flowerdew, J. (1993). An educational, or process, approach to the teaching of professional genres. *ELT Journal, 47*(4), 305–316.

Flowerdew, J. (2002). Genre in the classroom: A linguistic approach. In A. Johns (Ed.), *Genre in the Classroom: Multiple Perspectives* (pp. 91–104). Mahwah, NJ: Lawrence Erlbaum.

Flowerdew, J. (2011). Reconciling contrasting approaches to genre analysis: The whole can equal more than the sum of the parts. In D. Belcher, A. Johns and B. Paltridge (Eds.), *New Directions in English for Specific Purposes Research* (pp. 119–144). Ann Arbor, MI: University of Michigan Press.

Flowerdew, J. and Wan, A. (2006). Genre analysis of tax computation letters: How and why tax accountants write the way they do. *English for Specific Purposes, 25*(2), 133–153.

Forey, G. (2014). Offshore outsourcing: The need for appliable linguistics. In V. Bhatia and S. Bremner (Eds.), *The Routledge Handbook of Language and Professional Communication* (pp. 382–399). London: Routledge.

Forey, G. and Lockwood, J. (2007). "I'd love to put someone in jail for this": An initial investigation of English in the business processing outsourcing (BPO) industry. *English for Specific Purposes, 26*, 308–326.

Forman, J. (2004). Opening the aperture: Research and theory on collaborative writing. *Journal of Business Communication, 41*(1), 27–36.

Fosen, C. (2000). Genres made real: Genre theory as pedagogy, method, and content. *ERIC Number*: ED442107.

Fraser, B. (2005) Whither politeness. In R. Lakoff and S. Ide (Eds.), *Broadening the Horizon of Linguistic Politeness* (pp. 65–83). Amsterdam: John Benjamins.

Fraser, B. and Nolen, W. (1981). The association of deference with linguistic form. *International Journal of the Sociology of Language, 27*, 93–110.

Freadman, A. (2002). Uptake. In R. Coe, L. Lingard and T. Teslenko (Eds.), *The Rhetoric and Ideology of Genre: Strategies for Stability and Change* (pp. 39–53). Cresskill, NJ: Hampton.

Fredrick, T. (2008). Facilitating better teamwork: Analyzing the challenges and strategies of classroom-based collaboration. *Business Communication Quarterly, 71*, 439–455.

Freedman, A. and Adam, C. (1996). Learning to write professionally: "Situated learning" and the transition from university to professional discourse. *Journal of Business and Technical Communication, 10*(4), 395–427.

Freedman, A. and Adam, C. (2000). Bridging the gap: University-based writing that is more than simulation. In P. Dias and A. Paré (Eds.), *Transitions: Writing in Academic and Workplace Settings* (pp. 129 –144). Cresskill, NJ: Hampton Press.

Freedman, A., Adam, C. and Smart, G. (1994). Wearing suits to class: Simulating genres and simulations as genre. *Written Communication, 11*(2), 193–226.

Freedman, A. and Medway, P. (Eds.) (1994a). *Learning and Teaching Genre*. Portsmouth, NH: Boynton/Cook.

Freedman, A. and Medway, P. (Eds.) (1994b). *Genre and the New Rhetoric*. London: Penguin.

Fulk, J., Steinfield, C., Schmitz, J. and Power, J. (1987). A social information processing model of media use in organizations. *Communication Research, 14*, 529–552.

Galtens, J. (2000). Lessons from the field: Socialization issues in writing and editing internships. *Business Communication Quarterly, 63*(1), 64–76.

Geertz, C. (1983). *Local Knowledge: Further Essays in Interpretive Anthropology*. New York: Basic Books.

Gerhart, B. (2009). How much does national culture constrain organizational culture? *Management and Organization Review, 5*(2), 241–259.

Ghadessy, M. (1993). *Register Analysis: Theory and Practice*. London: Pinter.

Giddens, A. (1984). *The Constitution of Society: Outline of the Theory of Structure*. Berkeley, CA: University of California Press.

Gillaerts, P. (2003). A textlinguistic and genological approach to the letters of application. *Hermes, 31*, 105–117.

Gimenez, J. (2006). Embedded business emails: Meeting new demands in international business communication. *English for Specific Purposes, 25*(2), 154–172.

Gimenez, J. (2016). Discipline-specific writing for business students: Research, practice and pedagogy. In J. Flowerdew and T. Costley (Eds.), *Discipline Specific Writing: From Theory to Practice* (pp. 126–143). London: Routledge.

Goffman, E. (1967). *Interaction Ritual: Essays on Face-to-Face Behavior*. New York: Pantheon.

Gollin, S. (1999). "Why? I thought we'd talked about it before": Collaborative writing in a professional workplace setting. In C. Candlin and K. Hyland (Eds.), *Writing: Texts, Processes and Practices* (pp. 267–290). London: Longman.

Gooch, J. (2005). The dynamics and challenges of interdisciplinary collaboration: A case study of "cortical depth of bench" in group proposal writing. *IEEE Transactions on Professional Communication, 48*(2), 177–190.

Goodman, M., and Hirsch, P. (2014). Electronic media in professional communication. In V. Bhatia and S. Bremner (Eds.), *The Routledge Handbook of Language and Professional Communication* (pp. 129–146). London: Routledge.

Goodwin, C. and Duranti, A. (1992). *Rethinking Context: Language as an Interactive Phenomenon*. Cambridge: Cambridge University Press.

Graham, M. (1998). Administrative writing: Bringing context to pedagogy. *Journal of Business and Technical Communication, 12*(2), 238–253.

Grice, H. (1975). Logic and conversation. In P. Cole and J. Morgan (Eds.), *Syntax and Semantics 3. Speech Acts* (pp. 41–58). New York: Academic Press.

Gu, Y. (1990). Politeness phenomena in modern Chinese. *Journal of Pragmatics, 14*, 237–257.

Guffey, M. and Du-Babcock, B. (2008). *Essentials of Business Communication* (Asian ed.). Singapore: Thomson.

Gunnarsson, B. (1997). The writing process from a sociolinguistic viewpoint. *Written Communication, 14*(2), 139–189.

Haas, C. and Witte, S. (2001). Writing as an embodied practice: The case of engineering standards. *Journal of Business and Technical Communication, 15*(4), 413–457.

Hafner, C. (2013). The discursive construction of professional expertise: Appeals to authority in barrister's opinions. *English for Specific Purposes 32*(3), 131–143.

Hafner, C. (2014). Embedding digital literacies in English language teaching: Students' digital video projects as multimodal ensembles. *TESOL Quarterly, 48*(4), 655–685.

Hafner, C. A. (forthcoming). Digital Discourses. In A. Phakiti, P. De Costa, L. Plonsky, and S. Starfield (Eds.) *Palgrave Handbook of Applied Linguistics Research Methodology*. Palgrave.

Hall, E. (1976). *Beyond Culture*. New York, NY: Anchor Books.

Halliday, M. (1978). *Language as Social Semiotic*. London: Arnold.

Halliday, M. and Hasan, R. (1976). *Cohesion in English*. London: Longman.

Hansen, C. (1995) Writing the project team: Authority and intertextuality in a corporate setting. *Journal of Business Communication, 32*(2), 103–122.

Hansen, R. (2006). Benefits and problems with student teams: Suggestions for improving team projects. *Journal of Education for Business 82*(1), 11–19.

Harris, S. (2003). Politeness and power: Making and responding to "requests" in institutional settings. *Text, 23*(1), 27–52.

Haugh, M. (2004). Revisiting the conceptualisation of politeness in English and Japanese. *Multilingua, 23*(1–2), 85–110.

Hemby, V., McPherson, B., Moore, W., Szul, L., Woodland, D. and Wilkinson, K. (2004). A meeting planning project: A major component in developing teamwork and collaborative writing skills. *Journal of Organizational Culture, Communications and Conflict, 8*(2), 27–45.

Henry, A. and Roseberry, R. L. (2001). A narrow-angled corpus analysis of moves and strategies of the genre: "Letter of Application". *English for Specific Purposes, 20*(2), 153–167.

Hewett, B. and Robidoux, C. (2010). *Virtual Collaborative Writing in the Workplace: Computer-Mediated Communication Technologies and Processes*. Hershey, PA: IGI Global.

Ho, V. (2011). What functions do intertextuality and interdiscursivity serve in request e-mail discourse? *Journal of Pragmatics, 43*(10), 2534–2547.

Hofstede, G. (1983). The cultural relativity of organizational practices and theories. *Journal of International Business Studies, 14*(2), 75–89.

Hofstede, G. (1997). *Cultures and Organizations: Software of the Mind*. New York: McGraw-Hill.

Hofstede, G. (2001). *Culture's Consequences: Comparing Values, Behaviors, Institutions, and Organizations Across Nations* (2nd ed.). Thousand Oaks, CA: Sage Publications.

Hofstede, G., Neuijen, B., Ohayv, D. and Sanders, G. (1990). Measuring Organizational Cultures: A Qualitative and Quantitative Study Across Twenty Cases. *Administrative Science Quarterly, 35*(2), 286–316.

Holmes, J. (2004). Intertextuality in EAP: An African context. *Journal of English for Academic Purposes, 3*(1), 73–88.

Holmes, J. and Stubbe, M. (2003). *Power and Politeness in the Workplace*. London: Pearson Education.

Hopkins, A. (2006). Studying organizational cultures and their effects on safety. *Safety Science, 44*(10), 875–889.

Hyland, K. (2002). Specificity revisited: How far should we go now? *English for Specific Purposes, 21*, 385–395.

Hyland, K. (2004). *Genre and Second Language Writing*. Ann Arbor: The University of Michigan Press.

Hyland, K. (2007). Genre pedagogy: Language, literacy and L2 writing instruction. *Journal of Second Language Writing, 16*(3), 148–164.

Hyland, K. (2016). *Teaching and Researching Writing*. New York, NY: Routledge.

Hyon, S. (1996). Genre in three traditions: Implications for ESL. *TESOL Quarterly, 30*(4), 693–722.

Hyon, S. and Chen, R. (2004). Beyond the research article: University faculty genres and EAP graduate preparation. *English for Specific Purposes, 23*(3), 233–263.

Ide, S. (1989). Formal forms and discernment: Two neglected aspects of universals of linguistic politeness. *Multilingua, 8*(2/3), 223–248.

Iedema, R. (2003). Multimodality, resemiotization: Extending the analysis of discourse as multi-semiotic practice. *Visual Communication, 2*(1), 29–57.

Iedema, R. (2007). Communicating hospital work. In R. Iedema (Ed.), *The Discourse of Hospital Communication* (pp. 1–17). Basingstoke: Palgrave Macmillan.

Jacobs, G. (1999). *Preformulating the News: An Analysis of the Metapragmatics of Press Releases*. Amsterdam: John Benjamins.

Jacobs, G. (2006). The dos and don'ts of writing press releases (and how learners act upon them). In P. Gillaerts and P. Shaw (Eds.), *The Map and the Landscape: Norms and Practices in Genre* (pp. 199–218). Bern: Peter Lang.

Jackson, M. (2007). Should emerging technologies change business communication scholarship? *Journal of Business Communication, 44*(1), 3–12.

Johns, A. (2011). The future of genre in L2 writing: Fundamental, but contested, instructional decisions. *Journal of Second Language Writing, 20*(1), 56–68.

Jones, R. and Hafner, C. (2012). *Understanding Digital Literacies: A Practical Introduction*. London: Routledge.

Jones, S. (2005). From writers to information coordinators. *Journal of Business and Technical Communication, 19*(4), 449–467.

Jones, S. (2007). How we collaborate: Reported frequency of technical communicators' collaborative writing activities. *Technical Communication, 54*(3), 283–294.

Kankaanranta, A. (2006). "Hej Seppo, could you pls comment on this!": Internal email communication in lingua franca English in a multinational company. *Business Communication Quarterly, 69*(2), 216–225.

Kasper, G. (1990). Linguistic politeness: Current research issues. *Journal of Pragmatics, 14*, 193–218.

Kent, T. (1991). On the very idea of a discourse community. *College Composition and Communication, 42*(4), 425–445.

Kent, T. (1993). Formalism, social construction and the problem of interpretive authority. In N. Blyler and C. Thralls (Eds.), *Professional Communication: The Social Perspective* (pp. 79–91). Newbury Park, CA: Sage Publications.

Knoblauch, C. (1989). The teaching and practice of "professional writing". In M. Kogen (Ed.), *Writing in the Business Professions* (pp. 246–264). Urbana, IL: National Council of Teachers of English.

Kock, N., Davison, R., Ocker, R. and Wazlawick, R. (2001). E-collaboration: A look at past and future challenges. *Journal of Systems and Information Technology, 5*(1), 1–9.

Kong, K. (1998). Are simple business requests really simple? A comparison of Chinese and English business request letters. *Text, 18*(1), 103–141.

Kong, K. (2006). Accounts as a politeness strategy in the internal directive documents of a business firm in Hong Kong. *Journal of Asian Pacific Communication, 16*(1), 77–101.

Kramer, M. (2010). *Organizational Socialization: Joining and Leaving Organizations.* Cambridge: Polity Press.

Kress, G. and van Leeuwen, T. (1996). *Reading Images: The Grammar of Visual Design.* London: Routledge.

Kristeva, J. (1980). *Desire in Language: A Semiotic Approach to Literature and Art.* Oxford: Blackwell.

Kuhn, T. (1977). *The Essential Tension.* Chicago, IL: University of Chicago Press.

Kwan, B. (2014). Communities in studies of discursive practices and discursive practices in communities. In V. Bhatia and S. Bremner (Eds.), *The Routledge Handbook of Language and Professional Communication* (pp. 443–460). London: Routledge.

Lakoff, R. (1973). The logic of politeness; or minding your p's and q's. *Chicago Linguistics Society, 8*, 292–305.

Lakoff, R. (1975). *Language and Women's Place.* New York, NY: Harper.

Lave, J. and Wenger, E. (1991). *Situated Learning: Legitimate Peripheral Participation.* Cambridge: Cambridge University Press.

Ledwell-Brown, J. (2000). Organizational cultures as contexts for learning to write. In P. Dias and A. Paré (Eds.), *Transitions: Writing in Academic and Workplace Settings* (pp. 199–222). Cresskill, NJ: Hampton Press.

Lee, C. (2004). Written requests in emails sent by adult Chinese learners of English. *Language, Culture and Curriculum, 17*(1), 58–72.

Leech, G. (1983). *Principles of Pragmatics.* London: Longman.

Lehman, C. and DuFrene, D. (2002). *Business Communication.* Cincinnati, OH: South-Western.

Le Maistre, C. and Paré, A. (2004). Learning in two communities: The challenge for universities and workplaces. *Journal of Workplace Learning, 16*(1/2), 44–52.

Lenassi, N. (2015). Some linguistic and pragmatic aspects of Italian business email. In E. Darics (Ed.), *Digital Business Discourse* (pp. 80–98). Basingstoke: Palgrave Macmillan.

Levinson, P. (2009). *New New media.* Boston, MA: Allyn & Bacon.

Li, D. (2000). The pragmatics of making requests in the L2 workplace: A case study of language socialization. *Canadian Modern Language Review, 57*(1), 58–87.

Lillqvist, E. and Louhialaa-Salminen, L. (2014). Facing Facebook: Impression management strategies in company-consumer interactions. *Journal of Business and Technical Communication, 28*(1), 3–30.

Lindholm, M. (2008). A community text pattern in the European Commission press release? A generic and genetic view. *Pragmatics, 18*, 33–58.

Linell, P. (1998). Discourse across boundaries: On recontextualizations and the blending of voices in professional discourse. *Text, 18*, 143–157.

Locher, M. A. (2004). *Power and Politeness in Action: Disagreements in Oral Communication* (Vol. 12). Berlin/New York: Walter de Gruyter.

Locker, K. and Kaczmarek, S. (2014). *Business Communication: Building Critical Skills.* New York, NY: McGraw-Hill.

Lockwood, J. (2017). An analysis of web-chat in an outsourced customer service account in the Philippines. *English for Specific Purposes, 24*, 26–39.

Louis, M. (1985). An investigator's guide to workplace culture. In P. Frost, L. Moore, M. Louis, C. Lundberg and J. Martin (Eds.), *Organizational Culture* (pp. 73–93). Beverley Hills, CA: Sage.

Lowry, P., Curtis, A. and Lowry, M. (2004). Building a taxonomy and nomenclature of collaborative writing to improve interdisciplinary research and practice. *Journal of Business Communication, 41*, 66–99.

Mabrito, M. (1999). From workplace to classroom: Teaching professional writing. *Business Communication Quarterly, 62*(3), 101–105.

Macken-Horarik, M. (2002). "Something to shoot for": A Systemic Functional approach to teaching genre in secondary school science. In A. Johns (Ed.), *Genres in the Classroom: Applying Theory and Research to Practice* (pp. 17–42). Mahwah, NJ: Lawrence Erlbaum Associates.

Maier, P. (1992). Politeness strategies in business letters by native and non-native English speakers. *English for Specific Purposes, 11*(3), 189–205.

Marchand, A., Haines, V. and Dextras-Gauthier, J. (2013). Quantitative analysis of organizational culture in occupational health research: A theory-based validation in 30 workplaces of the organizational culture profile instrument. *BMC Public Health, 13*(1), 1–11.

Markman, K. (2015). Utterance chunking in instant messaging: A resource for interaction management. In E. Darics (Ed.), *Digital Business Discourse* (pp. 61–79). Basingstoke: Palgrave Macmillan.

Martin, J. (1992). *Cultures in Organizations: Three Perspectives.* New York, NY: Oxford University Press.

Martin, J. and Rose, D. (2008). *Genre Relations: Mapping Culture.* London: Equinox.

Maslow, A. (1943). A theory of human motivation. *Psychology Review, 50*, 370–396.

Matsumoto, Y. (1988). Reexamination of the universality of face: Politeness phenomena in Japanese. *Journal of Pragmatics, 12*, 403–426.

Mawer, G. (1999). *Language and Literacy in Workplace Education.* London: Longman.

Maznevski, M. and Chudoba, K. (2000). Bridging space over time: Global virtual-team dynamics and effectiveness. *Organization Science, 11*, 473–492.

McLaren, Y. and Gurău, C. (2005). Characterising the genre of the corporate press release. *LSP and Professional Communication, 5*, 10–29.

Meier, A. (1995). Passages of politeness. *Journal of Pragmatics, 24*, 381–392.

Meyer, L. (1996). The contribution of genre theory to theme-based EAP: Navigating foreign fiords. *TESL Canada Journal, 13*(2), 33–45.

Miller, C. (1984). Genre as social action. *Quarterly Journal of Speech, 70*, 151–167.

Miller, K. (2015). *Organizational Communication: Approaches and Processes.* Stamford, CT: Cengage Learning.

Miller, V. and Jablin, F. (1991). Information seeking during organizational entry: Influences, tactics, and a model of the process. *Academy of Management Review, 16*, 92–120.

Mills, C. and Hoeber, L. (2013). Exploring organizational culture through artifacts in a community figure skating club. *Journal of Sport Management, 27*, 482–496.

Morgan, G. (1986). *Images of Organization.* Beverly Hills, CA: Sage.

Morgan, G. (2006). *Images of Organization.* Thousand Oaks, CA: Sage.

Mulholland, J. (1999). E-mail: Uses, issues and problems in an institutional setting. In F. Bargiela-Chiappini and C. Nickerson (Eds.), *Writing Business: Genres, Media and Language* (pp. 57–84). London: Longman.

Mumby, D. (2013). *Organizational Communication: A Critical Approach.* Thousand Oaks, CA: Sage.

Myers, G. (1990). *Writing Biology: Texts in the Social Construction of Scientific Knowledge.* Madison, WI: University of Wisconsin Press.

Nathan, P. (2013). Academic writing in the business school: The genre of the business case report. *Journal of English for Academic Purposes, 12*(1), 57–68.

Nelson, S. (2003). Engineering and technology student perceptions of collaborative writing practices. *IEEE Transactions on Professional Communication, 46*(4), 265–276.

Newstrom, J. and Scannell, E. (1998). *The Big Book of Team Building Games: Trust-Building Activities, Team Spirit Exercises, and Other Fun Things.* New York, NY: McGraw-Hill.

Nickerson, C. (1998). Corporate culture and the use of written English within British subsidiaries in the Netherlands. *English for Specific Purposes, 17*(3), 281–294.

Nickerson, C. (2002). Taking an interdisciplinary approach in the analysis of multinational business discourse. In C. Candlin (Ed.), *Research and Practice in Professional Discourse* (pp. 641–662). Hong Kong: City University of Hong Kong Press.

Nickerson, C. and Van Nus, M. (1999). Teaching intercultural business communication research. In M. Hewings and C. Nickerson (Eds.), *Business English: Research into Practice* (pp. 25–34). Longman.

Ober, S. (2004). *Fundamentals of Contemporary Business Communication.* Boston, MA: Houghton Mifflin Company.

Ochs, E. (1992). Indexing genre. In C. Goodwin and A. Duranti (Eds.), *Rethinking Context: Language as an Interactive Phenomenon* (pp. 335–358). Cambridge: Cambridge University Press.

Ochs, E. (1993). Constructing social identity: A language socialization perspective. *Research on Language and Social Interaction, 26,* 287–306.

Ochs, E. (1999). Socialization. *Journal of Linguistic Anthropology, 9*(1–2), 230–233.

O'Connor, E. (2002). Storied business: Typology, intertextuality, and traffic in entrepreneurial narrative. *Journal of Business Communication, 39*(1), 36–54.

Odell, L., and Goswami, D. (Eds.) (1985). *Writing in Non-Academic Settings.* New York, NY: The Guilford Press.

Onrubia, J. and Engel, A. (2009). Strategies for collaborative writing and phases of knowledge construction in CSCL environments. *Computers and Education, 53,* 1256–1265.

O'Reilly, C., Chatman, J. and Caldwell F. (1991). People and organizational culture: A profile comparison approach to assessing person-organization fit. *Academy of Management Journal, 34*(3), 487–516.

Orlikowski, W. and Yates, J. (1994). Genre repertoire: The structuring of communicative practices in organizations. *Administrative Science Quarterly, 39*(4), 541–574.

Oxford, R. (1990). *Language Learning Strategies: What Every Teacher Should Know.* Boston, MA: Heinle & Heinle Publishers.

Pacanowsky, M. and O'Donnell-Trujillo, N. (1983). Organizational communication as cultural performance. *Communication Monographs, 50,* 126–147.

Palmeri, J. (2004). When discourses collide: A case study of interprofessional collaborative writing in a medically oriented law firm. *Journal of Business Communication, 41*(1), 37–65.

Pan, Y., Scollon, S. and Scollon, R. (2002). *Professional Communication in International Settings.* Malden, MA: Blackwell Publishers, Inc.

Pander Maat, H. (2008). Editing and genre conflict: How newspaper journalists clarify and neutralize press release copy. *Pragmatics, 18,* 87–113.

Paradis, J., Dobrin, D. and Miller, R. (1985). Writing at Exxon: Notes on the writing environment of an R & D organization. In L. Odell and D. Goswami (Eds.), *Writing in Non-Academic Settings* (pp. 281–308). New York: Guilford.

Paré, A. (2000) Writing as a way into social work: Genre sets, genre systems, and distributed cognition. In P. Dias and A. Paré (Eds.), *Transitions: Writing in Academic and Workplace Settings* (pp. 145–166). Cresskill, NJ: Hampton Press.

Paretti, M., McNair, L. and Holloway-Attaway, L. (2007). Teaching technical communication in an era of distributed work: A case study of collaboration between U.S. and Swedish students. *Technical Communication Quarterly, 16*(3), 327–352.

Parks, S. (2001). Moving from school to the workplace: Disciplinary innovation, border crossings, and the reshaping of a written genre. *Applied Linguistics, 22,* 405–438.

Peacock, M. (2002). Communicative moves in the discussion section of research articles. *System*, *30*(4), 479–497.

Peacock, M. (2006). A cross-disciplinary comparison of boosting in research articles. *Corpora*, *1*(1), 61–84.

Peacock, M. (2010). Linking adverbials in research articles across eight disciplines. *Ibérica*, (20), 9–33.

Perkins, D. and Salomon, G. (1989). Are cognitive skills context-bound? *Educational Researcher* *18*(1), 16–25.

Peters, T. and Waterman, R. (1982). *In Search of Excellence: Lessons from America's Best-Run Companies.* New York, NY: Harper & Row.

Pilegaard, M. (1997). Politeness in written business discourse: A textlinguistic perspective on requests. *Journal of Pragmatics*, *28*, 223–244.

Pogner, K. (2003). Writing and interacting in the discourse community of engineering. *Journal of Pragmatics*, *35*, 855–867.

Prior, P. (2004). Tracing process: How texts come into being. In C. Bazerman and P. Prior (Eds.), *What Writing Does and How It Does It: An Introduction to Analyzing Texts and Textual Practices* (pp. 167–200). Mahwah, NJ: Lawrence Erlbaum.

Rehling, L. (2005). Teaching in a high-tech conference room: Academic adaptations and workplace simulations. *Journal of Business and Technical Communication*, *19*(1), 98–113.

Reither, J. (1993). Scenic motives for collaborative writing in workplace and school. In R. Spilka (Ed.), *Writing in the Workplace: New Research Perspectives* (pp. 195–206). Carbondale, IL: Southern Illinois University Press.

Rentz, K., Arduser, L., Meloncon, L. and Debs, M. (2009). Designing a successful group-report experience. *Business Communication Quarterly*, *72*(1), 79–84.

Richards, J., Platt, J. and Platt, H. (1992). *Longman Dictionary of Language Teaching and Applied Linguistics*. Essex: Longman.

Roberts, C. (2010). Language socialization in the workplace. *Annual Review of Applied Linguistics, 30*, 211–227.

Roebuck, D. (2006). Improving Business Communication Skills (4th ed.). Upper Saddle River, NJ: Pearson, Prentice Hall.

Rogers, P. (1998). National agendas and the English divide. *Business Communication Quarterly*, *61*(3), 79–85.

Rogers, P. (2006). Introduction to the special issue: Communication challenges from new technology. *Journal of Business and Technical Communication*, *20*, 246–251.

Rogers, P. and Lee-Wong, S. (2003). Reconceptualizing politeness to accommodate dynamic tensions in subordinate-to-superior reporting. *Journal of Business and Technical Communication*, *17*(4), 379–412.

Rogoff, B. (1991). Social interaction as apprenticeship in thinking: Guided participation in spatial planning. In L. Resnick, J. Levine and S. Teasley (Eds.), *Perspectives on Socially Shared Cognition* (pp. 349–364). Washington, DC: American Psychological Association.

Russell, D. (1997). Rethinking genre in school and society: An activity theory analysis. *Written Communication, 14* (4), 504–554.

Samraj, B. (2002). Introductions in research articles: Variations across disciplines. *English for Specific Purposes*, *21*(1), 1–17.

Sarangi, S. (2002). Discourse practitioners as a community of interprofessional practice: Some insights from health communication research. In C. Candlin (Ed.), *Research and Practice in Professional Discourse* (pp. 95–135). Hong Kong: City University of Hong Kong Press.

Sarangi, S. and Candlin, C. (2003). Trading between reflexivity and relevance: New challenges for applied linguistics. *Applied Linguistics*, *24*(3), 271–285.

Sarangi, S., and Roberts, C. (1999). The dynamics of interactional and institutional orders in work-related settings. In S. Sarangi and C. Roberts (Eds), *Talk, Work and the Institutional Order: Discourse in Medical, Mediation and Management Settings*. Berlin: Mouton de Gruyter.

Schein, E. (1987). Coming to a new awareness of organizational culture. In E. Schein (Ed.), *The Art of Managing Human Resources* (pp. 261–277). New York, NY: Oxford University Press

Schein, E. (1992). *Organizational Culture and Leadership* (2nd ed.). San Francisco, CA: Jossey-Bass.

Schneider, B. and Andre, J. (2005). University preparation for workplace writing: An exploratory study of the perceptions of students in three disciplines. *Journal of Business Communication, 42*(2), 195–218.

Schnurr, S. (2013). *Exploring Professional Communication: Language in Action*. London: Routledge.

Schnurr, S., and Chan, A. (2009). Leadership discourse and politeness at work: A cross-cultural case study of New Zealand and Hong Kong. *Journal of Politeness Research, 5*(2), 131–157.

Schön, D. (1983). *The Reflective Practitioner: How Professionals Think in Action*. New York, NY: Basic Books.

Scollon, R., Scollon, S. and Jones, R. (2011). *Intercultural Communication: A Discourse Approach*. Chichester: John Wiley & Sons.

Seibold, D. R. and Kang, P. (2008). Using critical praxis to understand and teach teamwork. *Business Communication Quarterly, 71*, 421–438.

Short, J., Williams, E. and Christie, B. (1976). *The Social Psychology of Telecommunications*. New York, NY: Wiley.

Sifianou, M. (1992). *Politeness Phenomena in England and Greece*. Oxford: Clarendon.

Sitkin, S., Sutcliffe, K. and Barrios-Choplin, J. (1992). A dual-capacity model of communication media choice in organizations. *Human Communication Research, 18*, 563–598.

Skovholt, K. and Svennevig, J. (2006). Email copies in workplace interaction. *Journal of Computer-Mediated Communication, 12*(1), 42–65.

Skovholt, K. and Svennevig, J. (2013). Responses and non-responses in workplace emails. In S. Herring, D. Stein, and T. Virtanen (Eds.), *Pragmatics of Computer-Mediated Communication*, Vol. 9 (pp. 589–612). Walter de Gruyter.

Sleurs, K. and Jacobs, G. (2005). Beyond preformulation: An ethnographic perspective on press releases. *Journal of Pragmatics, 37*, 1251–1273.

Sleurs, K., Jacobs, G. and Van Waes, L. (2003). Constructing press releases, constructing quotations: A case study. *Journal of Sociolinguistics 7*(2), 192–212.

Smagorinsky, P. and Smith, M. (1992). The nature of knowledge in composition and literary understanding: The question of specificity. *Review of Educational Research, 62*(3), 279–305.

Smart, G. (1993). Genre as a community invention: A central bank's response to its executives' expectations as readers. In R. Spilka (Ed.), *Writing in the Workplace: New Research Perspectives* (pp. 124–140). Carbondale, IL: Southern Illinois University Press.

Smart, G. (1998). Mapping conceptual worlds: Using interpretive ethnography to explore knowledge-making in a professional community. *Journal of Business Communication, 35*(1), 111–127.

Smart, G. (2000). Reinventing expertise: Experienced writers in the workplace encounter a new genre. In P. Dias and A. Paré (Eds.), *Transitions: Writing in Academic and Workplace Settings* (pp. 223–252). Cresskill, NJ: Hampton Press Inc.

Smart, G. (2006). *Writing the Economy: Activity Genre and Technology in the World of Banking*. London: Equinox.

Smart, G. and Brown, N. (2002). Learning transfer or transforming learning? Student interns reinventing expert writing practices in the workplace. *Technostyle, 18*(1), 117–141.

Smart, G. and Brown, N. (2006). Developing a "discursive gaze": Participatory action research with student interns encountering new genres in the activity of the workplace. In N. Artemeva and A. Freedman (Eds.), *Rhetorical Studies and Beyond* (pp. 241–282). Winnipeg, Manitoba, Canada: Inkshed.

Snyder, L. (2009). Teaching teams about teamwork: Preparation, practice, and performance review. *Business Communication Quarterly, 72*(1), 74–79.

Soroko, E. (2012). The presentation of self in letters of application: A mixed-method approach. *Journal of Employment Counseling, 49*(1), 4–17.

Spack, R. (1988). Initiating ESL students into the academic discourse community: How far should we go? *TESOL Quarterly, 22*, 29–51.

Spencer-Oatey, H. (2000). Rapport management: A framework for analysis. In H. Spencer-Oatey (Ed.), *Culturally Speaking: Managing Rapport Through Talk Across Cultures* (pp. 11–46). London: Continuum.

Spencer-Oatey, H. (2008). Face, (im)politeness and rapport. In H. Spencer-Oatey (Ed.), *Culturally Speaking: Communication and Politeness Theory* (pp. 11–47). London: Continuum.

Spilka, R. (Ed.) (1993). *Writing in the Workplace: New Research Perspectives.* Carbondale, IL: Southern Illinois University Press.

Standing, G. (2011). *The Precariat: The New Dangerous Class.* London: Bloomsbury Academic.

Stevens, M. and Campion, M. (1994). The knowledge, skill, and ability requirements for teamwork: Implications for human resource management. *Journal of Management, 20*, 505–530.

Storch, N. (2005). Collaborative writing: Product, process and students' reflections. *Journal of Second Language Writing, 14*, 153–173.

Suchan, J. and Dulek, R. (1988). Toward a better understanding of reader analysis. *Journal of Business Communication, 25*, 29–45.

Swales, J. (1990). *Genre Analysis: English in Academic and Research Settings.* Cambridge: Cambridge University Press.

Swales, J. (1998). *Other Floors, Other Voices: A Textography of a Small University Building.* Mahwah, NJ: Lawrence Erlbaum Associates.

Swales, J. (2004). *Research Genres: Exploration and Applications.* Cambridge: Cambridge University Press.

Tekin, B. C. (2008). The construction of Turkey's possible EU membership in French political discourse. *Discourse and Society, 19*(6), 727–763.

Tench, R. (2003). Public relations writing—A genre-based model. *Corporate Communications: An International Journal, 8*, 139–146.

Thompson, I. (2001). Collaboration in technical communication: A quantitative content analysis of journal articles, 1990–1999. *IEEE Transactions on Professional Communication, 44*(3), 161–173.

Thurlow, C. and Poff, M. (2009). Text-messaging. In S. Herring, D. Stein and T. Virtanen (Eds.), *Handbook of the Pragmatics of CMC.* Berlin and New York: Mouton de Gruyter.

Thornbury, S. (2005). *Beyond the Sentence.* Oxford: Macmillan.

Thurlow, C., Lengel, L. and Tomic, A. (2004). *Computer Mediated Communication: Social Interaction and the Internet.* London: Sage.

Townley, A. and Jones, A. (2016). The role of emails and covering letters in negotiating a legal contract: A case study from Turkey. *English for Specific Purposes, 44*, 68–81.

Tribble, C. (1991). Some uses of electronic text in English for academic purposes. In J. Milton and K. Tong (Eds.), *Text Analysis in Computer Assisted Language Learning* (pp. 4–14). Hong Kong: Hong Kong University of Science and Technology and City Polytechnic of Hong Kong.

Upton, T. A. (2002). Understanding direct mail letters as a genre. *International Journal of Corpus Linguistics*, 7(1), 65–85.

Upton, T. A. and Connor, U. (2001). Using computerized corpus analysis to investigate the textlinguistic discourse moves of a genre. *English for Specific Purposes*, 20(4), 313–329.

Van den Berg, P. and Wilderom, C. (2004). Defining, measuring and comparing organizational cultures. *Applied Psychology: An International Review*, 53(4), 570–582.

Van Nus, M. (1999). Can we count on your bookings of potatoes to Madeira? Corporate context and discourse practices in direct sales letters. In F. Bargiela-Chiappini and C. Nickerson (Eds.), *Writing Business: Genres, Media and Discourses* (pp. 181–206). London and New York: Longman.

Vergaro, C. (2004). Discourse strategies of Italian and English sales promotion letters. *English for Specific Purposes*, 23(2), 181–207.

Vickers, C. (2007). Second language socialization through team interaction among electrical and computer engineering students. *Modern Language Journal*, 91, 621–640.

Vygotsky, L. (1978). *Mind in Society*. Cambridge, MA: Harvard University Press.

Warren, M. (2013). "Just spoke to …": The types and directionality of intertextuality in professional discourse. *English for Specific Purposes*, 32(1), 12–24.

Warren, M. (2016). Signalling intertextuality in business emails. *English for Specific Purposes* 42, 26–37.

Warschauer, M., Zheng, B. and Park, Y. (2013). New ways of connecting reading and writing. *TESOL Quarterly*, 47(4), 825–830.

Watts, R. (2003). *Politeness*. Cambridge: Cambridge University Press.

Wee, L. (2003). Linguistic instrumentalism in Singapore. *Journal of Multilingual and Multicultural Development*, 24(3), 211–224.

Wegner, D. (2004). The collaborative construction of a management report in a municipal community of practice: Text and context, genre and learning. *Journal of Business and Technical Communication*, 18(4), 411–451.

Wenger, E. (1998). *Communities of Practice: Learning, Meaning and Identity*. Cambridge, UK: Cambridge University Press.

Weninger, C. and Kan, K.H-Y. (2013). (Critical) Language awareness in business communication. *English for Specific Purposes*, 32, 59–71.

Wickliff, G. A. (1997). Assessing the value of client-based group projects in an introductory technical communication course. *Journal of Business and Technical Communication*, 11, 170–191.

Winsor, D. (1989). An engineer's writing and the corporate construction of knowledge. *Written Communication*, 6, 270–285.

Winsor, D. (1996). *Writing Like an Engineer: A Rhetorical Education*. Mahwah, NJ: Lawrence Erlbaum.

Winsor, D. (1999). Genre and activity systems: The role of documentation in maintaining and changing engineering activity systems. *Written Communication*, 16(2), 200–224.

Winsor, D. (2000). Ordering work: Blue-collar literacy and the political nature of genre. *Written Communication*, 17(2), 155–184.

Winsor, D. (2003). *Writing Power: Communication in an Engineering Center*. New York, NY: SUNY Press.

Witte, S. (1992). Context, text, intertext: Toward a constructivist semiotic of writing. *Written Communication*, 9(2), 237–308.

Yates, J. and Orlikowski, W. (1992). Genres of organizational communication: A structurational approach to studying communication and media. *Academy of Management Review*, 17(2), 299–326.

Yates, J. and Orlikowski, W. (2002). Genre systems: Structuring interaction through communicative norms. *Journal of Business Communication* 39(1), 13–35.

Yeung, L. (1997). Polite requests in English and Chinese business correspondence in Hong Kong. *Journal of Pragmatics*, *27*, 505–522.

Yli-Jokipii, H. (1994). Requests in professional discourse: A cross-cultural study of British, American and Finnish business writing. In *Annales Academiae Scientiarum Fennicae*, Vol. 71. Helsinki: Suomalainen Tiedeakatemia.

Yu, M. (2003). On the universality of face: Evidence from Chinese compliment response behavior. *Journal of Pragmatics*, *35*, 1679–1710.

Zachry, M. (2000a). Communicative practices in the workplace: A historical examination of genre development. *Technical Writing and Communication*, *30* (1), 57–79.

Zachry, M. (2000b). Conceptualizing communicative practices in organizations: Genre-based research in professional communication. *Business Communication Quarterly*, *63*(4), 95–101.

Zhu, C. and Engels, N. (2014). Organizational culture and instructional innovations in higher education: Perceptions and reactions of teachers and students. *Educational Management Administration & Leadership*, *42*(1), 136–158.

Zhu, C., Devos, G. and Li, Y. (2011). Teacher perceptions of school culture and their organizational commitment and well-being in a Chinese school. *Asia Pacific Education Review*, *12*(2), 319–328.

Zhu, W. (2004). Writing in business courses: An analysis of assignment types, their characteristics, and required skills. *English for Specific Purposes*, *23*(2), 111–135.

INDEX